COURT
VISION

COURT

VISION

UNEXPECTED VIEWS ON THE

LURE OF BASKETBALL

IRA BERKOW

WILLIAM MORROW

AN IMPRINT OF HARPERCOLLINSPUBLISHERS

HarperCollins books may be purchased for educational, business, or sales
promotional use. For information please write: Special Markets Department,
HarperCollins Publishers Inc., 10 East 53rd Street, New York, NY 10022.

FIRST EDITION

Designed by Joanne Metsch

Library of Congress Cataloging-in-Publication Data

Berkow, Ira.
Court vision : unexpected views on the lure of basketball / Ira Berkow.—1st ed.
p. cm.
Includes index.
ISBN 0-688-16842-6
1. Basketball—United States. 2. Celebrities—United States. I. Title.

GV885.7.B45 2000
796.323'0973—dc21   99-045201

00   01   02   03   04   RRD   10   9   8   7   6   5   4   3   2   1

To Shayne

CONTENTS

ACKNOWLEDGMENTS

I take full responsibility for any flaws that appear in the contents of this book. If, however, the reader has sweet thoughts about it, if it has succeeded in ways that I had hoped and strived for, then I am gratified, and must gladly share some of the credit.

I wish to thank Bill Adler, whose nimble brain conceived the original idea for this book. I wish to thank Zach Schisgal, the book's editor, whose equally agile head and hand made wise and proper suggestions for inclusions and exclusions.

I wish to thank friends Dick Goldstein and Audrey McGinn who were kind enough to read the book in manuscript and made typically senstitive and judicious comments to improve it.

I want to express appreciation to David Fisher for a variety of creative thoughts regarding those to be interviewed. And I wish to express appreciation to those who made special efforts for me on behalf of some of those interviewed: Cindy Berger, Leslie Dart, Carol Matthau, Lon Rosen, Paul Silverthorne, Leslie Sloan, Mark Volpe, Susan Wallace, and Christopher Walsh.

INTRODUCTION

The question was posed to Edward Villella, the retired ballet dancer who soared through the air onstage in a manner reminiscent of Michael Jordan on a basketball court: Is there a basketball player active today who might have made a great ballet dancer? "The young kid with the Lakers," Villella said, referring to Kobe Bryant. "Like all great ballet dancers, he can go forward and backward at the same time." And Villella explained.

I asked Grover Washington Jr., the Grammy Award–winning jazz saxophonist, if any of his favorite players reminded him of musical instruments. Yes, he said. Julius Erving, for example, would be a piano. "Because," said Washington, "the whole orchestra is in the piano."

Sharon Stone said that she studied Magic Johnson's moves on the basketball court for her role in *Basic Instinct*. It seemed a wholly unlikely pairing—Magic's blind passes, for example, with Sharon Stone's steamy scenes—but she made her beguiling case.

Saul Bellow understands why more reporters were present— and for good reason—at the retirement announcement in Chicago of the basketball icon Michael Jeffrey Jordan than were in the gallery for the first day of the Senate impeachment hearing of President William Jefferson Clinton.

And Colonel Brian Duffy, the astronaut, said that the closest he came to preparing for the scary uncertainty of a flight into space was when he had two free throws to shoot with the game tied in the closing seconds of a high school state tournament game in Massachusetts.

These are just a few of the insights, impressions, feelings, and memories about basketball collected in this book from some of the more intriguing, articulate, and original people in America. In recent years the game has truly taken its place as a cultural phenomenon, and not, of course, just in the United States, but worldwide.

Twenty-seven of these people are included in *Court Vision*, ranging from artists to scientists, actors to politicians, educators and religious leaders to psychiatrists, architects to lawyers, musicians to critics, novelists to chefs, news people to business people. None of them have any direct connection to basketball beyond an interest or knowledge or perception. None own a professional team or play for one or had necessarily made his or her mark in the sport. I was interested in finding people of noted achievement who can step back and see the game freshly. I wanted to see it through their eyes and minds, and based on the expertise of their particular field.

I was always intrigued by the Japanese movie *Rashomon*, in which several people view one incident through surprisingly different interpretations. I wondered what it would be like to sit at a basketball game with the people I have asked to participate in this book and see the same sport—if not the same game—through their unique viewpoints.

For as long as I have been a sportswriter—I began professionally in 1965 with the *Minneapolis Tribune* (now the *Star-Tribune*)—I have been interested in seeing things in an uncommon way. Many times, the views of highly creative people in a wide assortment of fields have provided that. One was Roy Lichtenstein, the pop artist. Among other things, he told me that he loves to watch football games on television and turns the knobs just a little to enjoy "the baroque entanglements."

Marcel Marceau, that sublime mime, once told me that he envisioned a javelin thrower thrusting back and getting his spear stuck in the mud, and a weightlifter so oppressed by his burden that he sinks into a split. And he appreciated the Harlem Globetrotters. "It is an act, of course, the way they fool very much the reflexes of their opponent. But the timing and the control is the greatest virtuosity."

And the poet Marianne Moore, in an interview I did with her years ago, told me she once taught typing and shorthand at the Carlisle (Pennsylvania) Indian School to a young Jim Thorpe. "James was the most pleasant athlete to watch," she said. "He was so limber and could perform wonderful feats with the grace of a leopard, and then take no credit for his achievement. A very unaffected person. And, you know, he wrote an old fashioned Spencerian hand, very deliberate and elegant." (While the last might, at first thought, have seemed extraneous to Thorpe's athletic achievements, it is my experience that many of the best athletes demonstrate the kind of concentration and attention to detail—they will not be hurried into the shoddy—that separates them from the rest of the pack.)

Walter Matthau often turns off the sound when watching basketball games and turns on recordings of Mozart. "It's remarkable how close the action is to the music," he said. At other times, Matthau watchs the game from the particular vantage point of one who spent a lifetime wagering on games. Once, Maureen Stapleton, who starred with Matthau in *Plaza Suite* and is one of his wife Carol's best friends, came by for a visit and went into Matthau's office in his home, where he was watching a game and rooting for his bet. She wanted to read him a short story.

"Maureen," he said, "there's two minutes to go in the game! This is work! Later!"

Some of the people in the book follow basketball less closely than others. But, as with Saul Bellow or Kary Mullis or Edward Villella, I am interested in anything they have to say, about anything. I respect and enjoy the cut of their minds. And since some basketball players are virtual household names, or have made an impact on our culture—from Bill Russell to Bill Bradley, from Wilt Chamberlain to Michael Jordan, from Larry Bird to, yes, Dennis Rodman and Latrell Sprewell—I felt certain that such people as Bellow and Mullis and Villella would have thoughts on the subject. And they did not disappoint. Each of those players that came up most often in discussion was, in retrospect, understandable. Each of them stood for something, or made a point larger, than the mere winning or losing of a basketball game. Some stood for pure excellence (Jordan), others for a weird audacity (Rodman) or the frustration of having cast a great shadow but of having often been considered in a rival's shadow (Chamberlain in relation to Russell), or the casting of light on a matter regarding a national crisis that had often been treated as taboo (Magic

Johnson's stunning public admission that he is HIV-positive), or one who succeeded with inexorable mind over matter (Bradley).

From my years as a sportswriter and from further talking with people in the game and with friends and acquaintances, I knew about others—beyond my own profession of news and feature writing—who did have an interest, sometimes profound, in basketball. Of those interviewed, two played college basketball: William S. Cohen, secretary of defense under Clinton, was a standout player for Bowdoin College (Maine), a Division III school, and Father Edward Malloy, president of Notre Dame University, was a fine high school player in Washington, D.C., and a scholarship athlete at Notre Dame. But during Malloy's varsity basketball career he was primarily a substitute player. Also, Governor Mario Cuomo was a strong recreation league player, a standout baseball player at St. John's University, and, briefly, a minor league baseball player (and, in his late sixties, continues to play recreational basketball).

The news anchor Tom Brokaw (in South Dakota) and Colonel Duffy were starting players on their high school basketball teams. Law professor and appeals attorney Alan Dershowitz was on the bench—and in the program, which he still has—for the Brooklyn yeshiva team that played a game in Madison Square Garden in 1954 against the Manhattan yeshiva team before the Knicks-Syracuse game. And the six-foot-tall Julia Child said she played in high school in Pasadena, California, but when she went to Smith College her basketball career ended because, she said, "they changed the rules" and made it harder if you were taller.

Some in this book have had firsthand experiences with some great athletes, and have met them on a different turf from sportswriters or fans. Karl (the Mailman) Malone, the formidable Utah Jazz forward, seeks financial advice from Donald Trump. Frank Stella discussed art and hoops with Dave DeBusschere, and compares the styles of some basketball stars to the styles of painters such as Picasso and Matisse and Léger.

Before his death, critic Gene Siskel reviewed movies with Michael Jordan, and they agreed to disagree, Siskel, meanwhile, drawing insights into the nature of Jordan.

Christie Hefner, CEO of Playboy Enterprises in Chicago, studied the way Phil Jackson dealt with, among others, Dennis Rodman as a way for the head of a company to engage successfully with personnel. William Goldman, the screenwriter and a fervent Knicks fan, compares elements of the Knicks to the movie he adapted, *Misery*. Kary Mullis, Nobel Prize winner in chemistry, compares a cannonball to an NBA player and wonders why the former comes down to earth with proper trajectory, and the other continues to sail through the air.

Johnnie Cochran gives his view of the changing athlete, and changing black athlete, from the time he grew up admiring Jackie Robinson to handling paternity suits against National Basketball Association players, some of whom have admitted to fathering multiple children with multiple women. And Chris Rock, with his inimitable, funny, and fearless social commentary, takes a like approach to basketball.

The prominent psychiatrist and enthusiastic recreational basketball player Dr. Isaac Steven Herschkopf has looked, to paraphrase Shakespeare, quite inside the heads of men, and, it follows, basketball players. The architect Richard Meier, among other constructive views, assesses a pair of Twin Towers.

And in his youth, Secretary of Defense Cohen went one-on-one with Jim Loscutoff, and learned to his chagrin why Loscutoff was known as the enforcer for the Boston Celtics. Secretary Cohen still plays pickup games during lunch hours at the Pentagon, as he did when he was in the Senate and the House, and has opinions on how one can determine whether a first-time opponent on the court is a Republican or a Democrat strictly by the way he plays basketball.

Woody Allen views a basketball game—a close one, anyway—as more dramatic than any play on Broadway. Erica Jong views basketball as the sexiest sport, Nikki Giovanni views it from a more nurturing angle (her recent poem, "Iverson's Posse," attempts to give hip-hop Allen Iverson guidance) and Seiji Ozawa, the conductor of the Boston Symphony, sees the artistry in a successful fast break on a basketball court as one with, say, a movement in

Beethoven's Ninth. And if each breaks down, he observed, they break down for like reasons.

While many of the accomplished and original-thinking and sometimes controversial contributors to this book viewed basketball from widely different angles and arrived at wholly different conclusions—though no different from, say, the members of the Supreme Court—I was also struck by the similarities that many of them perceived. While individual talent and genius are certainly greatly valued and appreciated by the contributors, the merits of teamwork, and of the player who "sees the court," as the saying goes, versus the insular hotshot, is a theme frequently depicted and identified with, whether it be in politics or music or a thrust into space.

This also gave rise to the title of the book, *Court Vision*. It is a term commonly used among basketball people, and means having a sense of where all the players on the court are at a given time. Even more, there is the uncanny ability of the best players to intuit where the other players—teammates as well as opponents—are going to be in the moments ahead of a play, to, in effect, see in advance. It is the chess player seeing several moves ahead, or the race car driver suddenly aware of a crash up ahead and in split seconds avoiding it by comprehending the movement of the crumpling cars.

In his book, *Values of the Game*, Bill Bradley explained this phenomenon in personal terms: "During a game, what I loved most was spotting an imbalance in the opponent's defense and getting the ball to the open man at the right time, in the right place, with the right zip. I loved sensing where a teammate was and following my intuition with a pass. I would notice when an opponent turned his head the wrong way, then throw the ball past his ears or behind his legs to a cutting teammate."

Several contributors cited Jordan as a paradigm, noting that perhaps the greatest all-around player in basketball history didn't win a championship ring until his sixth season in the NBA, or until he either learned to be a team player or gained confidence in his teammates. Several of the contributors credited their success to their own ability to be team players and pass off important projects or assignments at the propitious moment.

There are numerous others whom I have greatly wished were in this book, but time and circumstances and some unaccountable predilections dictated ultimate inclusion.

In my last two years of high school and my first two years of college, I worked summers as a garbage collector for the city of Chicago. I loved the job. I loved working in the alleys alongside adults, loved finding out about their lives, and enjoyed working outdoors—once the smell from the back of the truck was conquered (gradually, to be sure). I was growing up, and these garbage collectors, who could be witty and wise, were instrumental. I know that when Larry Bird left Indiana University after only a few months there—I suspect Bobby Knight's authoritarian attitude had something to do with it, though Bird still won't say for sure—he went back to his home in French Lick, Indiana, and got a job on a sanitation truck.

Shortly after he took the job as head coach of the Indiana Pacers in 1997, I interviewed him in his office in Indianapolis. I had known him for years as a player, but I never happened to mention that we had something in common. I said I had worked on a garbage truck, too, and that I had really enjoyed it. I said that people I tell this to can't believe that I loved the job. Bird, known for his stoicism on the court, brightened. "I loved it, too!" he exclaimed. "In fact, if I had to go back to it tomorrow, I wouldn't mind it at all."

Bird and I shared stories about the men we worked with, and the things we learned from what they did and what they had to say. I recall this because while I know from direct experience that plumbers and schoolteachers, typists and docents, truck drivers and electricians—and sundry journalists, I might add, and garbage collectors—may very well have as unusual and pristine a view of a subject, any subject, as those I chose to interview about basketball, I thought it would be even more compelling and entertaining for the reader to get those outlooks from people with whom many of us are generally familiar.

The interviews took place from November 1998 to October 1999. Jordan had retired from the game shortly before, but, of course, remained indelible in the minds of basketball observers, and beyond. (His legacy of brilliant play seemed safe for years to come—or at least until publication of this book. *Sic transit gloria*, after all, is a concept forever in the wings of every endeavor.) And the whereabouts of Rodman—did he hook up with another team? was he ensconced in a tattoo parlor?—remained in question, as, it appears certain, they will for the length of his life. And there was the shocking news of the sudden death of the towering, massive, still youthful seeming Wilt Chamberlain, "the Big Dipper," at age sixty-three, to congestive heart failure.

A personal note:

One day a few years ago I received a phone call.

"Hi, Ira," said the deep male voice.

"Hello," I said.

The caller asked how I was, but I didn't quite connect to who he was.

"The voice is familiar," I said, "but I can't exactly place it."

"I'm T.D.H.," he said.

"T.D.H.?" I repeated.

"Tall, dark, and handsome," he said.

"Sorry, I'm still at a loss," I said.

"It's me, Wilt," he said.

"Oh, Wilt!" I said. "If you had just said T and D, I would've got it. But the H threw me off."

There was a hearty laugh at the other end of the wire. "Well, two out of three's not bad," he said. "I would've taken it shooting free throws."

Though there is occasional mention in the book about the women's professional game, college and high school basketball, and international competition, I have focused primarily on the NBA because it is currently the most accessible in terms of the widest national knowledge and associations to basketball.

In the ensuing process, I not only expanded my perceptions of basketball and the people who play it, but I widened my universe on a host of other subjects as well. It was an adventure—going into, for me, uncharted territory, but with basketball as a kind of compass.

I learned a great deal, and learned it with pleasure. I hope the same holds true for the reader.

COURT
VISION

WOODY ALLEN

BORN Allen Stewart Konisberg on December 1, 1935, in New York City, Woody Allen has become one of America's most respected filmmakers. *Annie Hall* won an Academy Award for Best Picture, and he for Best Director, in 1977. Allen has also had a highly successful career as a stand-up comedian, actor, and writer. He won an Academy Award for Best Screenplay for *Mighty Aphrodite* in 1996. He has had several bestselling collections of short stories published, including *Without Feathers* and *Getting Even*, with most of the stories appearing first in *The New Yorker*. He has had season tickets to Knick games for nearly thirty years and attends games regularly, sitting unobtrusively, often with his wife, Soon-Yi, at courtside. The following interview was conducted in his film studio on the ground floor of a hotel-apartment complex on Park Avenue. His shirt, slacks, and shoes were casual and neat and apparently nondesigner, a wardrobe that may well have been unchanged since the 1950s.

● ● ●

Q: What do you look for in a basketball game?

A: Drama. Drama and aesthetics. I'm more interested in those aspects than in who wins or loses. I've always been that way. For me to see the Knicks blow out the other team, I find this uninteresting. I couldn't care less about that. I like it when the Knicks win, but I like them to win in the last four seconds or something.

And sometimes even if the Knicks lose the game, if it's a beautiful basketball game, if it's aesthetic, I go home more satisfied. If I go to a game and it's one of those where they are playing Milwaukee or someone like that, and I can leave five minutes before the game is over because the Knicks are twenty-three points ahead, or something, then it's no fun for the evening. But if it's a tight game, then even if the Knicks lose I feel I've gotten a better evening of theater than I have watching them just win.

Q: How does a dramatic basketball game compare to dramatic theater?

A: Basketball is more interesting. In the theater you are almost always ahead of the writer, and in a basketball game you can't be ahead because you don't know that if there is one second left whether the guy is going to make a three-pointer. So the tension is tremendous. What happens is when you get to know the players, just as a fan, and the Knicks are playing Chicago or something, and then you see the game unfold and it's the last fifteen seconds and the score seesaws three times. That's something you can never get in theater. You always sort of know, "Well, Willy Loman is going to die at the end and it is great." But you're just always ahead of the writer. You see it played out and it's wonderful, but you know the outcome of it. Even in a play you've never seen before, the outcome is reasonably understandable to you before it happens. You know where it's going. But in basketball, never.

Q: I understand you once told Gene Siskel that he was lucky to live in Chicago. He was surprised that you, a dedicated New Yorker, would say something like that, until you told him that he was lucky to be able to watch all those Bulls home games—that is, in the Jordan era.

A: What it is, is this. Years ago when the Knicks had their great team—DeBusschere and Reed and Frazier and Monroe and

Bradley—I went to every single game. It didn't matter if they were playing the last-place team, and it didn't matter if they were winning or losing. I wanted to see the Knicks play because it was a great thing of beauty to watch Walt Frazier play basketball, or Earl Monroe play basketball. If you were in Chicago and you get to see the Bulls with Michael Jordan, it doesn't matter who they're playing. It's just a joy to watch them play and him play. I don't have that with the Knicks now. Now, the best that's happened over the last years with Oakley and Starks is that they'd win, but it would be a kind of brutal, hard-nosed, blue-collar win. Starks would be fighting, and Greg Anthony would get into a brawl. Rick Barry once said that all that brutality takes away from the finesse of the game. As a New Yorker I like the Knicks to win, but there was no beauty to it, no aesthetic satisfaction. So when I'm sitting at a game, and in a fourth quarter Reggie Miller would throw in sixteen points—as he did in a playoff game at the Garden—it was so exhilarating to watch that, even though the Knicks lost. It was such a demonstration of the art of basketball.

Q: If you had been a pro basketball player, who would you like to have been? Who would you like to have played like?

A: I guess Earl Monroe. He's the most fun that I've had watching. I think Michael Jordan was definitely a greater player, but Earl Monroe was the most fun because he caught the jazz spirit of the game. He made it so aesthetically joyful to watch.

Q: Do you think he was an artist?

A: I do. I thought he was absolutely an intuitive artist. It's that natural thing that he doesn't even know he has. It's just that he can't step outside himself, and appreciate himself, the same way that Brando can't watch Brando on the screen and know what everybody is fussing over. Marilyn Monroe said years ago, "I wish I was a guy so I would know what it would be like to fuck me."

[*Laughter.*] That's the feeling that you get with Earl Monroe. He can never fully appreciate himself. He was just a great, natural hunk of poetry.

Q: A hunk of poetry?

A: That's what it is. That's what you see with Brando. You see Brando in the middle of *On the Waterfront*, in the movie, or in the play in a New York theater about a New Jersey dock. There is this big hunk of poetry in it. Brando's not like any longshoreman you know, and he doesn't move like one, doesn't sound like one, but it's pure poetry. The same thing with Earl Monroe. And both took risks. Sometimes they failed, but more often they succeeded.

Q: Could you describe for me how you saw the way Earl Monroe played?

A: He was just a joy to watch because he was so graceful, but in those jerky motions he had. He was like on dangling coat hangers. He was all bones and lanky and dangling like those skeletons that dangle, the dancing dolls on Broadway. He would come down the court, always with that high dribble and that great look on his face. Now, Frazier was such a beautiful-looking man, with great posture. Monroe was more like a beast. He would have that fiery look in his eyes and come downcourt twisting his body this way and that. Then he would dart into a group of guys and spin and pivot and duck under and turn around. It looked like his hands and feet were going off in every direction at the same time. The ball would go up and he would make the shot. He made it so many times. One of the sportswriters once said that his misses were more exciting than most people's baskets. That's true. Your heart was always in your mouth because he had those bad knees. He just looked so bad when you saw him. I've seen him do so many things. I saw him not miss a shot all night, just 100 percent for the night. I saw him in a shootout with Kevin Porter, when Porter was with the Bullets.

The two of them had a shootout at the end of a game that was almost comical. The two teams just about sat and watched. Porter would come downcourt and do a move and then make a shot. Then Monroe would take the ball downcourt, spin, and score. This went on and on. They must have exchanged seven or eight baskets in a row. Their teammates would just feed each of them.

Q: You once said that when Monroe takes off with the ball and races the length of the court, he resembles an animated cartoon character whose feet never touch the floor.

A: It's like a great dancer. For some reason, there are a million guys who can dance wonderfully and have great technique, some as good or better than Fred Astaire, but when you see Fred Astaire dance there is something in him that is above and beyond the technique. You look right through the others. But with Astaire, there is something in his attitude, his personality, that is special. Monroe was like that, a complete star. He had fun turning on the audience. He held himself as a star. He behaved like one.

Q: A number of years ago you accepted an assignment by *Sport* magazine to write an article on Monroe. You had it arranged to meet Monroe, you went to his home, but he never showed up. How did you feel about that?

A: I would excuse him anything, and if that is the way he is, that's the way he is. It doesn't matter to me. You just sort of accept it. When someone is so great at something, you just figure, "Well, he needs this to be great." I mean, that's the way his personality is. You know, you draw the line if the guy is hurting somebody, but he was out playing tennis, so I chatted with his girlfriend. She was a very beautiful woman.

Q: You still wrote the article, a kind of *Waiting for Godot*. And I remember you describing Earl's girlfriend as being packed into her jeans with an ice cream scoop.

A: Oh, she was just beautiful.

Q: I happened to speak to Monroe a few months ago and asked him why he didn't make it for your interview. He told me that he was getting a haircut. He said, "And you know how it is in barbershops, guys just were talking and talking and when I finally got out of the chair, it was too late to meet Woody." Years later, and he seemed sort of apologetic.

A: Well, his girlfriend told me he was playing tennis. It didn't matter at all. He had a great night that night at the Garden. I can't recall what he scored, but I know it was a good shooting night. I mentioned it in the article. And I had a good time at the game.

Q: Didn't you film him for one of your movies, but you didn't use the piece?

A: I used the whole Knick team at the time. Earl was on the team. It was a little scrimmage thing.

Q: Why were you unable to use it?

A: It was for *Annie Hall*. It just took too much time for that particular joke. I cut a million jokes out of every movie. This was just one that got cut. But it wasn't him alone.

Q: Walt Frazier once told me about an afternoon at P. J. Clark's, where he used to go for his pregame meal, and he said that he was eating and at a nearby table a guy was reading a newspaper that he held up and which shielded his face. When Frazier looked up the guy quickly raised up the newspaper. It was as though the guy was staring at Frazier and then when Frazier looked in his direction the guy shot up the paper, as though he didn't want to be caught staring. Frazier recalled that this happened several times. He said that the guy was you.

A: It could have been me because I was often there. But I wouldn't have been watching him. I would probably have been hiding myself. Now Frazier is a completely different type from Monroe. They were two genius guards and Frazier had total elegance. That erect posture, that slow confidence, never arguing a call, just quietly going about his business. It got to be where the fans got pissed off that he didn't take the ball away from the other team when they wanted him to. He just waited for a more timely moment in the game. He was so adept. I believe the other athletes once voted him the most coordinated athlete in any sport. He just so elegant, so smooth. The Rolls Royce. And on the court he was serene. Earl was like hot jazz and Frazier was cool.

Q: You compared Monroe to Brando, could you compare Frazier to an actor?

A: I compared Earl Monroe to Marlon Brando because they both had the same fire inside. When I think of Frazier in this regard I think of Fred Astaire. Someone who would just be at home in a top hat, white tie, and tails. If Frazier were dressed like that, he would carry it perfectly. Whereas Monroe is the torn T-shirt and jeans type. He's just a different person for me, but they are both worth the price of admission. And the Knicks don't have anything like that now. That's why when Sprewell joined the team all of us were hoping that they'll start to focus the team in that direction. That's what you want. You don't want workmanlike basketball. For those people to whom winning is everything, any kind of championship would make them happy. But I remember in the 1970s when Golden State won the NBA title. They were not interesting to me. They were the Cinderella team of the year or something, but they didn't mean anything. I would have felt the same way if the Knicks had beaten Houston a few years ago. I would have felt local pride but it was workmanlike basketball. The Knicks would come out and Starks would play his good but unaesthetic game, and Oakley would do all the hard labor under the boards. And they would go down to Ewing in the last quarter every play, as they do now.

If Ewing was on and everything was on, they would win. I find the same thing with Allan Houston. I think he's an amazing shooter, as good a shooter as you can get. But it's not nearly as much fun to watch as, say, Tim Hardaway of the Miami Heat. He's got that thing. That bad-boy thing. He's a fine ballplayer, a superb executor. Tim Hardaway has got some of that real potential to thrill you. He's always shorter than you think he is and he's the guy who can make the buzzer-beater shot at the end of the half. And he's not afraid to shoot in the last three minutes or two minutes of the game. I love that.

Q: Sprewell has demonstrated that he's not afraid to take those shots either.

A: Players like him shoot and suffer for it if they miss, or they make it. That's what I love about Reggie Miller. I was always a great fan of his, despite all the Knicks fans hating him. I always loved him because he couldn't care less what they think of him. You could boo him the whole game. Doesn't matter to him. He does what he's there to do. He makes those shots. He makes those foul shots and when the time comes at the end of the game he's not afraid to shoot the ball. He's got enough drama to make himself the winner or the loser. When he shoved Michael Jordan out of the way in the playoffs in 1998 and made a big three-pointer at the end of a game, that was sensational.

I think over the years you can consistently go to him in the last five seconds of the game, and it's a surprise when he doesn't come through.

Q: Probably because he thinks he's going to make it. Never in doubt . . .

A: Right, he always thinks he's going to make it. Some confidence.

Q: You said you like Charles Barkley a lot.

A: I love Barkley. He also has it. He's got a completely different personality, but it's huge. He's funny. He's great. He's got a lot of humor, a lot of wit. He's a guy who is totally in your face in a charming way, and he's willing to say, "Who cares if I don't get a ring." It doesn't matter for a second to him all these fan clichés and these broadcasting clichés. He's no bullshit player. He's always sticking it to the other players.

Q: But occasionally in bad taste, like spitting on a fan.

A: It's sort of refreshing. Some of those fans really have it coming. I've seen some pretty awful fans say some pretty awful things—personal things. I'm suprised sometimes that the guys take it that calmly. I don't mind when they needle the players, but I'm surprised at how vicious it can become.

Q: In the play *The Bleacher Bums*, the fans would shout to the married outfielder on the visiting team the phone number of his girlfriend in Chicago.

A: That's vicious. Well, I always empathized with Barkley. He's one of those players who has delivered over the years. Now you see him in his waning years, but when he was at his peak, he was a terror, a rebounder, a three-point shooter, a major scorer, a dominant force. If I was making up some all-time great teams, Barkley would probably be one of the starting forwards. It would include Karl Malone and Elgin Baylor and Larry Bird. I loved Bird. He was clearly the hayseed as genius. Again, it's a function of individual personality. You thought of Bird as the guy who would be sittin' and whittlin' somewhere on a farm. He just also had that sense of drama.

He was a textbook basketball player who was not boring. He did everything. It was a joy to watch his technique, like watching a great piano player who has astonishing technique and where you can appreciate the execution of his game. There was no weakness in his game.

Q: Maybe a little on the defensive end, but he played team defense.

A: And he was outstanding at that. There are certain guys that have instant authority and maturity as winners when they come into the league. Magic had it, but he had a little flash, too. Bird had no flash. Bird was just, "I'm here and you guys have been here ten years. I'm running this." Someone who has that now, I think, is Tim Duncan. Duncan was a rookie in 1998 but he looked like he was completely mature.

Q: Before Duncan joined San Antonio, the Spurs were said to be David Robinson's team.

A: And then it became Tim Duncan's team. He's a no-nonsense player. He was not caught up in any kind of extra baggage like a guy like Iverson—who I think is as exciting a guard as there is in basketball. But you get a lot of baggage—he has this image of having tough guys around him in a kind of entourage and he had brushes with the law—and you have to wonder if he is ever going to be a guy that will move teams or contribute in a great way to championship teams. But Tim Duncan I thought was an immediately mature player. He wants to win and he executes beautifully.

Q: What do you make of Rodman?

A: First of all, he's a great rebounder. All the rest I think is a bad aesthetic choice. I think he's been smart enough to use it to make him money, but it's just the wrong choice for me. It would be like if a movie came out that was a stupid movie and it made $100 million. That's fine, but that's not my taste. While I don't find Rodman's aesthetic choice mine, Barkley's is. The problem with a kind of guy like Rodman is that he can only really help a team if he is in a very, very disciplined context. So if you are on Detroit with Isiah Thomas and Bill Laimbeer, they can get something out of Rodman. In Chicago, with a real organization, they were just too serious to let him screw around too much. Otherwise, he's a maniac.

Q: But a great rebounder.

A: I think you have to think of him as a Hall of Fame player. He has distinguished himself from other rebounders and other ballplayers, but I used to think that I had no aesthetic taste for Muhammad Ali as a fighter. I'm a big fight fan and I was always a purist. I thought all of that talk and the hands-down style and the Ali Shuffle was undignified and beneath a fighter of his ability and stature, and not something that Joe Louis or Ray Robinson would have done. I believe Muhammad Ali would have beaten Joe Louis, but I think what happened was that Ali turned boxing a little bit into wrestling. I don't like that. So if you see a guy like Prince what's-his-name?

Q: Naseem Hamed?

A: Yeah. It's like all heavy-handed bullshit. You've just got to go in and fight. That's why Mike Tyson was such a breath of fresh air, when he came along.

Q: No robe. No socks. No frills.

A: He would just come in and fight. It was fun to watch him fight because he was tough and strong. So I don't really find any of that marketing stuff with Rodman fun, but he is a great player. I can't think of any rebounders over the years who were better.

Q: DeBusschere?

A: He was great, yes. He was like Larry Bird in a sense. He really didn't have a weakness in his game. He could take long outside shots, he could score when you needed scoring. He was a smart ballplayer.

Q: The Knicks of the championship years of the early 1970s did have an interesting group of players.

A: What was so great was the mixed chemistry. They had hard-nosed players like DeBusschure and Reed on the team, and poetic players like Frazier and Monroe, who were just simply geniuses.

Q: What about Bill Bradley?

A: He was a very solid player, a very heady player. He was great moving and playing without the ball. I never found it too much fun to watch, though.

Q: As a film director, can you relate in any way to basketball coaches?

A: I can only relate to this aspect of it: those guys must have big problems when they inherit a team. In many, many films—most—you know the director has got to be father to one person and the friend to another and the lover to a third one and try to keep everybody happy and keep the star from being too temperamental and this one doesn't want to do this line and this writer is complaining about keeping it in. . . . And coaches have got to mediate between, you know, various personalities as well. I've had to do less of that because I'm usually in my own film, and I cast my friends. So I don't usually have a mutinous situation.

Q: When you watched the Knicks of the 1998–99 season founder, what would you have done to change it if the situation were similar to a movie you were making?

A: I would recast. I've always thought that the problem with the Knicks, win or lose, was casting. When they won games, they still were not the most exciting team.

Q: What of the last few years?

A: Since they won the championship, in '73, even the tail-off years with Monroe and Frazier were still fun to watch. The casting was good, even though they lost. But I don't feel this current team has been fun to watch, win or lose. It's because their franchise player has been Patrick Ewing, who I believe is a truly great player. I'm one of those people who think he's always maligned by sportswriters and fans. But he's been the whole franchise. Without him over the last thirteen or fourteen years, they would have just been languishing in the basement year after year. But the teams with him never play interesting basketball.

What you need is a team that's guard-oriented, and they haven't had that since Walt Frazier and Earl Monroe—really first-class guards. And so it's always more fun to watch the guard-oriented teams with Stephon Marbury or Allen Iverson or Reggie Miller or Jason Kidd or John Stockton or Gary Payton, really wonderful, exciting guards—any of the standout guards over the years. When you get all the pieces together, as the old Knicks did, then it's great entertainment. That's why I like the Lakers. They are exciting to watch, even though they don't have it totally together. Glen Rice is an exciting shooter, and Shaq is fun to watch.

But if it was just Shaq without Glen Rice and Kobe Bryant, it's not so pleasurable for a fan. It's watching the big guy because of his size get points—size and skill. The same with Patrick. He'll kill you with his ability, but he needs supporting players, and the Knicks have never had that.

Q: What was your feeling when the Knicks signed Latrell Sprewell?

A: I think the fans were crazy about that. Most fans in New York were excited to get Sprewell and were disappointed that they hadn't worked him into the lineup properly. But that's what they really needed. All of a sudden New York with Sprewell had the closest thing since Bernard King, who brings real excitement to the crowd.

Q: Did you have a visceral feeling about Sprewell in regard to his having choked his coach at Golden State?

A: It was a terrible thing to do, but I thought the guy paid his dues for it. You don't want to ruin his life. He did a bad thing, was suspended for it, and it cost him a fortune—what, six or seven million dollars? He was vilified in the papers and screamed at by everybody. All right. You don't want to execute the guy for that. He did it and he paid his dues. If he's ready to be a respectable citizen, fine.

Q: And being a team player?

A: The team player thing is something I never personally was that crazy about. Sure, you like a well-oiled machine, but not a dull machine.

Q: There seemed to be a problem with the Knicks when Sprewell and Alan Houston were on the court at the same time, since both essentially play the same position, shooting guard. Sprewell's presence seemed at times to put Houston in a funk. What did you make of that?

A: I don't know why they wouldn't mesh. I don't see that as the two of them playing together being mutually exclusive. They have a team that is so antithetical to what Sprewell does—his fast-paced game—that they either shouldn't have gotten Sprewell or they should refocus their team because Ewing, I feel, is going. He's still a terrific ballplayer, but how many more years can he go and still make a heavy contribution? The team should be running, and passing the ball fast. I also like Marcus Camby. He's got great moves, and he's a beautiful player to watch. He can go full court, and his spins and shots are quite pretty for a guy that's around seven feet tall. And he's some shot-blocker. If they kept Houston, Sprewell, and Camby and built the team around them, they'd be a lot of fun. It might take them a while to get winning, but they'd be interesting.

The Nets are a team that I find aesthetically fun. Now, why they had such a miserable year is because they just never had a legitimate point guard. They were interesting with Keith Van Horn and Kerry Kittles, and I think they'll be much better in the future with Stephon Marbury as their point guard.

Q: What do you make of team prayers after games?

A: I find it absurd. These guys suddenly huddle after a game and they have their prayer session. "It was up to God. . . . I want to thank God for this." It's giving too much credit to God for their own brilliance. All I can think of is that they're praying for a salary increase. What else is there? I don't put any stock in it in basketball players. I don't like it in the Academy Awards. Jews were praying all though the 1940s. Let me tell you, it doesn't work. Instead of huddling in prayer after a game, I think the players should be working on their free throws.

Q: What turned you on as a basketball fan to begin with?

A: I liked the game as a boy. I remember the old Knicks, with players like Carl Braun, and I'd go to the Garden a certain amount. I liked it when Joe Fulks came to town—he was a great jump shooter. Then around 1967 I would watch the Knicks on television and started noticing the level of the game going up. I don't know if it was the twenty-four-second clock or what, but the games had become more exciting.

Q: Because the Knicks were building their championship team at that point, with Reed and Frazier and Barnett in particular?

A: We didn't know it then, but yes. I remember the first year Frazier came, in '67, and they played him sparingly at the end of games. The minute he was sent in he just had this authority. It wasn't like some tentative rookie. He came in like a winner, carried himself like a winner. He stole the ball, passed it, he would dribble behind his back, you couldn't get it from him. He was just wonderful. And the Knicks then were developing stars. On a team, like in a movie, you need stars and a supporting cast. You can't just have a supporting cast. If a movie came out tomorrow and there were five good, solid people in it, you would enjoy the movie and you'd tell your wife, "You should see this." But it's not the same if that movie also had some new star, like Ben Affleck, or an established star like Robert De Niro.

But basketball wasn't my favorite sport by any means. I loved baseball and boxing. Willie Mays and Sugar Ray Robinson are two of my all-time favorite athletes. They had a magic flair. I envied their gifts and at one time I said that if I could live life over as someone else it would be wonderful to be Sugar Ray Robinson or Willie Mays. With my luck, however, I would undoubtedly wind up being John Maynard Keynes.

But I did play some basketball when I was a kid. I was famous for my air ball.

Q: Your air ball?

A: Yes. Famous for my air ball. I consider myself a role player, that in the last seconds of the game—when a game is on the line and the score is close and they need someone to turn the ball over—they sent me in. If a team needed an air ball, I was the one they sent into the game. That was my contribution.

Q: So you never considered becoming a pro basketball player?

A: My height was insufficient for a serious career. But to this day, if I play in a game with kids eight years old and under, I'm a tremendously effective shot blocker.

WILLIAM COHEN

WILLIAM S. COHEN, born on August 28, 1940, in Bangor, Maine, was confirmed as secretary of defense under Bill Clinton in January 1997. He is a former Republican congressman and senator from Maine, and, among other committees, served on the Senate Armed Services and Governmental Affairs committees from 1979 to 1997. He is the author or coauthor of nine books, among them two books of poetry, *Of Sons and Seasons* and *Baker's Nickel*; two nonfiction books about government and Washington; and a thriller cowritten with Gary Hart, *The Double Man*. Secretary Cohen was a Maine all-state basketball player for Bangor High School in 1958, and a starting guard on the Bowdoin College team, graduating with a major in Latin in 1962. In 1962 he was inducted into the New England Basketball All-Star Hall of Fame, and in 1987 he was selected by the National Association of Basketball Coaches for the Silver Anniversary All-Star Team, which honored college players who later made outstanding contributions in other fields.

●　●　●

Q: You had said that you played basketball in the gym of the House of Representatives and the gym in the Senate. Do Republicans play any different from Democrats?

A: To be counterintuitive, you would think that the Democrats would like to pass and Republicans shoot. I saw no such distinctions. [*Laughter.*] They believe in local control. It's kind of a Republican philosophy of government that power should evolve to the local level and the individual should be allowed to aspire to his highest potential without the assistance of government. I think Democrats become Republicans on the basketball court.

Q: Can you tell the difference on the court between one or the other?

A: Not really.

Q: I've played in pickup games with doctors, and one can usually tell which ones are the surgeons and which ones are the pediatricians. The surgeons are much more aggressive, and argue a lot of calls, while the pediatricians say, "Oh, pardon me, did I foul you?"

A: When you're talking about politics, it's different. Everybody is out there with an equal amount of aggression.

Q: When you play, are you more concerned with defense or offense?

A: I had a friend who said to me, "Secretary of defense, never! Secretary of offense, always!" I've played a lot of offense, was so-so on defense, but it was mostly always offense.

Q: As secretary of defense, do you watch a basketball game now with the notion of a battle going on between the two teams, as in attacking a goal and defending it?

A: In team sports, there's a game plan. When you're talking military it's still a game plan, but it's a war plan. It's either how to prevent a war from taking place or what happens if you have to go to war and how you structure your forces, what happens if, what are the contingency plans, what is the escalation. All of that is not identical to a game plan, but it's training and practice. The United States has the most highly trained military force in the world and it's because it practices every day. For example, trained forces go off these carriers every day during the month of August. Out in the Persian Gulf you had the USS *Lincoln*. The temperatures with combined heat and humidity were 150 degrees in August.

They still launched 2,000 sorties, aircraft taking off and landing, in that month's time. So they are practicing every single day for the time that they have to actually get into the game. What do they do when they come up against it, they go one-on-one, air-to-air combat. What do they do when they're just going up against a target that's sending up a surface-to-air missile? So the training and practice and teamwork—if you've ever been on an aircraft carrier, you've got 6,000 people, a small city, on a single carrier and they all have something to do and it's all teamwork. So you have game plans, you have war plans, and there are lot of similarities but also lots of differences.

Q: Of the coaches that you have observed, who in your view would make a good general?

A: I think Red Auerbach, the old Celtics coach, would have made a good general. He was a tough guy. I think Pat Riley of the Miami Heat would be very inspirational and a high motivator. I'm not sure about Larry Bird. I'm not sure how his coaching style with the Indiana Pacers would translate into being a general.

Q: Too laid back?

A: Yeah. We have laid-back generals, don't misunderstand me. That's not necessarily the deciding characteristic, but they have to be in command positions. I haven't seen Bird that much, and of course he was a great player, but I'm told he's a great coach as well. It appears to me that he just kind of sits back and watches the players go through their motions.

Q: I have a sense that he was determined to be the anti–Bobby Knight coach.

A: I think to be a good general you obviously have to be aggressive, but controlled. I think that what the military looks to is a leader who has the requisite level of aggression, but the leadership characteristic of calmness as well. So they want somebody who's strong, but calm. If you get somebody who's strong and excitable, it doesn't necessarily translate into competence down the ranks.

Q: You mean, just because you might kick a chair across the basketball court, or kick your son who is playing for you in the shins when you are critical of him?

A: Whatever. I don't think those kinds of things translate well.

Q: But Auerbach's style, which was sometimes emotional, would?

A: I grew up in New England and so I followed the Celtics during the Auerbach era and I observed how he handled the talent that the team had, how he was able to mold them into a team over the years. Those teams of Bill Russell and Bob Cousy and Bill Sharman and the Jones boys and John Havlicek won I don't know how many championships in a row.

Q: I recently happend to look it up. It was eight championships in a row, and nine in eleven years.

A: Well, just taking the talent. You have a lot of talent in the NBA, but taking that talent and year after year it showed consistency, it showed the players had confidence in Auerbach and he had the ability to motivate them. There was just this kind of magnetic quality about him. I remember one time he actually had a confrontation with my father.

Q: Your father?

A: Yes. My father was a baker in Bangor, Maine, where I grew up. We were in a restaurant delivering rolls and rye bread, and Auerbach happened to be sitting in the restaurant and my father was talking to the owner of the restaurant. My father's name was Reuben. The owner said, "Reubie, are you going to the exhibition game down at the Auditorium?" The Celtics were playing somebody that night. My father said, "Nah, they're all fixed anyway." Auerbach came out of his booth and came over and just confronted my father, saying, "What the hell are you talking about, they're all fixed?" It was interesting to watch the dynamic there between the owner of the restaurant who had to make a choice whether he was going to support Auerbach or my father. Obviously, he had to support my father because my father was coming in to deliver the rolls each day, and Auerbach would be gone the next day.

But it was one of those moments where Auerbach was offended that in any of those exhibition games any team would toss in the towel.

The restaurant owner actually tried to mediate. It was not a hostile thing. It was just Auerbach saying, "We play this game straight. We fight hard." It was pretty lighthearted, actually, but it got his attention. That was impressive to me. He didn't take that. Somebody else might have ignored it. But Auerbach picked it up and wanted to challenge it. He was definitely a competitor.

Q: How have you seen the game change, and does it in any way mirror society?

A: In terms of ability, it's a different story altogether in terms of the players being bigger, faster, stronger, more graceful and athletic. That's all changed dramatically since it's become a predominantly black game.

I remember watching the Celtics in the days of Russell and Frank Ramsey and there was more discipline in the system, and I think that it's justified in looking for metaphors in basketball in terms of what society is looking for today. They like the slam dunk. When I was in college, they couldn't do it. It wasn't allowed. And I don't remember seeing it in the NBA. But you look around at society and you say, "Look who's going to the wrestling matches." And you've got Jesse the Body—or the Mind—Ventura as governor of a state. I don't want to say that basketball today is less imbued with the fundamentals because the good teams always have good fundamentals. But I believe there is an emphasis on the more violent aspects of the game rather than, say, a concentration on shooting fouls.

I think people are looking for a faster, more violent way of life. Faster cars, future shock, video games, several episodes at once on a television show. It's quick, quick, quick, and not too much staying with one program or format. I think we're seeing some of that in our athletics, but the violent aspect, I believe, has become more accepted, if not promoted. That's where you get the slam dunk, which can rattle the rim and shatter the backboards.

I think that began with Darryl Dawkins—he called himself the Chocolate Thunder. At one point, the idea of ripping down the basket became a test of strength.

I come back to poor foul shooting as a reflection of changes in our society. I look at Shaq in particular, but he's not isolated. Many of the players today spend a lot of time at the foul line, both in practice and in the game, but they don't have that dedication to foul shooting anymore. There are exceptions, and Michael Jordan is one of them. It's just jumping and leaping and driving. It's all great. It's just part of the transformation of our society, I guess, but games are won and lost on the foul line.

I've heard theories such as the size of the hand of modern-day players and they can't get a feel for the ball. But players like Jordan dispel that. I think it's just a question of their not putting enough time in. The big guys especially. I think these guys figure they're like the home run hitters. They're getting paid for making the driving, slashing moves to the basket. That's what brings people out of the stands.

But I remember a few years ago that Shaq was so bad at the line and then he got not so bad. They went out and got some instructor and for about three or four weeks he just practiced with him. He started to come around and at least made one for two, and sometimes even a little better. But when he shoots the ball he still just drives it right into the basket on a line.

Q: Is Dennis Rodman an example of what you're talking about?

A: In some ways. Rodman is part of the fringe element of society, I guess. He does in fact reflect that. When he's good, he's very good. When he's bad, in terms of his behavior, he's pretty bad. But the tattoos, the rings, all of that off-court stuff has its message on court.

Q: And Allen Iverson?

A: I assume all young people go through various stages. At one point the shaved head was a statement, now it's giving way to Kobe Bryant returning to the days of the Afro or, in his case, a semi-Afro. I think players go through cycles as far as dress code, personal appearance, and such. But I think nothing should be made more of that than Michael Jordan starting the shaved head.

Q: Was the Sprewell incident an example of anything? I had never heard of a player attacking his coach.

A: I never heard of it before, either. It could be just an isolated case with him. But look at other sports. You've got Roberto Alomar spitting in the face of the umpire. You have periodic bursts like that, but the problem is you've got bigger, stronger guys who are getting more and more competitive. With the games getting rougher and rougher, you're going to see some of that. With respect to Sprewell and his coach, you've got a lot of young players getting big money who don't have the maturity, who have gotten to that top level but may come off less than great at times. You've got Tyson in the boxing ring. I think there are more exceptions to the rule. But you do have a lot of young players who make tremendous amounts of money who have not really come up the line and sort of earned it in the good old-fashioned way. They get it up front, where before they had to really prove themselves first. One player who I think has handled it well is Kevin Garnett. He signed right out of high school at seventeen or eighteen years old and he looks like he's doing all the right things. He seems to be doing just fine.

Q: Do you still play basketball?

A: I play a bit. We've got some pretty good players here in the Pentagon. We have a young captain who played guard for the Air Force Academy and several others who can really play. Every once in a while I venture out to what they call the POAC—it's the Pentagon's athletic club. We have pickup games three-on-three or four-on-four, and I do that occasionally, when I've taken leave of my senses. I go out and embarrass myself with them. Usually I stay out at the three-point range, and there are times I even astonish myself in that I still have a little bit of shooting touch left.

Q: What do you recall about your playing days in organized basketball?

A: I played high school and college ball and I had dreams and aspirations of one day playing pro, but two things held me back: size and talent. I'm five-eleven, and weigh about 170. But I played an awful lot. I was even an instructor at Bill Sharman's basketball summer camp.

Q: What player in the pros most resembles your game?

A: Jerry West. [*Laughter.*]

Q: Jerry West?

A: I've been mistaken as a double for Jerry West, except I'm about at least four inches shorter. I used to go to the West Coast and people would say, "Mr. West, this is your parking spot." I got a kick out of it because he's put on a few pounds, but in his youth we looked pretty much alike. But in terms of on the court, how about Dolph Schayes? Does that ring a bell? I have a two-handed set shot.

Q: Few people were shooting a two-hand set shot by the late 1950s and early 1960s when you were playing. Isn't that right?

A: A two-handed set shot was obsolete in college when I was playing, but I shot it. I was able to shoot it from very far and got it off very fast. Dolph Schayes was kind of a role model for me, though he was about six-eight or six-nine. But he had a very long, high-arcing two-handed shot that was very soft. And I admired it. Schayes was a good driver as well, while I was more outside. But the shot did let me drive on occasion, and there was one time when I got benched in college because I took a half-court shot. I was going in for a fast break and I was so confident of my two-handed set shot that I drove all the way under the basket and came back out to about twenty-five feet and shot it from there.

I was showing off for the guys in the stands. They were yelling not to take the easy layup. Bowdoin College was not known for its basketball team, believe me. We were known for our hockey teams, and all the hockey fans would come over between periods of the hockey game and watch the basketball games. They'd be having a few beers in between and get in the stands and kind of cheer me on to shoot the two-handed set shot from downtown. I was showing off.

Q: Did you make the shot?

A: I did. And then the coach benched me. The coach was Bob Donham. He was a former Celtic player, very old school, very straight arrow.

Q: Who were you playing?

A: I don't remember the team, but I remember sitting on the bench afterward.

Q: Did you play much after college?

A: When I was at Boston University Law School I used to play in pickup games with Jim Loscutoff, and sometimes we'd play one-on-one.

Q: Jungle Jim Loscutoff, the old Celtic?

A: Yeah.

Q: You must have got some bruises out of that.

A: I did. I did. He used to be known as "The Hammer." When we played he was then retired from the Celtics and was coaching at Boston State College, a school which is now defunct.

Q: What did you perceive or appreciate about what separated you from Loscutoff—that is, from your experience what were the differences between an amateur and a professional?

A: He was quite big for his day—six-five, about 240 pounds. And of course size makes a big difference. But people often don't remember that early in his career, in college and in the pros, Loscutoff was a pretty good shooter. Then he had back surgery and was never quite the same after that. And in later years they'd put him in when things got rough and he had the potential to hurt people. So his talents weren't as obvious in the middle or late years as they had been earlier. But he was still a good shooter, and very strong, and he was fairly quick. Surprisingly so.

Q: I understand Bill Bradley would occasionally shoot around in the Senate gym. Did you ever play with him there?

A: I didn't play with Bradley. I always tried to get ball games with him, but we never played together. I think most pro players—most pro athletes—don't like to go out and play after they've retired from their career games. We used to have nightly games in the House and the Senate. I think most professional athletes when they hang it up don't want to go back. Number one, their skills may have gone down a bit, but number two, they want to keep the image where it was. As you get older the skills start to deteriorate and you'd rather be remembered for how good you were than how bad you are today.

Q: And sometimes the retired pro player who is back on the court in a pickup game can be a target. Red Holzman once told me that he quit playing pickup games even when he was still in the pros because guys would try to do some damage—like knocking off the reputed fast gun—even if they didn't have the skill.

A: I tried that one time with Loscutoff. I learned a lesson.

Q: What was that?

A: We were playing a game outdoors and Loscutoff was catching a pass from Lou Tsioropoulos, another former Celtic. Loscutoff had to jump to catch the ball and I stood my ground and hit him as he came down. I knocked him backward a bit, and I thought that was a major accomplishment, except that he hit me with a forearm and drove me across the macadam court. He said, "Don't ever try that again." I said, "Yes, sir!"

Q: And the lesson?

A: You don't mess with these guys.

Q: You did receive a basketball honor a few years ago, didn't you?

A: Kind of, yes. I was named by the National Association of Basketball Coaches to their silver anniversary team. But that is misleading. It was taking athletes of that year—1962—who went on to do other things. My teammates for the silver anniversary were John Havlicek, Terry Dischinger, Billy Packer, and Dave DeBusschere. It was a terrific group. I had to give the acceptance speech in front of about two thousand coaches and others who were attending the Final Four in New Orleans. I stood up and looked around at those four other guys sitting near me on the dais—all great ballplayers—and I said, "I'm honored to be here. Thank God they still believe in affirmative action in the NCAA."

EDWARD VILLELLA

DWARD JOSEPH VILLELLA, born in Bayside, New York, on October 1, 1936, is often said to be America's most celebrated male dancer. He was a principal dancer with the New York City Ballet under the direction of the celebrated George Balanchine from 1957 to 1979, where he originated many roles, among them *Tarantella* and the role of Oberon in *A Midsummer's Night Dream*. A graduate of the New York Maritime Academy, with a bachelor's degree in marine transportation, he lettered in baseball and was a collegiate welterweight boxing champion. He is a Kennedy Center honoree, and in 1997 President Clinton presented him with the National Medal of the Arts.

Mr. Villella is the only American ever to be asked to dance an encore at the Bolshoi Theater in Moscow. He danced for President Kennedy's inaugural as well as for Presidents Johnson, Nixon, and Ford. His wife, Linda, is a former Olympic figure skater. They have three children. His autobiography, *Prodigal Son: Dancing for Balanchine in a World of Pain and Magic*, was published in 1992 and reissued in 1998. Villella is currently artistic director of the Miami City Ballet.

* * *

Q: It has been said that basketball is closer to ballet than any sport. Do you agree?

A: In certain ways. The timing, the understanding of the other player's capabilities and intentions, the look in the eyes of each guy as they're anticipating what's going on. I once danced a ballet, *Pas de Deux*, by Tchaikovsky, with five different ballerinas in one week. I would look them square in the eyes when the dance started and I knew what performance was going to come out of them. I knew what my responsibility was—how strong I have to be, how gentle, how much I have to take command, that kind of thing—and I get the feeling that the basketball players are that connected and are that physically attuned as well. I think the great teams have mentally attuned their minds and eyes, the eyes of the soul, or whatever—the windows of the soul are an extenstion of all of what they are and what they're about. So at that moment it's mind-driven. For me, that's what ballet is about. It's this incredible physical activity, but it's mind-driven. Every part of it.

Q: When you were talking about these five different ballerinas in a week, what exactly did you see when you looked into their eyes? What did you expect, or anticipate?

A: It's really the approach to the steps. The language is the same. We speak the same language. Like the basketball players. It's about that individual because like the spoken word, you can say "I love you" five thousand ways—it's just how you do it.

Q: Like "I LOVE you!" or "I love you?"?

A: It's that kind of thing. But first of all you have to know that person, what she can do, what capabilities she has, how you've worked with her in the past. Watch Tim Hardaway on a fast break and he may give the ball to Alonzo Mourning differently from the way he'd give it to Dan Marjele. They've practiced together a lot. Hardaway has a knowledge of their speed, their hands, their drive. In the ballet, you know your partner because you've rehearsed with her and you've been colleagues for years and years, so you have an instinctive understanding, and that's what I was relating to the basketball guys. They have this instinctive aspect about them. They look in each other's eyes and they know the guy is going to go to the hoop and here comes this or that.

I'd look into the eyes of these dancers and I would know their personalities, but now I could know what their energy level was, what their awareness was, and so on. I would know what was about to come. For instance, Patricia McBride, delicate, sweet, lovely, and I would look in her eyes and she would say, "Okay, Eddie, let's dance—you take care of me, I'll take care of you." Melissa Hayden—I would look in her eyes and she was a wonderful, wonderful, confident, tough dancer, and she would say, "Okay, honey, here we go. You want to compete with me? Here we go."

Suzanne Farrell had one of the most alluring and magnetic qualities onstage. She had technique. There were people—just like Michael Jordan, I guess—people who could jump higher. And there were people who had stronger techniques, but not the quality that she projected onstage. She was a unique talent.

Allegra Kent actually needed some work before she went onstage because going onstage for Allegra was not as easy as it was for me. I couldn't wait to get onstage. I elbowed my way on: "Get out of my way! Give me the ball!" There were other people whose nerves and sensitivities don't give them the comfort of just plunging onto a stage.

Q: Bill Russell, the great Celtics center, was so nervous before big games that he vomited.

A: Yes, stuff like that. There are people you can't talk to for an hour or two before the performance. They just don't want you in their presence. They don't want anything around them. They've got to prepare in their own way. And that's Allegra.

Q: Tim Hardaway has been an all-star point guard for the Heat. Is there a dance in his game?

A: He's the all-around player—inside-outside, ball handler,

shooter, passer—whew, that's a ballplayer! You like a dancer like that because they can do it all for you, no matter what the moment is or the style. But I think Tim Hardaway is a little too tough in his movements, a little too thick in his stuff. It's the glide that is needed. There are people like Joe DiMaggio, who I grew up with, who have the style, who had that phenomenal gait. Yogi Berra said, "I never saw a ball fall in front of him." And the jump and anticipation on the fly ball. He had it. That was a rare talent. But in general, ballet dancers are more like wide receivers in football.

In my eyes, Scottie Pippen is like that. Lean and fluid. He has a grace, has a style, he's economical. That's the thing you look for in great dancers. There's never a wasted gesture. The timing is always available. You're never off the music. You don't hit the note, you split the note. Boom! You syncopate. You can take time and let's say this time is from here to there. Now, you subdivide the time so you can hit it right before the note, you can hit it on the note, or you can hit it after the note, depending upon how fine you want to get and what the effect is that you're seeking. We call it phrasing. You just play with the music, but then you have to understand how it was written, and why it was written that way, but also how it was choreographed and why it was choreographed that way. So it leaves you with the slightest bit of area that you can make a timing comment. That takes a long time to achieve. It's like these guys with the behind-the-back passes, the no-look passes, and all that sort of thing. You achieve that as time goes by and you get finer at anything that you do.

Q: You danced for George Balanchine for most of your professional career. And you have observed Pat Riley close up. Can you draw any parallels between the two men?

A: George Balanchine changed the face of classical dance. He did it by taking the existing vocabulary and concepts of dance and without destroying tradition invented new forms. He wasn't just a choreographer, he was an inventor in the art of ballet. He took the basic elements of dance, the turning of hips, limbs, how every position of the body is placed, and did something different, something unique with it. That's what I mean by saying that he took the tradition and vocabulary of classical dance and extended it. I feel Pat Riley has done something similar with basketball.

I'm hardly an expert on basketball; Riley's record indicates that he took existing forms and made innovations. He introduced new definitions, new offenses, and brought them to the next level. The Miami Heat as a team was nowhere until he arrived on the scene, and now they are a consistent playoff threat, and he did it in very short order. He was a winning coach with the Knicks and with the Lakers before that. That suggests that Riley really knows the game and, like Balanchine, has the ability to attract and recognize talent.

Q: Is it fair to say that, even though you were an artist, you approached the dance more as an athlete?

A: Well, there's a lot of the athlete in it. It's a physical occupation and it's like athletics except that we have other rules and regulations that guide us. Specifically, everything we do is preordained. You don't just do a hook shot. It's got to go through line and form and structure and timing and philosophical and stylistic and period and all of those things. You've got to have all of those things working for you as you are driving the athletic part of yourself. But again, it's all mind.

Q: In comparison to basketball, there are some rehearsed plays, of course, but they don't always work out the way they are designed on the chalkboard.

A: But basketball is much more improvisation than dance, certainly. It's rare that we step out and improvise, but you never know what the tempi are going to be like, what the lighting is going to be like, if the stage is slippery, if it's cold or it's too warm, if you've done a matinee.

Q: You have talked about the importance of "muscle memory" for a dancer. Would the same hold true for a basketball player?

A: Oh, it's critical. Number one, you don't want to be thinking about what you're doing while you're doing it. You have to have a conditioned reflex. So as much as your mind is driving your movements, your muscles also have to be so finely tuned and aware and in shape in that muscle memory anticipates the gestures, so you're ready for the gesture before it's on you. There's that alley-oop play in basketball when the pass to the leaping player is timed so perfectly that the catcher grabs the ball at the top of his jump and then just jams the ball down into the basket. It's one guy looking at the other and saying with his eyes, "Hey, baby, I'm going to the hoop. You start throwing." On defense, there's a similar kind of awareness. You have to know when to switch off and who's going to take who. To me it's like a corps de ballet. A corps de ballet is all the people moving without accent—that is, we are speaking a physical language without accent. Everybody on the team, as it were, understands the language absolutely perfectly.

Q: You were a welterweight boxing champion in the merchant marines in 1957. Did you find any boxers who were artistic to watch?

A: Sugar Ray Robinson was incredible. Not only did he have style, but he had a phenomenal mind. And a lot of the great athletes do. Someone like Sugar Ray Robinson didn't go out there and just throw punches. You see punchers, and you see what they do, and it's not the same. In the end, the best performers have the best minds. And if I go to watch a ballet performance, I go to watch somebody's mind, to see what they're doing with the role, with the steps, with the musicality. Big deal if somebody does a lovely technical thing. Great. But to me, that's more acrobatic than dancing, but it's the steps between. How do you get from one gesture to the other? It's the continuity of the gesture that's real dancing to me. Not just that you make the shot as a basketball player, but what are the three or four moves that you make, the two head fakes and the crossover dribble—all that kind of stuff—to get you where you want to go, where you can be most effective.

Q: How often do you go to Heat games?

A: Maybe three times a year. For me, it's just a question of time. I'm buried with what I do, like everybody else. It's a luxury to watch a game from time to time. Pat Riley and his wife invite us to watch the game on the floor. Actually, it's Pat's wife, Chris, who I'm friendly with. I had the pleasure of sitting at dinner with her when they first came to Miami, and since then we've bumped into each other at a gala or some affair, and they've been sweet to say, "Hey, listen, if you'd like to come and see the game, let us know."

Q: Have they gone to the ballet?

A: I believe she has. I doubt if he has.

Q: Have you ever seen athletes, like Herschel Walker, dance a ballet? [*Walker, when he was a Dallas Cowboys running back, danced in a Dallas ballet.*]

A: I didn't see it, but stuff like that mostly has—what can you say?—well, it attracts attention. It makes people think and so on, but for an athlete to be a ballet dancer, to be any semblance of a ballet dancer, it would take probably five years. You know, this is a physicality and an art form that has such a fine, fine challenge. Again, we move through very specific positions and that's what gives us this similarity. That's why we look alike, because we have a physical alphabet and we have a physical vocabulary. It's incumbent upon us to take alphabetic vocabulary and make it into poetry.

Q: But basketball, of course, has its own language, and yet for a ballet dancer to become a basketball player you believe it might be very difficult?

A: Oh, there's no question, but I think that ballet dancers just aren't that big. I'm about five-seven. There have been some who were six feet and over. Peter Martins of the New York City Ballet is six-two. But most aren't that tall. If you look at the last two great Russian dancers—Baryshnikov and Nureyev—both of them were about my size, or shorter.

Q: Why did they stand out?

A: Talent.

Q: [*Laughter.*] Anything else?

A: So many different things, but primarily it's understanding what you are doing theatrically, not only technically. But a basketball player doesn't have to act until he's scored three points. Then you jump up and down and dance. Or you're a football player and you score a touchdown and you dance.

Q: What do you make of those celebratory dances?

A: [*Laughs.*] First of all, I'm thrilled that they want to dance. But then I think, they could use a lesson.

Q: Do you remember the Icky Shuffle? That little dance done on the sidelines by the Cincinnati Bengals running back a few years ago, and a small chorus line of teammates?

A: He went from left foot to right foot, back to left foot and back to right foot. It was really fascinating. It was full of complication and syncopation. [*Laughs.*]

Q: It seems some of these athletes don't know what to do with themselves after they score a basket, or a touchdown. I remember Paul Brown, the coach of the Bengals at one time, talking to his team about celebrating after a touchdown. He said,

"Look, fellas, when you get into the end zone, act like you've been there before." It appears that they do more jumping than dancing. Is there a difference in jumping between a basketball player and a ballet dancer?

A: We work at it in a very technical way. We don't just jump. I'm sure the basketball players aren't just jumping. There's a lot of positioning. But I've noticed that basketball players never point their feet when they jump. If you're going to jump, you use calves, thighs, whatever. Now you're pushing away from the floor, so you use your feet to push away. You snap that ankle and point the foot for that last thrust. But most of the basketball players jump with feet parallel to the ground. They get up high—whew, they do!—but they could get up even higher. We use the foot like you use a hand. What we try to do is get the same articulation in our feet that we have in our hands. It's totally ignored in athletics.

In our field, we have two generalities in terms of jumping. One is the straight-up-and-down jump, the other is the traveling jump. We have hang time, like the basketball players, but it's a split second because we have so many other things that are going on. You've got to time it to the music and whoever is coming next to you or with you. But what you need to do, if you have that power of the jump to hang—which a few people can do—is to attack the preparation to take the time to hang in the air. You can't do a slow preparation and hang in the air and land. Now you're late. So you attack the preparation, hang in the air, and now you're on time. It's full of those little intricacies.

Q: In a conversation we had many years ago, I asked you which of the athletes you were aware of at the time would be the best ballet dancer if he had started young. And you said Gale Sayers, then the great running back for the Chicago Bears. What about today?

A: Of course, you'd have to start around ages eight and ten, as I did. I wanted spiked shoes for baseball then, and my mother got me a pair of ballet slippers. My sister was a little older than me and taking ballet lessons and my mother didn't want to leave me alone, so I accompanied them. That's how the ballet started for me. Who would I envision doing that kind of thing and succeeding in the ballet? I'd say that young kid with the Los Angeles Lakers.

Q: Kobe Bryant?

A: Yeah. What agility! And this guy is so economical in his moves, so smooth. He's got timing. He can change direction. He can go in two directions at the same time, which is another thing that ballet dancers work really hard at.

Q: Two directions at the same time?

A: When you're going backward, your body is going forward.

Q: Oh?

A: Our whole technique is based on turnout, on rotation. If you think about rotating the major joints—the ankle, knee, hip, and shoulders—and if you think that as you are rotating, you just take your right ankle and move that foot forward and rotate the ankle so the ankle is rotating forward and out. Then you take the knee and you do the same thing with the knee. The same with the hip and the shoulder. So now your whole body's focus is forward, but you've got to move backward. And then there's the turnout. The left side is rotating to the left, the right is rotating to the right, and the whole turn is to the right, but you can't bring the left side with you. The left side has to still rotate to the left to maintain the line and form and structure of the gesture. It's full of a lot of crazy stuff.

Q: Basketball players are generally considered among the best-conditioned athletes. How do you compare them to ballet dancers?

A: We prepare for an hour and a half in what we call a company class. It's an articulation of the entire technique. That prepares us to rehearse for six hours. And whenever I used to work with athletes, everybody would be nervous. I'd say, "I'm the ballet dancer, you're the athletes. I'm physical, you're physical." And then I asked how they prepare. Then they'd show me a few things. I'd say, "Well, let's see, we do that, too, but we do this and that and that and we add this." They look and say, "What? You do all that?"

Q: What about weight training? Athletes are increasingly getting into that.

A: The only weights we do is with the ladies.

Q: How so?

A: We pick them up and put them down.

Q: Are you still dancing?

A: I'm sixty-two years old. I danced for twenty-two years. I have nine broken toes, stress fractures in both legs, an operated knee no longer operable, two artificial hips, a bad back, and a bad neck.

Q: So what's preventing you from dancing?

A: The audience.

CHRIS ROCK

Chris Rock was born on February 7, 1966, in Brooklyn, New York. His weekly late-night talk show, *Chris Rock,* begun in 1994 on HBO, continues to win widespread praise for its originality, its daring, and, not least, its humor. In 1989 Rock joined the cast of *Saturday Night Live* and, until his departure in 1993, emerged as one of its stars. His 1997 book, *Rock This,* was a bestseller. A critic for the *New York Times* decribed Chris Rock as "probably the funniest and smartest comedian working today."

Rock's 1996 HBO comedy special, *Bring the Pain,* won an Emmy Award, and he followed that most recently with the HBO comedy special *Chris Rock: Bigger and Blacker.* He has appeared in several movies, including *Dogma* with Ben Affleck and Matt Damon and *Lethal Weapon 4.* Rock also was the guiding developer for *The Illtop Journal,* a quarterly humor magazine based at Howard University and modeled after the *Harvard Lampoon,* which, he said he hopes will serve as a training ground for young black comedy writers.

* * *

Q: Did you play basketball very much when you were growing up?

A: Very little. I was in the same homeroom class as Pearl Washington, at Boys High in Brooklyn. He kind of ran the school. He was like the principal. He came in when he wanted to. He left when he felt like it. He was Pearl. The best basketball player I've ever seen was Pearl Washington in high school. I once saw Pearl Washington shake a whole school to the ground. He made five guys fall down. He did a move that made each one of them fall down and then went in for the easy layup. But his weight was a problem. And his work ethic.

Q: He didn't practice too much?

A: He didn't have to. College came easy to him. It came easy until he got to the pros.

Q: He was an outstanding college player at Syracuse, and he was a number one draft pick for New Jersey, but he didn't quite make it in the pros.

A: It's weird. Who would have ever thought Mark Jackson would be a better pro than Pearl Washington? They were guards in the New York area at around the same time—Pearl from Brooklyn, Mark from Queens. Pearl was a year ahead of Mark in school and he was clearly the bigger star. Mark had to work harder at it. It came a lot easier to Pearl. Mark is still a terrific player for the Pacers, and he's in his what, tenth or eleventh season in the NBA. Pearl played three seasons and was gone.

Q: Are there comedians who you could equate with that? Were there guys as funny as you?

A: Oh, they're all funnier than me.

Q: But were there guys who didn't have the professionalism or the perseverance or even the confidence that you had in order to rise?

A: I'm more in the Mark Jackson vein. I'm a Mark Jackson comedian. I don't really do a lot of things. What's a good quality for a comedian—to do a bunch of voices? I can't do a bunch of voices, to mimic or do all those dialects. That's a great quality for a comedian. I don't possess that thing. I can't do impressions. That's another great thing for comedians of today's era. I don't do that. So you do what you can do. I know how to write jokes, so I just write and write, write, write and make up for my short-comings.

Q: And when you watch Mark Jackson, what do you see?

A: Mark Jackson's not the fastest player. He's not the best defensive player, but he sees the whole court. He sees the court probably better than anybody in the game. And he's not the best shooter, but when it's time to shoot his shot, it's the most funda-mental shot you're going to see. And if the guy guarding him is smaller than he is, he's going to take him to the basket and post him up. He's one of the smartest players there is.

Q: When you watch a Latrell Sprewell or Allen Iverson or Chris Webber or Jalen Rose, who are said to be players in the so-called hip-hop generation, can you relate to them? Now, Mark Jackson somehow is not hip-hop—maybe a little too old for that designation—but he has done some funny gyrations on the court, a shimmy when he's made a good pass, or an airplane motion when he's scored on a good drive.

A: He's a little over the top on occasion. A little bit. Who do I identify with? I identify with Chris Mullin. I had him on my show. He's thirty-three years old. I'm thirty-three, so I'm the same age as Mullin and Jackson and those guys.

Q: But a lot of white people don't necessarily understand the hairstyles, for example, of Sprewell and Iverson, the cornrows and that kind of thing.

A: Whoever the best player is pretty much dictates everything.

Q: But what about from a culture standpoint? When you see the players, what do you look at as a young black man? What do you see in the Sprewells, and maybe the Tim Duncans and the Grant Hills? What are your thoughts on the range of these people and the cultures?

A: I don't know. It's not quite a question.

Q: Well, it ended in a question mark.

A: It ended with a question mark, but I don't know what to say to that.

Q: Can you see culture and background in the way these people—any of them—play the game?

A: I see culture in the style, in the baggy shorts now and the cornrows, but it's always been that way. It's the street game.

Q: But what about the way, say, Iverson badmouths his coach, Larry Brown, in Philadelphia?

A: Iverson was taken out of games. He wants his time. We're in the age of more media. Michael Jordan badmouthed Phil Jackson, too. Do you think Michael Jordan liked coming out of games?

Q: Can basketball be funny? What's material in basketball for you?

A: I always say that the most dangerous play in basketball is the open white man. It's because there is nothing more surefire, nothing makes me scream louder—Reggie Miller when he's open, too, but generally a white guy open behind the arc is frightening. Like Chris Mullin. The ball's going in, he's knocking it down.

Q: But not Chris Dudley.

A: Chris Dudley tries to wipe all that away. I've got to hand it to him.

Q: Chris Dudley can hardly make a free throw.

A: I've got to hand it to him for not following stereotypes.

Q: What about Jayson Williams of the Nets?

A: He's a really funny guy. He's got a lot of charisma. One of the funnier characters in the league. We went out during the lockout and tried to raise money for the hungry NBA players. We got some pretty funny responses. It was pretty much, No. No one gave us anything. But we did piss off some players. Everyone was pissed off.

Q: You do comic riffs—you start with an idea and it seems you improvise as you go along. Do you see that in basketball? Can you relate to that in some way?

A: Some guys improvise. It's good when you're in trouble. But the best ad lib is the one you thought of the day before.

Q: So you're prepared.

A: I'm very prepared. Coaching is everything. The NBA is very much like college. It's really a coach's league. Everybody thinks it's a player's league, but you can't judge anybody who hasn't been in a decent system. You really can't. Look at Milwaukee. It's the same team as the year before, and they didn't make the playoffs the year before. New coach, and they're in the playoffs. George Karl implemented a system—much better defense—and now they know how to play. Philadelphia the same thing. And

Sacramento. My God! I mean, there's a few of them. On the other side, look at the Lakers. As good as they are, there is no system there. The teams that go the farthest are teams. It's a nine- or ten-guy effort. And when you look at the NBA's final four, they're all teams: Indiana, Portland, San Antonio, the Knicks. There's not a big overwhelming star. Nobody is really—who's the best guy in the playoffs? You can't even say. Tim Duncan? Reggie Miller? Latrell Sprewell? Isaiah Rider? They're all playing great ball, but so are their teams.

Q: What about Shaquille O'Neal? Why can't he win?

A: Shaq is probably the most dominating player in the game. He's really unstoppable, though he's got to work on his free throws. But he hasn't won because he's only been on one team so far. And that's Orlando. The Lakers haven't been a real team, just a bunch of talented individuals. The Lakers are like a weird comic book, where Superman and Iron Man team up. It's not real. It's a ratings thing. It's just a thing to sell more comic books that week. Superman and Iron Man have a fight. But they don't really fight. The Lakers have all these stars, they've got Shaq and Kobe Bryant and Glen Rice and they're all going in opposite directions. The Lakers are no team right now. They've got no point guard. I saw Magic Johnson the other night and told him, "There's no doubt in my mind you're better than Derek Harper right now." He didn't say anything, he just nodded. Magic, who hasn't played in whatever. He's better than Harper and what's the other guy—Fisher.

Q: The Rodman experiment failed them, too.

A: Rodman is just sad, man. The greatest rebounder in the history of the game. Hall of Famer. Yeah, he's not Russell or Chamberlain, but he's shorter than those guys. I think Allen Iverson is the best player in the game. You can say Shaq, but he's a center. Playing center is like hitting home runs from second base. A guard is always the best player in the game, a guard or a forward. Rodman, I don't know. He needs a father. When he had Chuck Daly he was fine. Now it's really sad, and he's old. He's not twenty-eight. He's what, thirty-six or thirty-seven? He's just a weird guy. He really got caught up in this whole thing. This whole show business. He got caught up in the new NBA.

Q: He considered himself an entertainer above being a basketball player?

A: They are entertainers. They're also basketball players. But Rodman is not playing not so much because of his behavior, but because he's old. The twenty-eight-year-old Rodman would be playing right now, and someone would put up with it. He wasn't in the best shape and he wasn't playing good, not because of the way he was acting.

Q: Did his act ever amuse you?

A: No. I loved him on the court. He was the best. The off-court stuff, I never really got it. When the Bulls beat Utah in the playoffs in '98, I thought he was the dominant player. He was like Lawrence Taylor. I've never seen a guy dominate so much without scoring. He was really the MVP of the series. But they'd never give it to him. But it's because of someone like Rodman that the NBA thrives and baseball dies—or dwindles. The NBA knows how to market Dennis Rodman, and basketball pretty much judges people on what they do on the court. If you commit a crime off the court, yes, that is definitely punishable. But basketball is a growing sport where other sports have leveled off. And what happened to Sprewell is an example of how the NBA handled a bad situation. You can't choke your boss. But you did your time, and he didn't play for a year. And he didn't get paid. Cost him something like seven million dollars. He paid his debt to society more than the average person would. It's safe to say somebody else would have probably got probation. You could go to jail, but it's a first offense. But you wouldn't lose seven million dollars.

Q: The other side of players like Iverson and Sprewell seems to be someone like Tim Duncan, who stayed in college four years and has never had any problems regarding the law or discipline.

A: It's just a different guy. People get mad about guys coming out of college before finishing four years. That's all racist. It's a big racist attitude. People quit school every day. No one gets mad at baseball players for not going to college. Or tennis players. John McEnroe went to Stanford for one year before turning pro. Nobody gets mad at golfers. Tiger Woods quit college after one year. He went to play with white guys. If he was going to play basketball with black men, people would have lost their minds. The whole country has a problem with young black men having fun and enjoying themselves. Jayson Williams is a guy who enjoys himself. He's a good guy, a good family man, funny. He talks to people and he appreciates what he's got.

Q: What about the white players? You mentioned Chris Mullin. What about the other white guy on the Dream Team, John Stockton?

A: Stockton's got a great game. It's a dirty game. Nobody throws more elbows. Nobody holds more shorts. But he's probably the best clutch shooter in the game.

Q: Do players make too much money?

A: Nobody makes too much money. The players are getting paid a lot of money, true. But the fewer amount of people who can do what you do, the more money you make. Point blank.

Q: And comedians, too?

A: If you can do what a lot of people can't do and want to do—or want to see you do. Should a teacher make more money than Charles Barkley? Probably. Charles Barkley does entertain millions of people, and a teacher has about thirty kids in her class. My little brother Andre, who drives a truck and hasn't been in school, he could teach tomorrow. He could get a teaching license. But he couldn't play in the NBA.

Q: What about Barkley? What about when he throws someone through a window, as he did when a guy was supposedly harrassing him in a bar?

A: That's his life. Here's the thing. They all get punished for it, so it's not really a bad thing. It's not like a bad message to kids or anything. They all get punished for bad acts or for breaking the rules or the law. Darryl Strawberry hits the pipe and he's out of the game. He gets punished. Kids see this. And I've never understood this "role model" business. Athletes aren't role models. Do you know what a real role model is? It's someone you'll follow when he fucks up. No one has ever worshiped a football player, basketball player, baseball player that sucked. If Charles Barkley doesn't play good, kids don't like him. If your parents are fucked up, you still like them. You give your parents like eight hundred chances. Your parents can beat you, and you still love them. That's a real role model. The kids will turn their back on Michael Jordan or anybody at the drop of a hat. No one is talking about Michael Jordan right now. What happened to Michael Jordan? He's playing golf. No one is screaming, "Michael, Michael!" Everybody is on to the new guy.

Q: What does that tell you about Michael, or people?

A: People let their entertainers entertain them, and when it's over, it's over. They move on. It's not like everybody makes it out to be. They're not the big role models that they're made out to be. What Jordan could teach us is that you have to work hard to succeed. Work hard and be competitive. That's the lesson we can get from Michael Jordan. But if Michael Jordan got on crack tomorrow, would everybody get on crack? No! Everybody with a

Jordan jersey would not go smoke the pipe. Most people would actually get rid of their Jordan jerseys.

Q: Did you ever have a Jordan jersey?

A: No. Pearl Washington, Syracuse, yeah.

Q: How tall are you?

A: I'm five-eleven. About 140 pounds. I never really played much basketball, but I love it. And I follow it. It's fascinating. Like watching Patrick Ewing in a diminished role with the Knicks although he didn't volunteer for it. But injuries and age caught up to him, the same as it has for David Robinson. And the Knicks— and the Spurs, probably, too—are a better team for it. We still need Patrick, though, people are nuts who say we don't.

Q: Who was your favorite player?

A: It would have to be Pearl in high school, but as far as the NBA, I loved Mo Cheeks. Me and my brother used to call him Mo Cheeks the Exploiter. He would just really exploit the defense. He had game, man. He was smart and quick and he just carried himself so cool. He was like one of the coolest players. Dominique Wilkins was fun to watch, too. Jordan goes without saying. I like Chris Webber's game. He's kind of straightened out his act, on and off the court. He's a young guy with tons of money. But he's growing up. Money changes everybody, but it changes people around them more than it changes them. If you hit the lottery, you're the same guy, but now everybody wants some money.

Q: Has that happened to you?

A: Yeah. Everybody asks in their own way and everybody needs whatever. It goes with the turf. Some people—some players—handle it better than others. The ones from stable families handle it better than the ones that don't, pretty much.

Q: That's what I asked you originally. When you look at some players, can you tell from their game or their behavior how they grew up, what the culture or even family background might have been like?

A: I can't tell. Maybe others can, but I can't.

Q: What about Magic and Bird? They were two guys from what might be perceived as very different backgrounds—black and white. And two guys who both with the similarity of playing a strong team game, both mature players even in their very first season in the NBA.

A: I think Magic is my favorite player ever. Michael Jordan can score the most. If you need forty points, nobody can get it quicker than Michael Jordan, but nobody can get you two points quicker than Magic Johnson. We need two. Nobody, not even Michael. Magic can just get two points via assists, via shot, via getting to the line. And nobody stops a run better than Magic. Bird was great, too. For a three-year period Bird didn't miss a shot. Everything he shot went in the basket. He was incredible.

Q: Is it hard sometimes for black guys to give white guys credit in basketball because they think it's their game in some way?

A: No, I don't think so. And if there are some who do, I don't know why they should. Everybody knows Bird was incredible. And Stockton—he even had more assists in his career than Magic, broke Magic's record. I enjoy all the parts of basketball. I even love missed dunks.

Q: Missed dunks?

A: Yeah. The other night I saw three of 'em. Guys go up to stuff and the ball hits the back rim and bounces away. Those are really great. Then you see the look on the guy's face who missed it. Shock and embarrassment. It's like they've slipped on a banana peel. I love this game.

ERICA JONG

ERICA JONG published her first book, a collection of her poems, *Fruits and Vegetables*, in 1971. Her novel, *Fear of Flying*, published in 1973, was a huge best-seller. The sexual candor of the book made her a provocative as well as controversial figure. Among her several other books was a highly acclaimed 1994 memoir, *Fear at Fifty*. Her most recent book, *What Women Want*, was published in 1998. She was born Erica Mann in New York City in 1942.

● ● ●

Q: Does basketball have sex appeal?

A: Absolutely. There is something very erotic about basketball. I've been to numerous games over the years, mostly Knick games at Madison Square Garden, and from the first time I saw a game I was struck by the bodies of these beautiful young black men, wearing almost nothing, with wonderful long muscular legs and great arms. They have a style and a swagger, and they know they're hot. That's part of the appeal, I think, about going to the Garden. I mean, for a woman. It's sexy to see these gorgeous young hunks jumping around for your benefit. I don't think Woody Allen would say that. But I think most women would. And I say beautiful black men because I see basketball as a game dominated by African-Americans in our country, at least on the highest levels.

And I think there is something really visceral about getting that ball in the basket. It makes you feel good. I'm sure hitting the tennis ball well, which I've never done, makes you feel good. But there's something very satisfying about that ball going through that hole. I wouldn't go so far as to say it recreates the sexual experience. I wouldn't make it so literal because I think that would wreck the whole metaphor.

But I liked throwing the ball through the hoop myself. Basketball has been important to me because it's always been important to my father. When I was a teenager, even younger, and living on the Upper West Side of Manhattan on Seventy-seventh Street, my father would take me to the park and teach me to shoot baskets. My father was a musician, a drummer in the 1930s and a songwriter who published songs. Then he went into the gift business. But he remains a musician at heart, and a basketball player. He's eighty-seven years old now and he still lives on the West Side. And he still shoots baskets when there's a hoop. He's a great athlete. He's a jogger and a treadmill person, and he stands on his head and he shoots baskets given half a chance.

I'm sure my interest in basketball began because of my father, my Oedipal connection to basketball—and by that I mean in some kind of fantasy way, not in any kind of reality. But in a way that you admire the parent of the opposite sex and are a little bit in love with the parent, which is part of being a healthy kid. My relationship with my father was always healthy.

So I've always watched basketball with great interest. And when I started going to games, I was shocked. The players were so tall they seemed miraculous to me. But beyond that, there is just something very appealing about the game, very erotic. All the things we do that turn us on have aspects of sexuality, maybe not in an overt way. Like writing. Like playing tennis. Anything that lets you go into the flow state where time is suspended and where you become completely absorbed in the activity, whether it's writing or playing a sport, or playing cards or painting a watercolor or writing a poem, time gets suspended, you live for the act of doing it itself. That's why sports relax people, because it takes them out of time and it takes them out of their daily worries and they're in a place where the brain waves are literally different in that state.

Did you ever read the book called *Flow?*

Q: *Flow?* No.

A: *Flow: The Psychology of Optimal Experience*, by the psychologist Mihaly Csikszentmihaly. He describes flow as the experience in which time seems suspended. You don't know how much time goes by. You feel totally complete and satisfied in yourself. Your brain waves are actually different than they are at other times. And all creative people go into that state when they're working—composing music, painting, writing, scientists when they're doing an experiment, and athletes when they are performing.

Q: In basketball, the term used to describe that kind of incandenscent state is "zone." Like, "I was in a zone."

A: Well, that's exactly what I'm talking about. And I guess one goes into that state in sex also. In that sense, it's familiar. It's similar because it's a suspension of time.

And there is a kind of rhythm to the activity when you're in a suspension of time. Which is why basketball is a pleasure to watch. When you're watching a good basketball game you could be watching the ballet or a modern dance. The pleasures are similar. You see people who have incredible skill and underneath that skill there is tremendous talent, which starts out being anatomical. They're just physically different from us. They're taller, they're more agile, more graceful. And they have a way of moving that's part skill and part talent.

I can't tell you that I watched one player more closely than another, but I did meet Wilt Chamberlain once. He probably was the sexiest man I ever met. We were both guests on a morning television talk show—I believe it was the *Today* show. He was not playing basketball at the time, but I will tell you a memory of Wilt Chamberlain that astonished me.

We were seated and talking in a very animated way. And then we stood up and his belt buckle was about parallel to my eyeballs. I thought, This is a different creature. I'm short, about five-three, and I often feel like a midget. But never more so than when I stood with Wilt Chamberlain. It's very funny when you're sitting next to somebody and your eyes are at the same level and then suddenly they stand up, and you realize he's twice as tall as you. How tall is he, anyway?

Q: He said he was seven-one, but most people around basketball believe he was about seven-three.

A: Because seven-one is more acceptable? He is an amazing physical specimen. But I think one reason I admire athletes so much is that I'm not one. I work out and I swim and I lift weights, but I'm not a natural athlete. I don't have that grace. I do it because I have to do it. I'm so in awe of people who have that talent, that body talent to be graceful and powerful. It's like another life that I never lived, and I'm in awe of it.

Q: You may recall that a few years ago Wilt published a memoir in which he confessed to having gone to bed with twenty thousand women.

A: Did he have a clicker on his belt?

Q: [*Laughter.*] I don't know.

A: How was he able to figure it out?

Q: I'm not sure, but I do know that that number, divided into the days of puberty and beyond until the publication date of the book came to about a woman and a half a day.

A: That's understandable—but I wasn't one of them.

Q: Why is it understandable?

A: Because he was so charming and self-possessed. Tremendous confidence. Bodily confidence. And that's very appealing, just as very, very beautiful people are very appealing because they seem beyond—they seem almost godlike. And it's not very hard for gorgeous athletes to get women, you may have noticed. Especially gorgeous, rich, successful athletes. I mean, look, fat little Jewish guys can get women if they have billions of dollars.

Q: Fat little rich Greek guys, too, and . . .

A: Right—Mick Jagger is not even so gorgeous anymore and women want to sleep with him because he's a famous rock star. So I don't think it's unbelievable that Wilt could have slept with so many women. But I do find it amusing that he should know the number. I think that when you're in the flow state, you shouldn't be thinking about statistics. [*Laughter.*] You should be a little more carried away than that.

Imagine. Wilt says, "You are number two thousand and one. Congratulations." But I would be a little wary of sleeping with such a person. I would immediately think, STDs. Sexually transmitted diseases. Wouldn't you?

Q: I don't think Wilt would have been interested in me. But someone said that after reading about his number of sexual liaisons it is finally understandable why he was such a poor free throw shooter: He never had time to practice.

A: But I guess his activities just go with being an athlete and the exuberance of it. But it's not the kind of person I would wind up with. Ever. I've always hung out with writers and intellectuals, but there's another part of me that wishes it hadn't been so.

Q: Did you ever meet any other basketball players?

A: I met Bill Bradley, but I met him as a politician, when he was senator from New Jersey. I never met him when he played for the Knicks. I think he's a very interesting character and an interesting man. He seems very modest and very honest and sort of straight. The times I've run into him I've enjoyed talking to him.

Q: Did he have the sex appeal that Wilt had? I should say, Did he have sex appeal?

A: People who are running for office don't look sexy to me. It's because they're in another state. I think there is nothing more awful than being a candidate. It's brutalizing. You get no sleep, you travel, you speak all the time, you always have laryngitis. I can't think of anything more awful. And you're always begging for money. Some people I know thrive on it. But when they're in their political mode and they're busy giving their speech to you about why you should work for their campaign or elect them or whatever, there's something so earnest about it. I don't find that sexy.

Q: You didn't meet Wilt as a basketball player, either. He was already retired. Right?

A: But he was an incredibly magnetic person. I could see why people would fall down dead for him.

Q: Maybe he should have run for president.

A: [*Laughter.*] I think that he wouldn't have been able to do it because I think we're going to want more chaste people in office in coming years. I think it's going to be tough. I think people are going to want politicans who don't have any history. Who are more neuter. And I don't think the country is ready for someone telling them, "Look, I'm an honest politician, I slept with twenty thousand women." No, I think that would not go in 2000. I think the country is in another place.

FRANK STELLA

FRANK STELLA, born May 12, 1936, in Malden, Massachusetts, is one of the premier artists of the twentieth century. His work, primarily abstract art both on canvas and in what is described as the plastic, or figurative, arts, has been exhibited or is in nearly every major art museum in the world, from New York to Paris to Tokyo. In the book that introduced his work to an exhibit of his at the Museum of Modern Art in the late 1980s, *Frank Stella 1970–1987*, there appeared this quote by him:

> I like to make paintings, and I work at that. I don't consider myself that different from anybody else. So I live in the real world and while I'm living in it, I'll be more or less like other people. At some points I'm going to cross common experiences. Some of them are going to stick and become a little bit peculiarly mine. . . . I don't worry about that. I worry about the paintings . . . the drive to make the art.

Stella is an alumnus of Princeton University, and has lectured at Yale, Cornell, and Brandeis. He has been a basketball fan for much of his life.

* * *

Q: Have you had a rooting interest in any basketball team?

A: I come from the greater Boston area, and came to New York in my twenties, and I always hated all the New York teams.

The most fun I've had in basketball was rooting for the Celtics against the Knicks. I was pretty involved in their championships. I did pick up interest in the Knicks when Bill Bradley joined the team, because I had gone to Princeton, too, though several years before he did. And when I had a knee operation the Knick trainer at the time, Danny Whelan, helped rehabilitate my knee. So I hung around, and got to know a few of the Knicks a little bit. And Bradley would occasionally get me tickets. But I used to sit in the Knick seats and root for the Celtics.

Q: Didn't you feel a little guilty?

A: Maybe a little. But when you're a Celtic fan, well, that speaks for itself. But at one point I almost actually rooted for the Knicks. My favorite moment with them was that spin move of Earl the Pearl's. It was so much fun to watch him do it. A beautiful kind of chromatic blur.

Q: I'm sure that everyone sees a basketball game differently. I once asked Roy Lichtenstein about watching sports, and he told me that he wasn't much of a fan but that he liked watching football on television because of the "baroque entanglements." And I'm sure every artist sees a game differently. What do you see when you watch a basketball game?

A: I played sports—I played lacrosse and I wrestled—so I know the games. I know what games are about. I see the whole thing, but I like the real beauty of it. I like it at the highest level because you know they're at the edge, and it's an exciting feeling to know that that's as far as you can go with it. You can't do it any better than the way they're doing it. And the pressure. You know, my favorite thing about basketball is how great the players are today. But the game has changed to a degree. I was talking with Dave DeBusschere, who's been retired as a player for the Knicks for some twenty-five years, and I said that the players today really have all the moves, and sweep by defenders. DeBusschere said,

"Yeah, they're faster and they go by, but if they have to put the ball on the floor, they wouldn't go by me." [*Laughter.*] He was saying that they don't dribble anymore. They take so many steps and it's not called today. It's a different game.

The game's changed a lot, and I'm not knocking that. They are great athletes, but it was a great game before, too.

Q: When you talked about the beauty of the game, from the standpoint of an artist, where do you see the beauty? Can you compare it to paintings or sculpture or anything else?

A: Yes. I can compare it, it's not hard. It may sound fatuous in a way, but it's the same thing. The beauty is in the coordination and getting it all together. The other beauty of it is that people don't believe it's true in painting or making art, but it is true. There are those moments when you really have to do it, and if you worry about it too much it's too late. That's the biggest thing.

Q: Can you give me an example of that? You don't mean something like you're on a deadline, do you?

A: No, no. It's not a question of deadline. It's a question of making it work. In other words, if a painting has to go, it has to go. It has to move. It has to finally go to the basket. It can't stay out there on the perimeter and get ready and do this and that and dribble. It's got the twenty-four-second clock, too. You've got to take it home. It's really true. All of the really best art does that. You feel engaged and you feel it's doing it. It's taking it with you and it's going somewhere, to the moment where you apprehend. I think the moment that you apprehend the art is very similar to the moment when you're excited. The ball is either going to go down and they're going to make the play or it's not going to happen.

There is a famous teacher and artist, Hans Hofmann. He did a series of paintings that he called Magnum Opus. He did them in his eighties, which makes them even more beautiful. They are the most direct, straightforward paintings that you can imagine. It's in your face. They are all like slamming the ball into the hoop. He does this in the paintings in what amounts to a gesture. He paints maybe a big brush stroke on the canvas and then he takes a huge chunk of paint and makes it into a slab and lays it right on top. He does this in several places and they are thick in pastel paints. He's into moving paint that's already on there—sort of wet paint. So it's paint into paint and moving fast. It's so fresh and vibrant.

There are Picassos that do that, and you can see it in Michelangelo in the way the sculptures are so present. You can see it in a lot of religious paintings in which the martyr—the hero—is sort of thrust forward and projecting through the painting. There is a famous Caravaggio painting in which the head of Holofernes is held right out in your face. It's the same way that Michael Jordan used to hold the ball out in front of him, palming the ball, and tantalizing his defender.

Q: That's quite an image.

A: But it's really true. And that has all the power of the players, and maybe even more. Now I would say that that's the best basketball painting, *Judith and Holofernes.* [*Laughter.*] It's in the Palazzo Barberini in Rome.

Q: Is it also true that in painting, like basketball, rhythm is important?

A: I think rhythm is the underlying aspect of art as well. A painting doesn't work unless your basic rhythm is there. And basketball is like tennis in this regard—I still play some tennis. If you don't have a stroke, it doesn't really matter how tricky you are or what spectacular shots you make on occasion. It's the mechanics of the strokes that allow you to stay out there, the consistency, and keep going and producing the better shot. Rembrandt's *The Night Watch* is an example. You could say that he really orchestrates what's happening on the court. There's the whole court, the full-court press, and everybody, the whole ensemble, is present and taking their positions and are ready to go. And looking at it you apprehend that everyone and everything is in the right place—the shapes, the colors, the people, the banners, the effect of light and dark. That's all rhythm.

Q: What about the colors for you at a basketball game? What do you take in?

A: I absorb it. I'm supposed to see everything, but in actuality in the games the excitement carries the color and you actually *feel* the color more than you actually see it. It forces the color into your body in a way.

Q: You take it all in in your pores? When you are painting or constructing a piece of art, is that the way you work, as well?

A: I think you absorb it and it comes out in your gesture later on. Your interpretation of the action and what is or was is programmed in some way into your own body. It comes out in some kind of unconscious way, or an un-self-conscious way, if not unconscious.

Q: In basketball there is both a conscious and unconscious—or un-self-conscious—level while in the act. I remember Earl Monroe telling me once that one of his pleasures is doing something on the court he never did before, and never knew he could do.

A: But you have to practice your skills to such a degree that those kinds of wonderful things can come out of your talent and experience. My father was a surgeon. One time when I was a kid I saw that he had left his glasses at home. When he returned that evening I said, "Dad, what did you do without your glasses? You had an operation." He said, "Frank, if you have to look, you shouldn't be doing it." Sometimes in basketball, if you have to look, it's too late to make the pass. Usually they look the other way when they make a pass. Magic Johnson was great at that, and John Stockton. You have to know what you're doing and where everybody is. It's being in control of your art, or craft.

Q: What are you working on now?

A: I'm working on something that involves shapes that I'm arranging near each other and the necessity of finding their relationship to each other. A lot of the forms I work on are woven. I was thinking that it goes back all the way back to the weave, the style of offense that Princeton used to use. But you move the shapes, as well as place them next to each other. They go in front and behind each other, as well as relate to each other laterally and vertically. So the weaving sometimes—the game is boring when they don't cross over, when they don't interrelate. If they are too static, the game doesn't have a flow and the motion doesn't have a weave.

Q: You said you were a fan of the old Celtic teams, in which Bill Russell was the centerpiece, literally and figuratively. As you know, he played thirteen seasons and the Celtics won eleven championships in that time. In your view, was Russell an artist?

A: He was. I don't know how he could have been so great. I think Russell is the most enigmatic player that I ever saw because you never really could tell how smart he was, but you had the feeling that in the end—and though he hid it—that he was always a little bit smarter on the court than everyone he played against. He never seemed to have a problem reading anybody. Never. Nobody ever fooled him. He had the bigger picture in his mind the whole time. He never got bogged down in the details. He was trying to make a big statement all the time, and in that game the big statement is winning. And he really controlled the flow, controlled the game with his rebounding and shot blocking—and threats of shot blocking—and made the game go his way. It was his game.

Q: Could you compare some painter or sculptor—some great artist—to Russell as far as his techniques or his mentality was concerned?

A: Matisse.

Q: Matisse? How so?

A: Because Matisse had that same kind of fluid thing controlling with the big gesture all the time. He had a lot of reach and he had a broad stretch—a big stretch—across the horizon of art, as it were. Russell brought to the game this kind of compressed and limited skill, but he made it a bigger game. He gave it a sense of panorama and almost a spectacle, but he had a big gesture in a really tight, confined game.

Q: What about Bill Bradley? Does he remind you of any painter?

A: If I were to make a comparison between Bradley's style of play and an artist, I'd pick Léger. Workmanlike but gifted.

Q: As I recall, Fernand Léger did abstract paintings of revolving things like pipes, wheels, tubes. He was an industrial painter.

A: Bradley was an industrial player. I don't buy the part that says Bradley wasn't as talented as most of the other players, that he stayed in the league because of his smarts. You know, Ivy League. But he really did seat-of-the-pants playing. He was always in the thick of it. And he could play rough if he had to. Elbows, hips, that kind of thing. While he wasn't as gifted as some, he was nowhere near the bottom half of the talent in the league. There were a lot of guys who looked more coordinated and were flashier, but they were nowhere near as talented. If you remember in that tournament in college at Madison Square Garden when he went up against Cazzie Russell, who was thought to be the best player in country, and Cazzie didn't prove to be a better athlete than Bradley.

Q: And Michael Jordan? If he were an artist, who might he be?

A: I'd have to say he was the Jackson Pollack of the game. He dominates and has the swooping gesture. He really has the kind of ways that say, "That's it! That's what I want to do." Pollack had that sense of liberation, that sense of the body and the gesture being together that everybody strives for. Everyone recognizes it as the ultimate gesture. Pollock had his critics, to be sure. A lot of it was patronizing, things like "Jack the Dripper." But what made his art great was his gesture, his speed, his freedom, that looping and so-called swirls of spilling the paint to become a painting. For me, Jordan had those kinds of moves.

Q: If the Knicks—or any team that didn't seem to be together as a team—were a piece of art that you were working on, what would you do to make it work?

A: I'm not that interested in the current Knicks. What can you identify with? They change the players every two weeks. It's really pretty much chaotic.
But to make it work, you take the parts, you dig them in, and you stir them around and try to get them going together. You've got to basically lean into it, but don't give up. You've got to find something to build around—I can't find a player on their team that you can build around. But I've had paintings that I was working on that weren't coming together. Happens all the time. There are paintings I'm working on now. I call them easel paintings, but actually they are more like sculptures. They are big physical pieces, but they are also like paintings. In one case, it was going along, and

it wasn't terrible, but it really was going nowhere. And there was one thing sticking out of the piece, a piece of stainless steel. And so I was walking around and suddenly I found another piece and I put that piece on top of the piece which was sticking out and made it stick out even more! It gave the piece a balance, a coherence, a rhythm. So taking something that was problematical and exaggerating it, that pulled it together and made it work.

Q: I once read a small book by Winston Churchill called *Painting as a Pastime*. And one of the things that struck me in the book was his description of how he started painting. He began with a little dot on the canvas. A woman friend came by, who was a painter, and saw what he had done and said something like, "No, you've got to have the big stroke, this kind of thing." And she took his brush and made a big, slashing stroke. She said, "Don't be afraid of the canvas." It was bolder than he had done, and, in her opinion, better.

A: I think bolder is okay, but it's not just bold. Bold is a bold gesture, but this gesture comes from something that's there and taking it to a more extreme. I mean, really exaggerating or reinforcing what's already there. Instead of eliminating it or covering it up in the piece of art I had just mentioned, I went with it.

Q: And Churchill also said that before he began painting he never noticed the shadows on buildings. Are artists' perceptions when observing anything, including a basketball game, more acute?

A: They are more acute about certain things, but think about all the things artists don't see that other people see. Like microbes. Or racing drivers, to take another kind of athlete, see far ahead in space as they're driving. But the acuteness of an artist's perception is seeing something in such a way that you feel it and incorporate it into your sensory perception and then finally your body mechanics, in handling the paintbrush or construction of a sculpture. If you get it ingrained in your body language, then you're on your way. Then you know it.

Q: If you could make one photograph or painting of one thing that you've seen in a game, if there was one moment that you just wanted to stop in time, some beautiful moment, some beautiful gesture, what would it be?

A: I like sitting down on the floor at a basketball game and you're right there when a player puts the ball down on the floor and he goes. Sometimes you don't know where he's going to go. It looks like he's going to the basket but sometimes he goes into a tangle of arms and legs and bodies and you don't even see the pass, but another player is slamming the ball down into the basket. It's a beautiful mystery. Reminds me of art.

KARY MULLIS

KARY BANKS MULLIS won the Nobel Prize for chemistry in 1993, for his discovery of polymerase chain reaction (PCR), which redefined the study of DNA and genetics.

He was born on December 28, 1944, in Lenoir, North Carolina, went to Dreher High School in Columbia, South Carolina, and the Georgia Institute of Technology, and received a Ph.D. from the University of California at Berkeley, where he was trained in biochemistry and physics. He now lives in La Jolla, California, with his wife, Nancy. Mullis may be the lone Nobel Prize winner who is also an avid surfer. A book of his essays on a wide range of subjects, *Dancing Naked in the Mind Field*, was published in 1998.

●　　●　　●

Q: As a scientist, do you believe you might watch a game differently from other people?

A: Being five-nine and a half, I watch it down at a lower level than someone like Kareem Abdul-Jabbar, or those guys. They watch it from the top. I was really excited about playing basketball until I got to high school and everybody else grew tall. I was about five-two when I graduated high school. I was a feisty little guard who never got to play varsity ball. The last time I saw a live basketball game was a Laker game a few years ago. But I do watch games on television when I can, especially the NBA playoffs. And

I see people floating through the air a lot of times and I say, "How the hell does somebody float?" It seems like when they jump up they should come back down on a parabolic arc like, you know, a cannonball or something.

Some of those guys can jump up and then go kind of horizontal for a little while. I don't understand how that works. It seems they are not really following a physical trajectory sometimes. Now whether that's the truth or not, it feels that way, anyway. They just keep on hanging up there. If they need to be another couple of feet along, they just float. I'm sure other people have seen it. You look at it and think, Hey, he didn't start coming down when he should have.

I guess as a scientist you could measure it. You could set up a television screen and analyze it. It's probably an illusion, but who knows? Everything that goes up comes down, and if it has a horizontal velocity, it follows a parabola, or that's what physicists believe. I've seen Michael Jordan float through the air. I've seen others do it. I don't know, maybe they're doing something illegal, like putting helium in their shorts. Or maybe they are capable of violating physical law by some kind of mental strength. You know, in my dreams I can do that. I've done it a lot in my dreams. So I know what it feels like not to come down, to jump off the ground and just stay aloft for a while.

But nothing's impossible, I don't think. If other people have the same illusion about them as I do, it isn't an illusion. Maybe they are in fact floating.

Q: From the standpoint of physiology, there are some who contend that blacks in particular have a different bone structure, most notably in the Achilles tendon, that allows them to jump higher than others. Do you subscribe to any view like that?

A: No. I have never studied a physiology difference, but it wouldn't matter. In physics, it doesn't matter what the thing is once it's off the floor. Or out of the cannon. It really should act in the air just like an inert object. It shouldn't matter whether it's a basketball player or a cue ball or whatever. If it goes up it should follow about the same path coming down as going up, the only difference in the two being almost insignificant when it comes to something as heavy as a person. Air resistance has a little bit to do with it, but not seriously. A person should act like an inert projectile once he's left the floor.

Let's say you can jump and go off at a forty-five-degree angle, or a sixty-degree angle, but whichever angle you go off at, that's the one you should fall down at. You shouldn't come down at some other angle than the one you jump at.

It's true that the higher you jump, the longer you stay aloft. But you still come down in a parabolic trajectory. But these players seem to jump up and then go flat for a while, like the parabola is interrupted by a flat place on top of it somehow. And it finally comes down hard after they stuff the basketball into the basket.

I know they talk about "hang time." It's not beyond complete belief that there is someone, or some people, capable of doing something with their bodies which is like what I do. When I'm asleep.

Like sometimes it seems people are capable of looking into the future. I mean, like a good race car driver. He is looking way out in front of him and making decisions for the second afterward, instead of right now. He's not looking right in front of the car, he's looking way down the track. He's already analyzed what's between him and there, and he's way out ahead of it. Now, basketball players probably have to do something similar.

They are also doing it in the sense that it's not like a whole bunch of cars, but it's a whole bunch of people and a player is trying to calculate in his head—without thinking of it as calculation—but feeling it, where everybody is going to be in one second, and how am I going to be in a place where they don't think I'm going to be. It looks the way it does when you disturb an anthill.

It's extremely organized, and it seems like they are in each other's little minds, and they aren't moving around in random ways. They're just taking in the whole scene immediately somehow. Ants probably do it by, I bet, some telepathic way because anthills are just one big organism.

It's like your left hand knows where your right hand is going to be for reasons that are not apparent to somebody who's not in you. These basketball players seem almost in their teammates' heads sometimes. They've been practicing and practicing and practicing so it's not like a brand-new move. But in fact every game is a brand-new game. And they seem coordinated with each other in what you would think of as an extrasensory way. It might be that they just can do it so fast that it looks like that. But they are professionals.

People talk about the game slowing up in the minds of the great players. In other words, their perception of it is that the seconds stretch out quite long, compare to what it looks like to us just watching it. It's like, "What the fuck just happened?" You know? They knew exactly what was going to happen just a second or two before it did. It's exactly the same thing with race car drivers. They are operating in the future a little bit, instead of the present.

Q: Can you equate this in any way to what you do as a scientist?

A: Sometimes when you're trying to solve a problem in science, you go to the solution instead of the route to the solution. You have an intuitive sense about what is going to be the answer long before you really have a notion of how to get there, but you just sense it. I think of it as being not a plotting, linear process when you're inventing things, and probably a really good basketball player is not plotting, but spread out over time, sort of bulging into the future. We don't really understand all that stuff, we just know it exists. Some people seem to be responding to the future as though it had already happened.

It may sound strange to many people, but not to physicists. We deal with that kind of stuff all the time—cause sometimes happens after an event, down at some micromolecular level. It's like time is not extremely well defined when you get down to the scale of atoms and things like that. It's fuzzy. It's not clear what happens first, and so the cause of an event can sometimes happen after the event. It's a mystery, actually, to our minds. But quantum physics itself is a mystery to us. Because on the macro scale—on the big scale like us—cause always precedes the event. Something had to happen to cause something else to happen. But that's just the way our mind interprets the reality that our senses are looking at. It's not necessarily everything.

We're still kind of in the Stone Age in terms of understanding what's going on around us. We're very comfortable in thinking that there's somebody who understands everything, but that's just not true.

Q: Then do you think in years to come that we will understand how someone like Michael Jordan or the other great players do what they do?

A: It's always possible. My feeling about reality is that none of it is completely hidden. It's just much more complex than we in the post-Newtonian centuries here comprehend. All kinds of stuff might be happening. Michael Jordan just might be floating. Until someone measures and proves that he's not, you don't really know. You just have to put a little laser or whatever on his center of mass and see what trajectory his center of mass follows. I wouldn't be a bit shocked if somebody were able to show physically that something that would be considered impossible for cannonballs was not impossible. Or for basketball players.

Once upon a time we thought the earth was flat. We thought that the earth was the center of the universe. But I wasn't a part of that. [*Laughs.*] I think I was washing dishes somewhere. But we have an extremely smug attitude in this century, and it's based on the fact that a lot of times most people don't understand how much of a mess the logic of science is.

The logic of science is not nearly as tight as many consider it to be. In the nineteenth century, the philosophy of science was that the universe was sort of a giant piece of clockwork, and that if you could know the original state of everything, then since we knew the dynamic laws that caused other things to happen, you could predict the future completely. By just knowing the position of all the particles, you should be able to—with a huge computer—predict the future. But we discovered something called quantum mechanics early in the twentieth century that said that that's not actually how it works. We were forced to adopt the concept that the universe was not a windup clock-like thing. In fact, the ultimate forces and particles in it were not subject, even at a very tiny scale, to the things like time and space.

Now it's clear from experiments that things are coupled to each other immediately over vast distances, like where the speed of light really should be a constraint, it isn't. Like simultaneously two things are connected that are too far apart for any kind of light to travel between them, and that generally consists of relativity at the speed of light. But a lot of weird stuff has been proven.

Things just kept coming up that were not understandable from any classical, physical point of view—classical meaning like going back to the laws of motion that were described by Newton in the eighteenth century, which is most people's view of the world. That is the way it looks until you see somebody like Michael Jordan float.

Most of the things in your life conform to the idea of conservation of mass, conservation of energy, whatever goes up comes down—it's always a smooth pathway when it's up in the air, unless it's going really fast and resistance starts affecting it. But, like, when we launch things toward Mars, and land within twenty feet of where we want it to, we've used those laws that were proposed in the twentieth century.

I'm just saying that when you get down to a small scale these days, physicists don't deal with Newton's old laws. You have to have a totally different set of laws that really allow for almost anything. Maybe Michael Jordan is following a different set of laws. [*Laughter.*] It doesn't seem like a big object like him would be able to violate the standard model of physical interaction that Newton proposed. But we know that little things can do it. Things like atoms do it all the time. Things smaller than atoms, in fact, come in and out of existence all the time, and nobody quite understands that in the sense of everyday reality, but physicists deal with it all the time. And many may laugh at the notion of it happening on a large scale—to a Michael Jordan—but they don't understand consciousness, either.

That is, Michael Jordan is not a cannonball. He's a conscious thing, and we don't really know precisely what that means. Science can't really define what consciousness is, although there is definitely philosophical opinions and groups of people who say, "Well, consciousness is just a really complex bunch of calculations, and it could happen that even a computer could be conscious at some point." Other people would say, "Bullshit."

But we don't really know all of the powers out there. There's all kinds of stories about people rushing into burning buildings and picking up three tons of girders off their wife or children. Or lifting up a semi truck. They are like superphysical acts that are performed under extreme conditions by certain individuals and probably never repeated by those individuals. Well, mildly superphysical things might be going on in every basketball game. And that's where we say, "That guy is great!"

There is something about this guy's greatness, and it could be like reaching into a burning building and snatching out your wife from underneath a ton of metal.

But you know, you wake up in the morning and we don't know how that happens, either. You just do.

Q: Do you have a favorite basketball player?

A: It would be just trite, like everybody else's players. I don't have any—well, you know, this crazy bastard? What's his name, with the green hair?

Q: Dennis Rodman?

A: Yeah. He adds a dimension to the whole game.

Q: Which is?

A: He makes more of a show of the game in addition to it being an athletic event. He brings this wild character into the mix that nobody in my high school would have ever had the nerve to have hair that color. But he said, "Well, I'll do it, plus date Madonna if I want to." That sort of thing puts some people off, but that's really entertaining.

Q: How about your hair? Would you ever consider—

A: I wouldn't plan to do my hair like that, but, you know, I'm sometimes outrageous as a scientist.

Q: So you can identify with Rodman in some way?

A: Yeah. I think I can identify a little bit with him. My favorite player? Yeah, I think I might vote for him.

GENE SISKEL

EUGENE KAL SISKEL, a film critic for more than three decades, was born in Chicago on January 26, 1946. He grew up in Chicago and the suburbs and went to Yale, where he received a bachelor's degree in 1967. He wrote a newspaper column for the *Chicago Tribune*, and made a national reputation on the popular, nationally syndicated television show, *Siskel & Ebert* with Roger Ebert, the movie critic for the *Chicago Sun-Times*. The two were contrasts in physical size, Siskel being tall and lean, Ebert shorter and stouter. They coauthored *The Future of the Movies*, published in 1991.

The following discussion was held in the small back room of the CBS Studio on McClurg Court in Chicago where Siskel had an office, a receptionist, and a producer. The office contained a round desk with papers scattered on it; squares of notes for upcoming screenings of films to be attended were tacked onto a cork bulletin board. There were numerous film books on the shelves. Siskel's thinning dark hair was neatly combed; he wore an NBA cap for the occasion, and a tan sport jacket, brown slacks, and loafers. He drew up a chair to the table. His speech was not as rapid-fire as one remembered it on his television show. The interview was conducted on Monday, November 16, 1998. Several months earlier he had undergone surgery for a brain tumor. His illness returned, and he died on February 20, 1999.

•   •   •

Q: Excuse the obvious, but is it thumbs-up or thumbs-down on basketball?

A: Overall, two thumbs-up, though some games can be real stinkers, too. But basketball games are often high drama. You can often expect the unexpected, and you don't have to be a film critic to appreciate that. But as a film critic for thirty years, I can't turn it off. When I come into a room I'm aware that incipient violence could be right around the corner. Or that someone can be coming through the door with a gun or an ax. When I walk out on the street I look at every site as the potential movie scene location. I also watch things in a basketball game that others may not. Like defense. Like the way the Bulls played it. The Bulls' defense coach, Tex Winter, calls them "Dobermans," because of their tenacity. I'd tell friends, Don't just watch the ball. With the Bulls, watch Michael Jordan and Scottie Pippen on defense especially. They play defense with their legs, as they fundamentally should, but also with their eyes and their arms. Long arms, shifty eyes. It's the eyes that invariably tell the story. Look at films, the camera catches the eyes. They laugh, they cry, they show fear, they scrutinize. In silent films, the eyes told everything.

Jordan and Pippen were uncanny in that they were able to guard a man and a half each. Together they defend three guys, or three lanes, if you will. That means that the fifth guy on the floor can virtually leave his man and freelance. When was the last time you saw what amounts to six guys on the court on defense?

People often ask me, "Are you a basketball fan or a Michael Jordan fan?" I tell them, "Both." You pick all the hackneyed phrases you want—"Poetry in Motion," etc., etc.—and they'd all be true. It's been an honor and a treat to have watched Jordan so many times over the years. And the even more shocking thing is that he has gotten better with age. He's an unbelievable physical specimen. When he was no longer flying to the basket he developed this amazing turnaround jump shot in which he twists his body and shoots over a defender while practically falling into the stands.

Q: Were you a basketball fan growing up?

A: Yes, I've been a basketball fan since I was a small boy, and shooting baskets in the driveway of our home in Glencoe, a Chicago suburb. I've never been a great basketball player, but I can shoot the ball, and from long distances. I'm fifty-two years old and stand six-two and a half, weigh 199 pounds, and can hit shots from half-court. Hit the rim, anyway. Not regularly, but on occasion.

I remember watching NBA games on television when growing up in the 1950s. My favorite player at the time was George Yardley. There's a wonderful trivia question: "Who was the first player to score over 2,000 points in an NBA season?" It was Yardley. I can still recall that in 1958 he scored 2,001 points for the Detroit Pistons to lead the league. He was called the "Bald Eagle," probably because he was bald. He was around twenty-nine or thirty then, but he seemed like an old man because he was bald. I took to him because I've always rooted for underdogs. I'm just by nature an underdog fan. Like I rooted for Wilt Chamberlain over Bill Russell. Russell was the people's choice. Russell won all the championships with the Celtics and Wilt seemed only to win the scoring and rebounding titles. But I felt he was an underdog and I believed him when he said, "Nobody likes Goliath." Well, I liked him. I felt the giant was getting picked on.

I've had front-row seats at Bulls' games in the United Center for the last five years—at roughly $500 a game, but I pay it because there's nothing like it for me. But like my mother once said when I bought my apartment and it was a lot of money, "What do you have it for?" That is, what's the point of making money if you aren't going to spend it on something worthwhile?

Because of my television visibility, a lot of players know me and sometimes chat with me about films. Basketball players see a lot of movies, they spend a lot of time in their hotel rooms and often watch SpectraVision, or they go to movie theaters at home or on the road.

There was a game between the Bulls and the Phoenix Suns and K.J.—Kevin Johnson—the Suns point guard, made a great drive shot along the baseline. I shouted, "Good drive, K.J." There was a timeout—I sit right across the court from the visitors' bench—and when the whistle blew to resume play, K.J. left the huddle and began to walk across the court toward me. The referee was holding the ball under the basket to begin play, but K.J. kept walking toward me. I wasn't sure what this was all about. I repeated, "Uh, nice shot, K.J." Maybe he thought I was riding him, but I was serious about complimenting him. He walked right over and stood in front of me. He said, "So you really liked *Richard the III*?" I had to laugh. He had seen my review of it and wanted to know if he should see it. I said, "Two thumbs-up, K.J."

Woody Allen came over to me in a restaurant and said, "You know, you wrote something pretty good, Gene. You gave fifty reasons to live in Chicago over New York." I said, "Wow. I forgot. What did I write? Coming from you, the ultimate New Yorker, fifty reasons to live in Chicago over New York. What were they?"

He said, "Fifty Bulls home games."

I've been to games with Spike Lee, and while I don't involve myself with the players during a game the way he does, I can make myself heard like any other fan, especially one rooting for his team. One player I regularly get on is John Starks, the Knicks guard. I was incensed when I saw him leg-whip Pippen and Dennis Rodman. Starks had fallen and seemed to intentionally trip both of them on different occasions. When he comes to the United Center and misses a shot, I've hollered, "Oh for one!" When he misses another, "Oh for two!" If he hits one, I say, "Better than two for eighteen!" I'm sure he isn't thrilled to be reminded that he made just two shots in eighteen attempts when the Knicks lost the seventh game of the 1994 NBA finals to the Rockets. One time I was on him like this and as he ran downcourt, he passed me and said, "You're getting to look like Ebert."

John certainly knows how to hurt a guy. It was funny, though.

Q: Does Roger Ebert have an interest in basketball?

A: Ebert tells me he envies my getting my Bulls seats years ago. He said it was like buying Microsoft at one. But he doesn't have nearly as great an interest in basketball as I do.

Q: Does he attend many games?

A: It just depends on what they are serving in the VIP room that day. [*Laughter.*]

One of the really interesting things for me at courtside has been to observe Phil Jackson, who has been a great coach with the Bulls. I view a coach like a movie director. You have to be watching everything, and sometimes all at once. One of the reasons for Jackson's success, I believe, is his maturity. He treats the players like adults, and does it with indirection and humor—and respect. And like a superb director, he's able to get the best out of people. Other coaches, for example, would just throw up their hands at some of the antics of Dennis Rodman. Jackson felt he needed Rodman— one of the great rebounders of all time—and maintained a semblance of discipline with him but did it kind of with raised eyebrows at Rodman's antics. I imagine it's how Billy Wilder directed Marilyn Monroe in *Some Like It Hot.*

I think it must be very difficult to manage many of these players because they've been coddled much of their lives and they're making a staggering amount of money. They are celebrated everywhere they go. That distorts a personality, even one that has been raised in the most solid of homes, which many of the players haven't.

And a film director is the ultimate authority for a lot of people, especially those on the set. But he has to impose his will. That's what Jackson did.

Q: What basketball movies have interested you?

A: There have been some decent basketball movies, but my favorite of all time is one that is never seen anymore because of some legal issues involving its rerelease. The movie is *Go, Man,*

Go!, the story of the Harlem Globetrotters, starring Dane Clark as Abe Saperstein, the founder and coach of the Globetrotters, and even had a young Sidney Poitier, as one of the basketball players. I saw it when I was ten or eleven years old and it gave me the first sense of the drama and the theatricality of basketball, and the joy of it. There was also an exotic element to it beyond the black-white element of the story, and that was the New York tone. Marty Glickman, the old Olympic runner and famous as a broadcaster in New York, did the narration of the games in the film. And in those days, the announcer would give the score after every basket. They don't now, but they did then, and Marty, in his New York accent, would say, "Basket good, twenty-four to twenty-two Trahttahs." I loved it.

A lot of times the movies you saw as a kid don't hold up when viewed as an adult. Nothing can be as good as a childhood memory. But I was able to get a copy recently of *Go, Man, Go!* and saw it again and, sure enough, it was good—good enough for me to recommend on my show. I saw flaws in it I hadn't seen as a boy, but I still loved it. I've been trying to get it released again. I think it would appeal to this generation, too.

Of all the NBA players who talk to me about films, Charles Barkley does the most. Whenever he's in Chicago playing ball he'll rattle off every picture that is in release and he wants to know what my opinion is. He wants to know up or down, but he knows every picture. He's really sharp about films. And, being Charles, he naturally has strong opinions on the subject. Michael loves movies, too, and we'll get together and I'll want to talk basketball and he'll want to talk movies, and he wins, as he usually does at most things.

Michael told me that the funniest movie he ever saw was *Friday*. So I got a copy of it and screened it. It's about a couple of kids sitting on a stoop in front of an apartment building and they're stoned and they're just yucking it up. Michael thought it was funny. I was bored by it. But I did give a positive review to his movie, *Space Jam*. I said that David Falk, Michael's agent, had threatened the loss of my courtside seats if I said I didn't like the picture. That was a jest. What I liked about it is that I would probably congratulate Falk for putting his talent in the right kind of picture, as opposed to the manager of Shaquille O'Neal, who put him into the absolute wrong kind of picture. The reason I thought Michael's picture was right for him was that it didn't have extended lines, and he was given simple amounts of screen time. His speaking parts were short, like in a commercial, which he is very good at delivering. And he played Michael Jordan, which is what people want to see. Michael represented a cartoon-like character, in other words, an image. Not like the movie Shaquille O'Neal made, *Kazaam*, in which he played a seven-foot genie. It was terrible. It flopped. Shaq's no actor, but if he had played himself, it would have been fascinating. I mean, how does he maneuver all that bulk? How does he get into a car? I think the audience would have gone for that.

Q: Could Michael be a legitimate actor in films?

A: I'm not sure, but I believe he'd make a great James Bond. He's stylish enough, and because Bond doesn't have to say much, if you think about it. There's a lot of action, and very little visible sex. There's some nudity, or partial nudity in the Bond films, but not much. Or as Jack Benny once used the phrase in explaining to me why a film would be rated R—"thrusting." You don't see that in a Bond movie. And it's usually the woman who says something provocative, some pun or something. Jordan, the first black Bond. Perfect.

I liked Spike Lee's movie *He Got Game*. It was a good father-son portrayal. In terms of basketball it was credible, and that's hard to accomplish. The problem with making a basketball movie these days is that we have seen everything in slow motion, and we know what's real and what is faked. Our whole visual intelligence has been kicked up through sports shows, highlight shows, and so a filmmaker can't fake it. It's got to be really good. I thought the strength of the Spike Lee movie wasn't the basketball, it was the drama.

Ray Allen, the guard for the Milwaukee Bucks who's featured in the film, handled the drama well, I thought. It's tough because when you are that big on the screen, any flaw is obvious, any nervousness—Oh, my God!—will leap off the screen. Spike Lee told me, "The basketball wasn't the tough part in finding someone, it was finding someone who could act," a basketball player who could act. Based on that movie, I think Ray Allen deserves to get more work.

You know, you either have it or you don't when the camera hits you. And basketball players get it when they are shooting free throws. That's their close-up. That's why they are so much more popular than other athletes, the free throw. Time out. Close-up on them. That's a good chunk of screen time.

And we see the eyes, the tension, the concentration in the eyes. We can identify with them in this way. It's a cliché, but there's a lot of truth to the saying that the eyes are the window of the soul. I'll tell you how important the eyes are from somebody more knowledgeable about film than me—Steven Spielberg. He said that in designing creatures like E.T. it was all in the eyes. E.T. is kind of ugly, but the eyes catch you. And that's why I think Willy the Whale was not as successful. You couldn't get both eyes in the frame at the same time. I couldn't relate to Willy.

Because of my relationship with movies and the players' interest in them, I'm able to ask them questions that intrigue me. Like the one I asked Michael after an opening-round playoff game in which he was routinely terrific: "When you drive home to Highland Park after a game like that, do you look into the rearview mirror and say, 'Yeah, you did it again'? He said, 'No, I might say, "I got the young guys off to a great start." ' "

What impressed me about that is his desire to do what he could for the team, as opposed to just elevating himself. He had that team focus even in a moment of personal triumph.

And sitting at courtside, you are privy to things, like remarks on the court. One time Jordan made a fantastic clutch shot against the Miami Heat, and their coach, Pat Riley, called to Jordan as he ran past him, "You rat!" It was like something out of an old James Cagney movie. But more. It was cinema verité at its best.

TOM BROKAW

Tom Brokaw is anchor and managing editor for the *NBC Nightly News with Tom Brokaw*, and has been since 1983. He is also a contributing anchor for *Dateline NBC*. His first book, *The Greatest Generation*, about men who fought and survived World War II and came home "to build a nation," was published in 1998 and became a number one national bestseller, selling more than two million copies. Among other awards, he has received a Peabody Award and an Emmy for his special reports.

Brokaw was born February 6, 1940, in Webster, South Dakota. He went to Yankton (South Dakota) High School and, after a year at the University of Iowa, enrolled in the University of South Dakota, where he was graduated in 1962. He began his career in journalism after college at KMTV in Omaha, Nebraska. That same year, he married Meredith Auld, who had gone to high school with him and was the captain of the cheerleaders when he was on the basketball team in the mid- to late 1950s.

●   ●   ●

Q: Do you go to many basketball games?

A: I go to a lot, mostly Knick games in the Garden. I took Jesse Ventura, the Minnesota governor, to a game there when the Knicks played Minnesota. Jesse is a big Timberwolves fan. When we sat down, I said, "You know, I grew up in a succession of small towns in South Dakota and basketball was my primary sport." It

was the game I played best. It was the first one my father introduced me to when I was about four. I said to Jesse, "This is just an
extension of all the things I cared about. This is my hometown
team and arena now. It's like going to a high school game for me,
but written large." What I've always loved about basketball is the
intimacy of the arena. It seems to me that no matter how large it
is, a basketball game is an intimate game. The floor is manageable
and accessible to fans. It plays right out before you. You can see
everything that's going on. You see it all.

And there is a kind of wonderful community about people in
a big arena like that that's lost, it seems to me, in a big football sta-
dium. I think it's true of the old days of baseball. You had that same
feeling in smaller stadiums, and that got lost, but they're trying to
recreate that now.

Q: Can you get this feeling of intimacy even at Madison
Square Garden?

A: I really do. It's curious. I have a number of friends there that
I wouldn't have known without going to games. I know where
they sit and I say hello to them. We've got guys in our area that we
talk to a lot and we share things. You know, they were excited
about my book. I know about their daughters getting married, and
we razz the refs together and we talk to some of the players, too.

Growing up, I suppose I thought I would live in a middle-sized
city somewhere in the Midwest, like Minneapolis and Omaha, and
I would be able to go to high school basketball games. It was so
much a part of my formative years that I couldn't imagine giving
it up. Now by extension I have it. It's just that it's the most famous
arena in the world.

Q: When you watch a game, do you ever reflect back on your
own playing days?

A: Yes. I reflect back and say, "I couldn't do that." [*Laughter.*]
For one thing, the speed of the game. I think I played a measured

white man's game, and I was a slow white man—even by white man standards. I'm as struck by the absolute quickness and speed of the game as I am by anything else about it. The ability players have on a breakaway to exert such enormous control over their huge bodies—that mass that they have control of—either going for the basket or in the assist or positioning for a rebound, or whatever they happen to be doing. It's just so stunning to me. I believe they are the greatest athletes in the world.

I was thinking about it just last night. I saw the Nets play the Knicks. And Keith Van Horn of the Nets at one point was in the middle of a tangle of bodies and there was a loose ball and he got it and executed a pretty, flawless behind-the-back dribble to get out of the jam. I only dribbled behind my back when I had an especially lumbering opponent against me who was eight feet away. In fact, I did use a behind-the-back dribble because I practiced every day after watching Bob Cousy of the Celtics do it in a game I saw on television. He was this kind of grainy black-and-white image on the screen. Cousy was my hero, a guard about my height—six feet tall, but he could do miracles with the ball. And the first time I tried that behind-the-back maneuver in a game—it was an uncommon move in those days—my coach benched me immediately. Said I was "hot-dogging it."

I liked the Celtics because of Cousy, but the professional team I knew most about was the Minneapolis Lakers, in the neighboring state. When I was thirteen I won a trip to Minneapolis because I was carrying newspapers for the Midwest edition of the *Minneapolis Tribune* and I sold enough customers to win a weekend visit. A friend and I rode the train all night into Minneapolis. This is when I was living in this really small town, Pickstown. I was a junior high basketball player and I loved the game. When we were in Minneapolis we read in the newspaper that the Minneapolis Lakers were playing that night at the old Minneapolis Auditorium. We literally ran about thirty blocks to the auditorium. We didn't know how else to get there, and we had a lot of energy. We paid, as I remember, fifty or seventy-five cents for a seat way up. But before the game we were able to wander around and there was big

George Mikan, the star of the team, standing off the floor signing autographs and talking to fans. It was the damnedest thing you've ever seen in your life when you think back on it. We went up and shook his hand and told him where we were from, and he said, "That's nice, a couple of South Dakota boys," and that was it. We were thrilled.

At a dinner before an NBA all-star game, which I presided at, Mikan was there and it was really wonderful to be able to say, "I actually met you in 1953," or whatever it was.

Q: He didn't happen to remember it, did he?

A: No, but it was enough for me to remember it.

It's hard to describe how much I played when I was in junior high and, you know, when I was a teenager. I had a backboard and a net my father made for me out on our garage. I was out there a lot. Even in the bitterly cold winter I'd go out and shoot. I took basketball so seriously and yet I was only going to get to a certain level, and my dad always had the right perspective. There was a state tournament game in Aberdeen in the northern part of the state and my parents drove eight hours through a terrible blizzard to get there. And they had brought my girlfriend—not Meredith at that time. The state basketball tournament in South Dakota is the single largest cultural event of the year in the state. It's carried on every radio station. In those days there were just two divisions, A and B. We were in the A class, and the whole arena was filled. So it was this big deal. I was like the sixth man. I got into the game and I was just tighter than a two-dollar drum. And the first thing I did when I got the ball was dribble it off my foot, and then I blew a layup. It was just a nightmare experience. I felt my whole life was coming unraveled before me.

In the second game of that tournament I had been benched by the uptight coach for some silliness I had been involved in off the court. So I sat on the bench and I was really angry about it. At one point, I looked up into the stands and by chance made eye contact with my mother. She offered a silent expression of great sympathy. My father, sitting beside her, began to smile, then he looked left and right to be sure no one was watching. When the coast was clear he subtly, but clearly, flashed the finger! And while the thousands around us were caught up in the frenzy of the game, he and I laughed.

What that finger meant was, well, it was all about perspective. Like, "Hey, it's not *that* important, Tom. This is not the end of your life. There are a lot of other things." It was a moment I'll never forget. It almost makes me clutch now because it was my dad who worked so hard all his life as a construction equipment operator and he was able to create a balance of what was important and what had less importance.

Of course I recovered, and in my senior year I was a starting guard.

After one of my rare starring performances, I came home all excited and was going to change into something more dashing for a grand entry to the postgame dance. My father was installing acoustical tiles in the dining room ceiling. He congratulated me on the game and added, "Give me a hand here; this will just take a minute." We finished well after the dance had ended. I was steamed. My father was amused in establishing family priorities. And some forty years later the memory of that game is faint at best but I still have a pretty good idea of how to install a new ceiling.

Though we won fourth place in the state in my junior year, we didn't make the state tournament my senior year. We lost in a qualifying round to Beresford, a school from a smaller town. We lost by one point, in a game we had been favored to win. The whole community was—God, if you didn't win, the next day— well, it seemed to define the kind of worthiness of the whole adult community, or a big piece of it. It was vitally important to almost everyone. This wasn't the case in my household because my mother and father were not locker-room parents. They were pleased that I was playing and all that, but they didn't live or die by the fortunes of the team. I worked downtown in a clothing store on Saturdays and if you lost a game or didn't do something particularly well, these grownups would come in the store and not talk to me because we lost the night before.

I got a letter the other day from a guy named Teddy, a former classmate of mine from my hometown. We had a mutual friend named Whistler who was the best player on our team. And at the end of his letter, he wrote, "I'll never forget when you and Whistler lost to Beresford, goddamn it."

I wanted to write back and say, "Don't do this to me. I just get to the point where I think I've buried that memory and somebody has to bring it up again."

We lost that one big game when I was a senior and I've gone on to a thousand different things in my life. And others have as well. A lot of them have had distinguished careers. But to this day, when we go back, we're not in town one hour before someone says, "You fuckers, you lost that game against Beresford." [*Laughter.*] Yes, they have never forgotten it.

Q: What do you think of that, this emphasis on winning? Which is surely not strictly indigenous to small towns in America, or America, for that matter.

A: I think it's fine. They had big expectations for us, and we let them down. They were really pulling for us. Now that I've become a fan, and I've gone through some terrible years—when I was working in Los Angeles and became a Rams fan and they'd always lose to the Vikings in the playoffs—it would drive me nuts. So I did understand it. It's kind of God's way of saying, "We know something about you. You've done all this other stuff, and we know when the crunch came you lost a big game."

Q: So it keeps you humble?

A: Does it ever! Something else about that Beresford game. Joe Thorne was the star guard of that team who kept us from going to the state tournament. He went on to play football at South Dakota State College. After school, he went into the Army with a commission, and went to Vietnam. If you look in those directories they have at the entrance to the Vietnam War Memorial, you'll see the name Lieutenant Josef Lloyd Thorne. He was killed in Vietnam in April 1965, just a month short of his twenty-fifth birthday.

Q: That kind of tragedy gives a certain perspective, too.

A: It certainly does.

Q: When you were growing up in the 1950s, basketball was popular in many areas in America, but it didn't capture the widespread attention and enthusiasm as it does today, especially the pro game. From a newsman's viewpoint, how do you see it?

A: We've led off the *Nightly News* with some basketball or basketball-related stories. There was Michael Jordan's retirement from basketball—both of them—and Magic Johnson's announcement that he had tested positive for HIV, and the incident in which Latrell Sprewell choked his coach. These are a few prominent examples. To begin with, I think Michael had a lot to do with the rise in popularity to where basketball is today. His skills and his personality have contributed enormously to it. But I think the sheer athleticism that the black athletes brought to the game made a big difference—the first black didn't make his appearance in the NBA until the 1950 season. They did change it, and Michael is the apotheosis of all that. But there were others before him who obviously began the change. Curiously, when I was a young man I was a huge fan of the Harlem Globetrotters. They were the opening bill that night when I went to see the Lakers when I was thirteen years old. But I knew everything about Marquis Haynes and Goose Tatum and all those guys. I paid attention to them. I remember once, they even came to Yankton, South Dakota, and played before only a handful of fans. I just couldn't believe so few people would turn out to see these greatly gifted athletes.

I think that as much as anything, all these great players—and I include Larry Bird, not just the black players—occupy a level that is so much different from anything else that we've ever seen in terms of just raw athleticism. I believe that a hundred years from now they'll be talking about Michael the way we talk about Babe Ruth, or others. I just think he's a wonderful human being. He has a great spirit which shows in every pore of his being and then the ability to go with it. You know, a lot of guys are very competitive, but God, to do the things that Michael can do . . . ! And then there's the grace and dignity about him. I was at the game at the Garden when he had just returned from playing baseball and he scored fifty-five points. When he hit his first two shots, I turned to Meredith and said, "This is going to be a long night for the Knicks. Michael's going to have a great night." If you had just played basketball a little bit, even way down at my level, you could just see it. He was on radar. And the confidence—well, he always has utter confidence—but at the end of the game, you'll remember, the Bulls were trailing by one and he came off the bench after a timeout and he looked at me. I've known him for a while and we hadn't said anything to each other or exchanged any expressions, but he walked right over to where I was sitting and he looked at me like, "Well, we'll see about this." The place was going nuts, but Michael was so confident. I looked at him and said, "No, it's not going to happen, Michael." And then he went up for the jump shot—and passed it to Bill Wennington under the basket and the Bulls won by one point! And Michael just turned and flew off the court. That is the ultimate.

Q: What did you make of the Latrell Sprewell incident?

A: I was furious about that. I was outraged. You just can't choke your boss, no matter how displeased you are with him. And maybe it does say something about a society that is sometimes out of control. A kind of symbol of that. But I recently saw again the documentary *Hoop Dreams*, which I think is one of the most important documentaries that has been produced in this country about American culture in the last fifty years. It follows these two inner-city boys in Chicago who become high school basketball stars and then their problems as they go on to college on basketball scholarships. It's about expectations and exploitations and the desperate nature of some of the lives of people in the inner cities. So I think that the life of a Latrell Sprewell had more than one side to it. And while his actions shouldn't be excused, maybe they can be explained in a more profound manner. And I was not opposed to his returning to the league. I believe in second chances.

And then there was that *Sports Illustrated* story about all these NBA stars and their out-of-wedlock babies. It was very disturbing. And I think there wasn't enough discussion on that. I've always hoped that it would come from within the league, and the players themselves. I thought Michael, for example—who wasn't one of those fathers—I thought he might address the issue. But he hasn't. These guys have got to get this thing under control. Michael's done some important things, particularly about promoting the need for education, but it has been only episodic.

Q: When did you retire from organized basketball?

A: When I went to Iowa, I played in a pickup basketball game with Don Nelson, who was also a freshman there. And it was clear that he was on an entirely different level from me. But to this day I keep a basketball net up at our house in Connecticut. And they put some wonderful new courts behind the Met—the Metropolitan Museum of Art, near where I live in Manhattan—and I go there and shoot around sometimes. And I still have my memories and sometimes I transport myself to my high school basketball days.

Q: As you do when you're at the Garden?

A: Absolutely. You know, a particular jump shot, a particular move. You think, God, I wish I had seen more of this when I was that age. I would have tried that, or why didn't we have more plays than the—what, three or four we actually had. Teams must have seen them coming a mile away. Of course, our opponents then had about as many as we did.

And when I see a guy blow a shot, or a pass, I sometimes cringe, for him *and* me. I feel for the guys who do it. I really do. Like Chris Childs missed an easy layup for the Knicks the other night. Oh, God! He just tries to shrug it off, but that's a painful, humiliating thing. The other thing about the exposure of making a mistake in basketball is that it's like dropping a pop fly in front of all those people, except in basketball it is all out there in the open and you don't have a baseball cap to pull over your eyes.

I'm always conscious of all those things and what it's like to do that because I did more than my share of it, frankly.

Q: Looking back on all the hours that you put into practice in basketball, do you think it was a waste of time?

A: No, I should have practiced more. [*Laughter.*] I would have been better.

DONALD TRUMP

ONALD TRUMP'S office is on the twenty-sixth floor of Trump Tower in Midtown Manhattan. The widely known real estate developer, he has also been involved in sports, owning a professional football team, the New Jersey Generals of the defunct United States Football League, and promoting professional prize-fighting bouts, including several involving heavyweight title fights with Mike Tyson in Atlantic City, where he owns three casino-hotels.

Seated behind a desk in his large but rather understated office—one was inclined to expect a greater degree of ostentation from a man who rarely shuns the spotlight—Trump wears his customary dark suit and red tie. Behind him, through the large window facing Fifth Avenue, is an impressive panorama of New York's Plaza Hotel and the General Motors Building, both of which he owns, and Central Park, which he does not own, though, given his penchant for purchasing, he might like to bid on.

Among his holdings are Trump Tower, Trump Parc, Trump Palace, Trump Marina, Trump World's Fair, Trump Taj Mahal, Trump International, Trump Pageants, which includes Miss Universe, Miss USA, and Miss Teen USA, and the Empire State Building. He is a special adviser to the President's Council on Physical Fitness, and has received the Ellis Island Medal of Honor and was inducted into the Wharton Business School (he is an alumnus) Hall of Fame.

Donald John Trump was born on June 14, 1946, in Queens, New York.

This interview was conducted in December 1998, just a few weeks before the labor dispute between the National Basketball Association and its players' union was settled.

*   *   *

Q: When you go to a game, does Donald Trump look at the players as dollar signs, and do you project yourself on the court in some way?

A: I look at players as winners or losers. I watch players over the years, and I just see certain players as winning-type players or losing-type players. Give you an example. I watched Charles Oakley for the Knicks over a period of years—the Knicks traded him to Toronto after the 1998 season, which I think was a risky trade. What I liked about Oakley was his attitude. The guy was a workhorse, getting rebounds, setting hard picks, diving into the stands for loose balls. Now, he's not going to be Michael Jordan, but he was just a tremendous worker. I loved his work ethic.

You look for different things in different people. It's sort of like prizefighters. There are certain types of fighters. There are rough guys, tough guys without huge talent, the finesse guys, but you have to look for the guys who have that special something.

And all the guys who make it to the NBA have something special, no doubt about it. They've gone from level to level and they've reached this pinnacle. And then there's one level more, the level of being a true winner or not. There was that famous triple-pump shot in the playoff game for the Knicks that didn't go in. It was Charles Smith, who got three straight rebounds under the basket in the last seconds against the Bulls and couldn't put one in, and the Knicks lost that game and the playoff round. Now Charles Smith is a very good guy, but at nearly seven feet tall it was disappointing for him not to put the ball in the basket. I was at that game, and it's true that he was going up against three great defensive players at that moment—Michael Jordan, Scottie Pippen, and Bill Cartwright—but I don't think Michael Jordan or Charles Oakley or Charles Barkley or some other players we know would have been triple-pumping under the basket at that point in the game. They would have sealed the deal.

On the other hand, I feel Patrick Ewing is a terrific winner, even though I know some others don't share that feeling because the Knicks with him have never won a championship. But without him they would have been nowhere over the past couple of years. I just never thought he quite had the team around him. It was always tough to win when you had Chicago and Michael Jordan and Scottie Pippen against you. Ewing got the Knicks 95 percent of the way there, but couldn't get that last five percent.

There was one game that was a kind of microcosm of his career. It was the seventh game of the playoffs against Indiana at Madison Square Garden. I was at the game, and it was a game no Knick fan will ever forget. Patrick had been fabulous for the entire game—I think he had 36 points or something like that. In the last second of the game, with a chance to win it, he laid up a finger roll drive and the ball hit the rim and bounced away. I can't blame him for that. He took the last shot under pressure—he assumed the responsibility of a champion, where a lot of guys are afraid to take that last, big shot—and even though he missed, I respect him for it. You couldn't get angry at Ewing because he was so good in the game. I can't blame him for missing that last shot.

But it's funny about heart, you can never tell who has it until you see them under pressure.

But making it in the NBA is impressive, given the incredible competition for the relatively few spots in the league. It's like supermodels or other successful people. Let's say supermodels. People say, "Oh, they're beautiful." But they are very smart. You don't just become a supermodel, or you don't just make it because of your looks. There are a lot of beautiful people. You make it because you have something else. You have to have a head. Once you get to a certain level of talent, there is something just a little beyond that you need to succeed.

When you stand in the driving range and you watch the pros hitting balls, you can't tell the difference between the best pros—I mean, we're talking about a hundred guys—and the rest of them. You can't tell the difference between the best guy and the hundredth guy on the range. It's only when the flag goes up that you can tell.

Q: Is it the heart or the mind or both?

A: Both. I think it's inbred. I think it's a gene thing. There are a lot of people who have talent but don't have the head, don't have the drive, don't have that something. Of the millions of kids who play basketball, only a handful make it to the NBA; it's a huge achievement. And then you see these guys in college and they play great and all. But it's a pyramid. Some of them step up to the next level and some don't. It's a very complicated thing.

Look at John Starks, at what he did. He banged around the Continental Basketball League and then suddenly became an all-star in the NBA. He's an interesting player because he wins games for the Knicks that they shouldn't have won. But I also think he loses games for them that they should have won. Like the seventh game of the 1994 championship finals against Houston when he shot, what—one for eighteen? I think Pat Riley should have taken him out, but he felt Starks could shoot himself out of the slump. Some people don't have hot games at all. And then he's had his bad moments, but that's not unlike a lot of people. That happens.

Q: What is it about basketball that you like?

A: My interest goes to basketball during the season, but I don't confine my interest in sports to basketball. What I like about sports is the competitive nature. I like the fact that there is a final result in a short period of time, as opposed to a lifetime of work before you realize if you are really there. And a basketball game is a two-hour version of life, and that's the beauty of it. You have a start, you have a middle, and you have a finish. The nice part is that you don't have to go eighty years. In two hours' time you have a winner. There is something nice and satisfying about that.

Q: Fans often say that professional athletes in the major team sports make too much money. Do you agree?

A: The answer is, they probably do, but if the owners are willing to pay it, who is anybody to say they are getting paid too much? I think the one player who probably isn't getting paid enough is Michael Jordan, and he gets paid more than anybody else. He just brings in so much money to the game, he's such a spectacular performer—and you talk about a winner! Sometimes he just carries his entire team. I was at the playoff game in Utah in 1998—Karl Malone and I are friends and he had invited me to the game—and that was the game where Jordan had the flu. He went wild. He couldn't miss a shot. He's got a jump shot where he doesn't jump straight up and down, but he's jumping literally back—he's ten feet off the ground, and he's very tall to start with. He releases the shot almost like he's lying in bed, and you're way the hell back trying to guard him. So I see this guy—literally three feet in front of me—and in the first half Utah was winning a little bit, and then all of a sudden Jordan goes fucking wild. He could not miss. And he's got like a 102-degree fever. He scored around forty points, most in the second half.

Another thing that really amazed me, sitting up so close under the basket, was how unbelievably rough it is under the basket. And here was Scottie Pippen, who, when you see him on television looks like a thin, frail guy. But he would go in for a layup and it was rough, you have no idea. He'd go in and these big guys are just whacking at each other—and I'm sitting right there and watching this. Holy shit! It's really a much different game than you see on television. It was literally football. It wasn't basketball, it was football.

And Pippen especially amazed me because they're rapping and smacking him and he's rapping and smacking them right back and he goes and gets his points.

But Pippen is not as frail as he might appear on television. He's actually built quite well. But some of these guys are tremendous physical specimens. When you look at Karl—the Mailman—you see the immense size. He has arms like tree trunks. Forget about the legs, they're bigger than tree trunks. Then you see him jumping and taking a jump shot and it's like butter. It's so soft and perfect to the touch. You really have to say this is an amazing athlete to have this sort of size and touch.

I met Karl in Atlantic City in 1997 when he attended the Miss Universe pageant, which I own. His wife works with and schools future beauty contestants, and she came up to me and introduced herself as Karl Malone's wife. I said, "Karl Malone?" and she said, "Yes, the Mailman." I liked him as a player but I had never met him. She said, "Mr. Trump, he's your biggest fan. Could we call him?" She got Karl on the phone and he came down. And we became friends. When he came to New York he called me and we talked about his contract. I think he's totally underpaid. He was making like $3 or $4 million a year and there were guys making $20 million who couldn't carry his jock.

A guy like Juwan Howard is making $20 million a year! Rookies coming into the league are making more than he is! Gimme a break! So I told Karl, You can play out your contract but when it's terminated you'll be thirty-eight years old. Not a great bargaining position. Or you could do the less honorable thing and say, "Fuck you! I have a contract but I want more money." So I know it's not nice and he didn't want to do it last year, but I see he's sort of doing it this year. But he is a very honorable guy. A lot of guys would have done that much differently.

He's got a five-year contract at a ridiculously low salary and he's playing it out.

Another honorable guy is Larry Bird. After he hurt his back he had a contract which stipulated that if he decided to announce his retirement after a certain date, he'd get paid for the full year, something like $7 million. But a week before that date, he went to management and said he was retiring. They said, "But, Larry, you understand if you wait a week you'll get $7 million. If you announce now, the contract says you won't get the $7 million." He said, "I know. I'm announcing the retirement now."

When I heard he was going to be a coach, I didn't see him as a coach. I thought of him only as a great player. But he's turned out to be an incredible coach with the Indiana Pacers. One of the reasons he's such a great coach is because the players have such respect for him. And he's not a hands-on coach. He lets his players play, and they feel good about it. And I watched the game where Reggie Miller scored the three-point shot that won a big playoff game against the Knicks, and Bird had absolutely no emotion.

It showed me that he was a cool cat. A lot of people who do well under pressure as he did don't have that much emotion. They don't go crazy, they don't go up and down. They don't lose it. I deal with a lot of people and I think enthusiasm is good, but a lot of times I do see that the calmer people tend to do better under stress. And when I saw Larry Bird take that shot for granted, I thought that was cool. And obviously there was nobody better under pressure than Larry Bird as a player. He was a total winner.

Remember that game against the Pistons when the Celtics were losing and there were two seconds left in the game. I mean the game was O-V-E-R. And then Bird steals the inbound pass and whips a perfect pass to Dennis Johnson cutting under the basket for the winning score. I thought Larry Bird as a basketball player was 100 percent genius. I don't know how he did on his SATs, perhaps not well, but as far as basketball brains is concerned, he's Einstein.

I know David Simon, of the Simon family, who owns the Indiana Pacers. In fact, I bought the General Motors Building over there from them. I questioned him about why he had hired Bird as a coach when a lot of people thought he was crazy for doing it. He told me, "Donald, Bird is a winner." That was enough.

Q: How did you feel about the threat by Commissioner David Stern to use replacement players if the union's players refused to agree to terms?

A: If the NBA would bring in replacement players, even though everybody knows they are not going to be as good, I think that will be the straw that would break the camel's back. The union's players would capitulate. You might have a far smaller audience, and they'd have lower ratings, but they'd be playing for far less money, so it all equates. They'd probably be making more money than they would after paying these guys all this money.

This is in the realm of fair negotiation. And David Stern understands this. He's a smart guy. He's got automatic business talent. He's a very formidable foe.

Q: Have any players asked your advice on investments?

A: Some. I've seen a lot of them lose money because they've gone into these harebrained ventures with these fast talkers who just take their money away like taking candy from a baby. I've recommended that some of the players see various groups on Wall Street for investments. There was one player who made a lot of money who was going to invest a huge amount in a fast-food franchise thing. I told him, "Look, if you make that investment I will never speak to you again. You will lose all of your money. The chances of that business failing are much greater than of succeeding." That was four years ago. Recently that company announced it was filing for Chapter 11 bankruptcy. The investors lost every penny. So the player called me and said, "You saved me my money." Some of these schemes don't just stop with the initial investment. They want more and more. That's what happens. They get you and then they say, "Put up a little more." And before you know it your pockets are empty, and they aren't filled again.

Q: Will the lockout have any lasting effect on interest in the game?

A: I think people got angry at the players, and to a lesser extent the owners. I think they feel the players are making so much money, why whine about it? But it's a terrific game and it'll bounce back. It's like baseball. People were angry at the players and owners, and then along comes McGwire and Sosa and suddenly baseball's back.

Q: Did you ever play basketball?

A: I played baseball. And I play golf—I'm a five handicap, even though I don't have a lot of time to play. And I played football. I played a little basketball, but I never liked basketball as much as a player. It was not my best sport. I figured basketball is a jumping sport, and I didn't like to jump.

GROVER WASHINGTON JR.

ROVER WASHINGTON JR., the goateed saxophonist, won his first of two Grammy awards in 1981 (and six Grammy nominations overall) for his album *Winelight*, which included the song "Let It Flow (for Dr. J.)." It was written for Julius Erving, the former soaring star of the Philadelphia 76ers. And Philadelphia is where Washington makes his home and has his company, G. W. Jr. Music. Washington was born on December 12, 1943, in Buffalo, New York. Besides his sax playing, he was also a composer, producer, and arranger. His band continues to tour in America and abroad. He played the national anthem before 76ers games many times. His favorite 76ers teams were the championship team of 1983 and the finalists of 1980 and 1982, which starred players like center Moses Malone, guards Maurice Cheeks and Andrew Toney, forward Bobby Jones, and Erving. He continued to follow the NBA and particularly the 76ers and their new young star, Allen Iverson. Grover Washington Jr. died unexpectedly on December 17, 1999. He was fifty-six years old.

●   ●   ●

Q: How did you come to write "Let It Flow"?

A: The 76ers were playing the Lakers in a playoff game in 1980. Now, I admired Dr. J. I thought he was the epitome of hard work, intelligence, and he just listens to that inner voice of his. He was a great ballplayer. And I remember distinctly this one time when he was coming down the left side of the court with the ball. There are about three Lakers in front of him. He goes up and he checks his watch for the time, he does his laundry while he's in the air, and everybody tries to stop him and he floats to the other side of the basket for a perfect reverse layup. I've never heard the crowd at the Spectrum respond with louder cheers than after that shot.

It changed the whole momentum of the game, and I think it let some members of the Sixers who had some doubt about their own abilities sort of stand up and be counted. When I saw that, I said, "He's got a song coming for that."

While I was writing it I was trying to find the right tempo, and how I found the right tempo was I got a basketball and I just started bouncing it. When you hear the song, listen to the bass drum. That's the basketball.

For the flow, I tried to put a couple of different components into it. First, like the melody, the sense of having something stable so that you can depart from that and improvise. A game plan, if you will. A work ethic. When it gets down to the improvisation, that is what I'm after. It's like the open-court play. It's the unexpected great pass. It's Moses Malone throwing that outlet pass. Or it's Moses drawing the defense to him and dishing off to Bobby Jones. It's like Andrew Toney challenging the other team, "Somebody come out here and stick me."

That is the essence of it—total teamwork. A total cooperative effort. There are definite parallels between teamwork that a basketball team uses and the teamwork a band has to use to get across to the audience. When I say parallels, it's everything from traveling together to playing with harmony.

Take traveling. In the afternoon the basketball team has a shoot-around to tune up for the game that night; in the afternoon the band has a sound check. You sort of get your game plan together.

And in the game, everybody has to contribute. It isn't the case of one star standing out in front and everybody else is in the back. Everybody has to have the chance to shine. So you get the fundamentals down, and then we come to musicality of teamwork, which is called improvisation. Certain things happen on the bandstand on the spur of the moment, and I can look in somebody's eyes and I can tell from what they just played what they were trying to do or say and I can answer them back some kind of way.

It's the same thing on a fast break in basketball. There's a lot of eye contact, even if it's just instantaneous. It means start running, fill the lane, and if you run you will be rewarded at the end of the play, finishing off the play. As far as the band is concerned, the first eight or sixteen bars of a song, yeah, you pay strict attention to what's on the score. That's the most important part, because it gets the audience's attention right away. It has to be strong. In a basketball concept, when you come out and play ferocious defense and you make things happen, that's how you get the other team's attention.

I've played only a little basketball in my life, but I played enough to know what it's like to be in a zone, as it is called, or being in a rhythm—feeling your shot. On the court when I used to play those times came rarely, but when they did it's like you're unconscious. Everything that you throw up or every pass that you make there's a benefit from it.

With my band, it's the same way sometimes. You know from the first note that this is going to be a real special night, and everything that everybody does complements everybody else, and it doesn't overshadow that the game plan is—that is, to make the best music possible and to relate to your audience.

Q: When you attend a game, do you *hear* the game in any way?

A: Oh sure. I hear rhythms. One thing I listen for are the squeaks of the sneakers. A lot of squeaking means a team is playing great defense. That's when the squeaks mean everything—especially when it's your team that's doing it. It means that everybody is in their game and they're focused. When a team is like that, it's like they're in that zone defensively. You will not let them score in your house. You will not let them embarrass you in your house.

It's like the rhythm that the drums and the percussion play. It's like all of the improvisation that's going on—people helping each other out on defense, double-teaming, and then getting back fast to cover their man. You have to change with every step because basically you don't know what is in the offensive player's head. But as long as you position yourself well, and as long as you're covered by your other teammates just in case the guy you're checking gets by you, then you are aware you have help either way you turn, and you can be more aggressive, take more chances, be more alive on the court.

There are some players that attract the eye more than others. Of course, there's Michael Jordan. But some of my favorites, in the grace and way they moved, were Connie Hawkins, and Elgin Baylor in his prime, and Earl the Pearl Monroe and Freddie Brown, with the Seattle Supersonics, who was beautiful to watch, with those big hands, and could handle the ball like a magician. And Scottie Pippen is one of my favorite players, a great defensive player. And I had a particular respect for Walt Frazier, when he was the star of those championship Knick teams. Frazier knows how to run a team, he knows how to disrupt things, he knows how to set things up, and he knows how to get his teammates into the flow of what's happening.

Q: In regard to point guards, what about Allen Iverson, who has been said to have immense talent but is undisciplined?

A: I really like his play, and I really think that it's too soon to make any kind of judgment on him because now he is just starting to come into his own. And he is just now beginning to have the kind of talent around him that can make him a better all-around player, and will make him want to be a better all-around player. And I think he has a newfound respect for his coach, Larry Brown. Now he is willing to listen to other people rather than going freestyle on his own. I think with that realization he found he can be more effective as a player in the open court as well as in the half-court defense.

Q: The 76ers had a player in the late 1970s named Lloyd B. Free, who changed his name to World B. Free, and who was an outstanding shooter but never was known for developing the rest of his game. Is Iverson in that category?

A: I think they are two different kinds of players. World had the body, he could go underneath the basket. He could bang. Iverson can't do that. And World had no conscience. He would just shoot the ball. I see where Iverson is now starting to look for the open man. Even like when he drives, he is starting to see that if he draws a double team, someone else is open, and he's looking now to give the ball to that man. I think Iverson's eyes are open for the first time for all the possibilities of what he can do within the framework that Coach Brown is espousing. The future is bright.

Q: How often do you play the national anthem before a game?

A: Not that often anymore because the band has been touring a lot. In the late 1970s and early 1980s we used to make our touring schedule around the basketball schedule. But it's a different day for us, just like it's a different day on the court for the 76ers.

Q: As the head of a band, do you watch the coach sometimes and observe what they do, and relate to that?

A: Oh definitely. It's like when you're picking songs to play at a concert. You have to be cognizant of the fact that one song should flow into the other, and it should always move up. It should have a flow leading up to a climax, in a sense.

And you pick certain tunes because you want to give everybody a chance to play, just like a coach will pick different plays so that everybody will get involved in the game.

Larry Brown has impressed me for years, because I think he incorporates that kind of thinking into running a basketball team. And every team he has coached, he has made them a better team.

I think Brown relates to his players, maybe because he's been there. You have to have some sort of bond between the coach and the player, and if the coach was a player—but, more important, a thinking man's player—then the players will pay more attention to him because he has been able to convince them that that's where they want to get to.

I've talked to numerous players and we ask each other questions about our professions. One question I've got is, What is the point of departure from the melody to the solo? I say that that changes every night. When you're on tour you don't do the same thing every night because you have a different audience, you're in a different place, you're in a different mental place, but you still want all of those same rules to apply.

With a basketball team, it's the same thing. There are certain things you want to accomplish on the court. There are certain things you want to accomplish on the stage. Basically they are the same thing. You want to give the appearance and the sound of a professional, well-oiled machine that gives everybody the credentials to stand out front, and you're having fun. That's the first thing. You've got to have fun while you're doing it because if you're not, the audience can feel it.

Magic Johnson was a great example of someone playing great basketball and having fun doing it. He had the smile and he had the exuberance. You loved watching Magic play. And that's what music does for you, too. It makes you smile and when everything is going right you feel right.

And sometimes you hear music and it's played correctly, but it's not quite right—it doesn't have the passion behind it. You cannot go on automatic pilot just because you found something that works. You have to keep experimenting with it every night. That's true for a band as well as a basketball team. You'd see different things from Michael Jordan and Julius Erving every night, things you never saw before. They were creative, and experimental.

Q: Jordan is said to be the successor to Erving as far as style and flight to the basket is concerned. How would you compare the two?

A: They were both great players, and stand in the long line of great players that made the game as popular as it is today. But first of all, they played different positions. And Michael had a lot more touches than the Doctor. Almost every time down the court Michael is going to get the ball. The Doctor only made his presence felt when he had to.

One of my all-time favorite players was Moses Malone. Here was a guy who brought his lunch pail to work every day, and he worked and worked and worked. When the season is over, he went down to Houston and he worked on his game every summer. And that's why Hakeem Olajuwon got so good. Moses and Hakeem, when Hakeem was in college at Houston and early in the pros with the Rockets, used to play one-on-one every day and Moses wasn't selfish about what he knew. He was willing to share that with other players. Well, the same with Julius. It's the same with a lot of players across the league. The best ones realize that it's not all about me. It's about the game.

Q: This might be a stretch, but if you were to compare some players to musical instruments, which ones would that be? Like Julius Erving.

A: If I had to compare Julius to a musical instrument it would be the piano. Because the whole orchestra is in the piano. He can play so many different positions. He plays so many different roles on a team. You've got to have your foundation, and I think that the piano would be that.

Q: Moses Malone?

A: Moses would be the bass. Because he's always there. And that great outlet pass, he starts things happening. That's what a bass player does. There's a different attack. There's a different intensity. The bass fits Moses to a T.

Q: Maurice Cheeks?

A: Maurice is the drummer. He's the heartbeat of the band, the heartbeat of the team. As Maurice went, so went the 76ers. A very unselfish player. Which means that he is the one who likes to do the same thing every time—by that, I mean, is in the pocket and is setting up the others so that everybody else can shine.

Q: And what part would the saxophonist play on a basketball team?

A: He would be the coach. [*Laughter.*] Because he's constantly yelling things, you know, hoping that, hoping that somebody else will pick up on it. Like when the saxophone is playing in the band I have then taken the whole band in my direction by the things that I play, and as long as they listen to me, they're going to go where I want to take them. From note to note they will know where I'm going and then when I turn it over, it's up to somebody else. So you can say that the coaching chair changes, like from the saxophone to the guitar, to the drums, to the keyboard, to the percussion.

Q: By the way, did Julius ever hear your song tribute to him?

A: He said he loved it, that it was a great tribute to the game, and he loved the fact that the title was taken from one of the television commercials he had done for Converse sneakers, which was called "Let It Flow."

Q: Did he say what he liked in particular about the song?

A: No, because my ears stopped when he said he liked it. That was enough.

COLONEL BRIAN DUFFY

COLONEL BRIAN DUFFY was selected by NASA to be an astronaut in 1985. He has made three flights into space, and commanded the space walks in each of them, though he himself remained inside the ships. He has logged more than 750 hours in space. He was the pilot on STS-45 (March 24 to April 2, 1992), the first of the ATLAS series of missions to address the atmosphere and its interaction with the sun. His most recent mission was commanding the crew of STS-92 in June 1999, the third space shuttle mission to assemble the International Space Station.

Colonel Duffy was born June 20, 1953, in Boston, Massachusetts. He graduated from Rockland High School in Rockland, Massachusetts, in 1971, and received a bachelor of science degree in mathematics from the United States Air Force Academy in 1975 and a master of science degree in systems management from the University of Southern California in 1981. He is a recipient of the Distinguished Flying Cross, Defense Meritorious Service Medal, Air Force Meritorious Service Medal, and NASA Space Flight Medals.

Colonel Duffy's interest in basketball was nurtured as a starting guard for his Rockland High School team. He stands just over six feet tall and weighs 180 pounds. He is married to the former Janet Helms and they have two children. The Duffys live in Houston, and he works at the Johnson Space Center.

● ● ●

Q: Do you still get butterflies when you are about to lift off into space? Is there still a fear of failure?

A: Oh, yes. And more than standing at the foul line with two seconds left on the clock, I'll tell you. But you learn a lot of lessons in basketball as you're growing up, and playing the game helps you out.

An astronaut and the guy on the foul line are, in some ways, in similar situations. They did a movie about a flight on *Endeavor* we made in January of 1996, in which in space we retrieved the Space Flyer Unit that was launched from Japan ten months earlier. The crew was filmed in the suit room—in our launch and entry suits—and before we headed to the launchpad. We usually have a few extra minutes to kind of cool our heels, and my pilot, Brent Jett, and I were talking. He said, "You know, this is pretty exciting." I said, "Yeah, it feels like just before the big game, before you're ready to take the court for the championship game."

That's what it feels like. You're getting ready for the big one.

So having played in other games before—in big games—you recognize that feeling and you know that you're going to be able to go out and handle whatever happens. You're trained to do it just as the athletes are trained to handle their jobs. You're trained to work under pressure and must be willing to step up and accept failure or success. They're all valuable lessons that you learn as a child growing up playing in the game, and you carry those same lessons with you the rest of your life.

Q: Did you play in important games?

A: Yes. You play in these tournaments where you're going for the state championship. They're all big games because if you lose you're out. I had the opportunity to be at the foul line in a tight game with little time on the clock and having to shoot the free throws under pressure to win or lose.

Q: Do you remember one in particular?

A: Yes. I remember we were playing in the Brockton High School gym, Brockton, Massachusetts. It was about five miles from my home. And I believe we were playing Barnstable. The score is tied, and there's about thirty seconds left in the game. So there I was standing at the free throw line. And of course the other team iced me. They called time-out.

We went back to the huddle. My coach, Bob Fisher, knew that there was a lot of pressure on, and this is what he did: he didn't talk about it. He said, "Okay, here's what we're going to do. Brian is going to make the two free throws and then this is the full-court press defense we're going to use because we've got to run the clock out." He just blew right by the fact that we had to make the free throws.

I was listening to him and I said, "Okay." We went out and of course I was nervous on the line and [*laughs*] I made both free throws.

Q: So you can relate that to when you're going to be launching and going off into space.

A: Very much so. Those are very similar feelings.

Q: Have you walked in space?

A: No, being a pilot type, we don't do the space walks. Mission specialists train and do those.

Q: But it has to be scary. I mean, you don't know if you're ever going to come back, if you're ever going to see your family again. Is that right?

A: Sure. That's always in the back of your mind. The operation is still far from routine. It's a credit to the entire NASA system that they make it appear routine, but it's not a routine task to take the equivalent of a ten-story building sitting there—which combines the shuttle, the tank with fuel in it, the solid rocket boosters on the side—and the whole thing weighing about four and a half million pounds, and get it going 17,500 miles per hour in eight and a half minutes. You have to come to grips with the dangers before you ever walk out the door to go do this. You have to come to peace with yourself because when you walk out the door you're going to work. You know you've got a job to do and you've just got to do it and you concentrate on what you're doing. You do what you're trained to do. Just like in athletics. It's a great analogy between teamwork on the athletic field and the teamwork that we do here.

Q: Being in Houston, do you see many Rockets games and if you do, can you use their work as a comparison to yours?

A: I see as many games as I can, mostly on television, but sometimes I'll attend in person. I've watched the way the Rockets play, as well as other teams. The Rockets are interesting because they now have several star players—Hakeem Olajuwon, Charles Barkley, and Scottie Pippen. Sometimes they work together, sometimes they don't. I think that the teams that work real well together play to everyone's strengths. Every person in any endeavor has strengths and weaknesses. So the teams that do well take the strengths of the individuals on that team and play to them. They try to avoid hitting the weaknesses. They try to minimize those.

When I was growing up in New England, I followed the Celtics, naturally. Especially the teams of Larry Bird, Kevin McHale, Robert Parish, Dennis Johnson—those guys. You're forever a Celtic fan if you're born there. And these guys definitely played to everybody's strengths. One of your greatest strengths is actually knowing your weakness. Like Bird. He wasn't the greatest defensive player, but he knew how to maneuver his man so that Parish or McHale could help him out.

Q: In basketball, what was your weakness and how did you work around it?

A: Well, I certainly wasn't a leaper. And I'm not the fastest guy in the world, and I wasn't the best shooter. My strength was my defense. So when we played another team in a big game, my coach put me on their shooter. My job was to stop their shooter. I'd get a few points along the way, but that wasn't what mattered. And my strength in defense was hustle and anticipation, trying to anticipate and study the other guy and see what he does and try to beat him to his move and take away what he wanted.

Q: As far as anticipation is concerned, do you use that in being an astronaut?

A: That's our job, to look ahead and anticipate what could go wrong and make sure that it doesn't. That's the life of an astronaut. That's the career of a test pilot, a fighter pilot—all those things that I've done in the past. It's a lot of the same skills. In basketball, I see a lot of NBA players with great anticipatory skills, but one of the best has to be Scottie Pippen. I've been able to see Pippen only a little since he joined the Rockets, but I watched him when he played for the Chicago Bulls. He's like a consummate player. He's a hard worker, a team player, he comes through in the clutch.

He's also a good defensive player. Barkley is very focused and very aggressive. Another one you have to recognize is Dennis Rodman, and the way he rebounds. The reason he's so successful is because he does anticipate and he does get to where he needs to be before the other people get there.

Q: Are you amazed at how these guys fly through the air, as one who flies through the air? In fact, you are one of the few human beings who has been able to soar higher than Michael Jordan.

A: The difference is—I have to ride something to fly through the air; those guys do it all by themselves. [*Laughs.*] And how they elevate, and stay elevated, does amaze me. Look at when Michael leaves the ground at the free throw line and dunks the ball. You look and say, How can he possibly do that?

Q: You studied aerodynamics. Do you have an answer?

A: He must have a secret wing that carries him up there. I don't know how he does it. I guess they're in free fall for a few seconds. We're in free fall for a few weeks.

Q: What about coordination? Is that a factor for an astronaut?

A: Hand-eye coordination is important. And you have to be organized as well. The complexity of the flight that you're planning requires that you be able to completely understand everything, anticipate what's going to happen, and successfully execute it and then move on to the next task. That's not a whole lot different from basketball, when you come down the court and you set up the play, you execute it, and then you get back on defense.

As a matter of fact, on my flight in 1996, on STS-72, we had at least one major event every day. That was really significant to the success of the mission. There was a rendezvous one day to grab that Japanese satellite, the next day was a space walk, the day after that was to deploy a satellite with the arm, the day after that was another space walk, the day after that was another rendezvous to get the satellite that we had deployed that hadn't finished its science. We were up there for ten days. After about day six or seven, we'd wake up in the morning and talk about what we were going to do and our rallying cry was, "Protect the lead!" Just like in basketball. We clearly had the lead going in. Everything had gone perfectly. We were 100 percent successful. We hadn't made any mistakes, and we wanted to make sure we were perfect all the way to the end. So our mantra was "Protect the lead!"

And sometimes it got hairy. Like with the space walkers. We had to be perfect on their tether protocol, to make sure they didn't float away.

Q: The "tether protocol"?

A: That's the term we use. Everything is tethered from space walker to shuttle and the tether has a little hook on the end of it.

Q: You'd hate to have these guys floating out into space.

A: Exactly right. That would be poor form. They would probably grade us down on that. [*Soft laughter.*] But the guys walking in space are concentrating on what they're doing, what they're trained to do. The fact that you're in a very hazardous, life-threatening environment increases your level of caution a little bit. But you still have to execute. You try to put the danger behind you.

Q: Was there a time in your three previous journeys in space when you thought, "This is curtains"?

A: Of course, you're at risk the whole trip. Even while you're sleeping because you're in the environment. But we have people at Mission Control who are watching the systems on the orbiter, and they could wake you if they needed to. But there was one time on my second flight that we had the guys that were doing the space walk—two folks were outside—and we were up on the flight deck running through all the procedure that we have to do to support them and it's dark out there and all of a sudden the whole vehicle shook very abruptly, as though we had been hit by something. We just looked at each other, like "What was that!"

Q: Like some meteor hit you?

A: Who knows? It could have been anything. When you're going at that speed—17,000 miles per hour—something coming 17,000 the other way within orbit, you'd have a 35,000 mile-an-hour collision.

Q: What was it?

A: We stared at each other for maybe a couple of seconds—there were six of us in the spacecraft—and no one said anything. And then someone said, "Does anybody know what that was?" [*Laughter.*] And then everybody said, "No." We called the ground and said, "We just had this event where the whole vehicle shook as if it was hit by something." We looked around for damage, but we couldn't see any damage to anything. What we ended up thinking was that there was some residual stress because we had a laboratory in the back—in the payload bay. There's a tunnel that connects the crew compartment up where we are to the laboratory, and maybe something has instantly unloaded and knocked back and forth. But we still don't know.

Q: When you were growing up and Larry Bird was the star player on the Celtics, there was a certain coolness to him, which he now demonstrates as a coach with Indiana. And since you were a Celtic fan, did you admire that characteristic in him?

A: I think you had to admire the way he did it. He certainly was the guy who wanted the ball when the clock was running down. He had the confidence in himself to be the go-to guy. "Let me win it or lose it. I'll take the game on my shoulders." I think that's pretty admirable.

Q: And you are the commander of the flights. Are you a sort of a Larry Bird when you go up there?

A: Basically. And the last "Protect the lead" was for me to land the orbiter. You know, it's a hundred-ton glider coming in. You've got one chance at it and we're coming in at three in the morning. So it's similar to a Larry Bird situation—"Give me the ball, coach!"

Q: Do you have a favorite player?

A: Now that Michael's retired?

Q: Was he your favorite player?

A: You can't help but admire him. But I think Larry Bird is my all-time favorite player, and I've met him, too.

Q: When you were an astronaut?

A: Yes. I gave him a tour down at the Kennedy Space Center in Cape Canaveral, Florida, when he was still with the Celtics and they were playing the Magic at Orlando one time.

The way it happened was, a friend of mine—another astronaut named Sonny Carter—was working at the Cape for us. This was about 1991. Sonny was an interface between the astronaut office and the hardware folks who were putting the vehicles together. The public affairs people at Kennedy Space Center had gotten a request from the Celts saying that they had some free time—I think they had come in a day early—just to have a tour. It turned out Larry Bird was one of them, along with a couple of the coaches. So they called Sonny and asked if he could handle this. He said, "I'm not the right person to do this. We need Duffy down here." I was in Houston, but Sonny knew I was a Celtics fan. So he called me and said, "You've got to get in the 238—that's our training plane—and come down here and do this tour." I hopped right into the plane and flew down to Orlando. And that's when I met Larry Bird.

Q: Do you remember what he asked you?

A: He was asking mostly what it was like to launch and what it was like to be weightless up in zero gravity. He was pretty fascinated by it. I said it's a unique feeling that you very quickly grow accustomed to so that it becomes normal. One thing I really like about it is that it seems like everything is easier in space, except for keeping track of things. If it doesn't have Velcro on it, you can't just put it in a place or put it in your pocket. It just floats away. It's real easy to lose track of things.

Q: What did you ask him?

A: I asked how he likes playing in the bigs and how he liked all the traveling. He said the traveling wasn't so great, but you know, he liked the team, he liked the guys, and he loved the competition. It was just small talk.

Q: Was he impressed with anything particularly?

A: He was impressed by the size of everything. You can't help but be. Everything is so huge. The crawler that carries the space shuttle out to the launchpad, for instance, is a big platform and has these treads on it like tank treads. But each one of the treads on this track weighs a ton. Just one little tread is 2,000 pounds. And there are a bunch of them, of course, on each of the tracks. He was surprised at this.

Q: Were you surprised at anything about him?

A: Yeah—at how big he is! He's huge! You don't realize how big he is, or the other players. You hear somebody is six-nine, or six-ten, and it sounds tall, but what you don't realize is that their shoulders and arms and legs that go into that size are huge, too.

We had another time when the Celtics came to Houston and I was asked to go to the game and then into the locker room. I bought my son, Shaun. At the time, he was seven or eight years old. So after the game we went into the Celtic locker room and a trainer met us who had also been on that tour at the Cape. He brought us in and Kevin McHale—who is about six-eleven—was on a training table. The table was about three feet off the ground, and he was stretched out laying back and they were working on his knee. We came in and they introduced my son to Kevin—he was really gracious. So Shaun was eyeball to eyeball with Kevin McHale as he was laying on this table. After about five minutes they were done working on McHale's knee and he says, "Well, excuse me, guys, I have to hit the shower." And he stood up. My son was standing right next to him and his head goes back as he's looking all the way up at McHale. It was like looking at the Empire State Building. It was really comical. It was one of those sights I'll never forget.

Q: How long have you been a basketball fan?

A: My whole life. It was really big in my hometown when I was growing up. It was the sport to play. We played it twelve months a year. We had summer leagues and I played organized ball from the time I was in elementary school. I didn't play basketball in college. But I did play baseball at the Air Force Academy. But I continued to follow basketball. I think the professional basketball players are the best athletes in the world. It's amazing to sit at courtside and see these huge men running faster than I can run. And when I watch a game I watch for team dynamics. How a team is clicking or not clicking on a particular night. I'm especially mindful of the third quarter. If the Rockets, say, had a poor first half, I watch to see if they adapt to the change. If they had a good first half, I watch to see how they adapt to the other team's change at halftime, presuming they make changes. And I look to see if the Rockets will maintain their lead and continue and drive through to the end.

Q: Do you still play basketball?

A: All the time. Actually, I've played regularly until recently, when I hurt my knee while playing and had to have arthroscopic surgery on it. But I'm coming back. My last crew was a six-person crew, and all of us played, so we had a built-in three-on-three. It was great fun and it was great camaraderie and good team-building for our flight. So protecting the lead came naturally.

REVEREND EDWARD ALOYSIUS MALLOY

FATHER MALLOY, the president of Notre Dame University, was born on May 3, 1941, in Washington, D.C. He went to DeMatha High School there and, at six-three and a half, was the starting guard on a basketball team that went undefeated in fifty-five straight games, a national high school record that stood for two decades (a teammate was John Thompson, who went on to play for the Boston Celtics and coach Georgetown University for many years). Father Malloy received a bachelor's degree from Notre Dame in 1963, earned a master's from the same school, was ordained a priest in the Roman Catholic Church in 1970, and received a Ph.D. from Vanderbilt. He became a professor of theology at Notre Dame and in 1987 was named president of the university.

Father Malloy is known widely as "Monk." Almost everyone calls him that, including the students when they see him on campus. He says, "It is a nickname, not a title." The name was given him by a friend named Bunky in the third grade. Malloy called him "Bunk" for short, and Bunk began calling him "Monk." He is the author of several books including, most recently, *Monk's Reflections*, part autobiography and part philosophical ruminations, which was published in the fall of 1999.

●　●　●

Q: Basketball has been called a kind of religion. Do you share the view that for some, basketball, or success in basketball, is more than just a game?

A: Athletics, not only in this culture, but in other parts of the world, has some features of religion. It has devotees, it has people who utilize fandom as their primary outlet, people who are pre-occupied by statistics and other kinds of gathering and memorabilia and identifying with the colors and the logo and team songs. I think that for some that's correlated with being part of a metropolitan area and having a kind of regional or local identity. It has some elements of religion in the sense that there is a stylized and ritualized way that you participate in all of this, and periodic tests of success and failure. You might say that a lot of people don't have any religion if they are not committed or involved in an organized religion, but some are looking for a substitute and athletics might be an available substitute. So could rock music or theater or art or some radical movement.

Q: There was a famous story about a black man in the South in the 1930s who was convicted of murder and received the death penalty and was put into the gas chamber and all the time he had proclaimed his innocence. As the gas jets were turned on he was heard to plead, "Save me, Joe Louis, save me!" I've heard similar things about Michael Jordan being raised almost to a deity.

A: Jordan was a super basketball player, but not a super baseball player.

Q: Some wonder if he's a super golfer.

A: Now, there's the whole question about what he does with his future. I think the test case for Michael Jordan from here on out is what kind of contribution does he want to make to the well-being of society, because he has a chance to do a lot of good. So the fact that people would look at any individual, whether it's

Bill Gates or Bill Clinton or Michael Jordan or anybody else, as kinds of deities because they are prominent and well-known and have a degree of success in a given field, has something to do with the psychology of a given individual. But I don't think there's very many people around who think of sports figures in those terms.

Q: After some games—the Knicks, among others, do it all the time—some of the players gather in a circle on the court and hold a short prayer session. Woody Allen says the only explanation can be that they are thanking the Lord for their high salaries. What do you make of such a display of public prayer?

A: There is an effort by the Fellowship of Christian Athletes and various evangelical groups to promote that sort of manifest display of religion connected to sports, and it could be an example of these athletic basketball teams that go around playing college teams at the beginning of the season. They ask to give a religious talk at halftime. So this is not spontaneous. This happens as a result of either organized groups or the interposing of a particular ministerial figure with a local team. I have no objection to it. But it's not something I would wish to have participated in if I were an athlete.

Q: Because?

A: It's usually the after-the-game phenomenon. At Notre Dame our teams have a mass before the game, in the locker room. We have prayer in the locker room afterward, but we try to make it less public and more directed to the members of the team praying for health and avoiding injury, and they pray for success as well. But I think that anybody who knows any theology knows that if both sides are praying, who is God paying attention to? It's like it has more to do with our sense of preparation and dependency, rather than legitimately expecting that God is going to favor one side over the other.

Q: Did you ever make the sign of the cross at the free throw line?

A: I did. It was something we used to do in grade school, and maybe in high school.

Q: Why did you stop?

A: It didn't seem as obvious that it was the right thing to do. It probably just happened by osmosis. I shot about 85 percent from the free throw line in high school, so maybe I was more confident later.

Q: No longer needed divine intervention in this area?

A: [*Laughter.*] I don't know. Maybe at the time.

Q: You received a basketball scholarship to Notre Dame out of high school. But for the most part at Notre Dame, you sat on the bench. What life lessons did you learn from sitting on the bench?

A: I learned that it's better to be playing than sitting.

Q: Anything else?

A: I learned quite quickly that high school is different from college. I learned that my particular set of skills did not fit the circumstance that I found myself in, although I could imagine a different scenario, at another school, where I might have played more. But that is not untypical of anyone sitting on the bench anywhere. They always think that if they had gone to another school, things would get better. They didn't for me, but it wasn't like I was frustrated.

Q: You weren't?

A: Well, you try to be as resilient as you can from day to day. You live in hope. You always think it will get better. Next year will be better than this one. You think that if you work in practice, somehow your set of talents will become appreciated. That's how you motivate yourself from day to day.

Q: But that didn't quite happen to you.

A: I played more as time went on, but I never got to the point where I was a prominent member of the team, or a member of the starting team. So there is always some frustration connected to that.

Q: If you had to do it over again, would you have gone to Notre Dame?

A: Sure. In retrospect, it was the best thing that ever happened to me because of the education, because of the people I met, because of the vocation to the priesthood that emerged out of that, because I've come back and played multiple roles in the same school. If I think of it, my time on the bench was a minor setback, and I just used that energy from not playing much and directed it somewhere else.

Q: Where did you direct it?

A: I was involved in student leadership at the dorm level, and I was involved in various activities of service. I went to Latin America, to Peru and Mexico, for three consecutive summers on service projects. It was working with the poor and relief efforts and helping in some minor medical care.

Q: As a priest, and knowing the game of basketball, do you feel when you watch a game or are involved in a game that you can in some way look into the souls of people who are playing? That is, can you tell the character of those people?

A: I still play pickup games on campus. And I've maintained a position for a long time which continues to be demonstrated to me that you have very quick insight into the character of people when they're in games. Especially in a team game like basketball. If you play basketball on the same team or against people on a fairly regular basis, their interest in and capacity for a team style comes to the fore. You see them dealing with anger, you see what kind of competitive juices they have, how they deal with frustration. I think there are insights that come, and the more you are with somebody, and the more you interact with them, I think it's very revelatory.

I can think of a lot of people I know who I've seen a direct correlation between what I saw for them in basketball and what I've seen them do academically, relative to their ability, how generous they are, how interested they are in other people or preoccupied with themselves. I think all of these things are very evident. Now if they are totally inept at a game, it probably doesn't happen. And if you're a superstar, you may not see the same thing because you just have such a capacity to rise above everybody else. But I think for the average person, you see that over time when you're playing either a pickup game or in games in leagues.

Q: By league games, do you mean like the NBA?

A: Yes, though the NBA is a stylized game that may not always be as easy to see, unless you watch somebody a lot. I think that over time you can get a pretty good sense of what makes people tick.

Q: How do you perceive the business of calling athletes "role models?"

A: Athletes can be only a selective role model. You can be a role model of how one deals with success and how one tries to represent a team or an area as a citizen. When it comes to the value of their life, their relationship with members of the opposite sex or their families, it has to be shown over time whether they are worthy of any kind of modeling, should they be given that recognition. But I would say the same about anyone else who gets a fair amount of media attention.

Q: Are there any NBA players who you are comfortable with viewing as a role model?

A: Grant Hill of the Pistons, for one. I happen to know his parents. From what I know of him, he has tried to live his life as someone who represents a very high set of ideals. He hasn't been connected with behavior that would be questionable in terms of use of alcohol or drugs or physical assault. I think he's articulate, and he seems to have a sense of balance about the role that athletics plays in his life. I'm aware that he is available for challenging young people to take advantage of their educational opportunities.

Q: Of the players you see in the NBA, are there any that might make a good priest?

A: [*Laughter.*] Someone I know personally. It's Pat Garrity, who plays for the Orlando Magic. Pat was a student here at the university and I had him in class when he was in his first year. He graduated with a very high academic average and in a tough course. I watched him develop as a player. I saw his relationship to his peers, and it's hard in a college setting to impress your peers unless there's some sincerity and genuineness there. He graduated being held in very high regard by Notre Dame people in general. He had a very successful college career, although the teams he played on weren't as good as they might have been.

Now he goes to the pros and the first stage, he's getting very little playing time. In some games, he didn't play at all. And then all of sudden he's given a chance to show what he can do. He had a couple of twenty-point games and some teen games. I've seen him make a transition.

Now one question I have about him—and John Paxson as well, who I know because he also went to Notre Dame before becoming a starting player on three Chicago Bulls championship teams—the question is: What do they do with their time and how do they relate to their peers in the pros. For me, it has a lot to do with values and interest of people who are basically intellectual as well as athletically gifted. I just think that that would be one of the most demanding and challenging things about playing professional sports. I think that when you're spending all your time in the company of people with a different orientation, that it's a real challenge to maintain your sense of self and integrity and interest.

Q: Bill Laimbeer is a Notre Dame alumnus who had a less-than-stellar reputation as a player with the Pistons. Basically, he was considered an effective but dirty player. Did you know him?

A: I actually talked with him more since he finished playing for Detroit than I did while he was playing. I watched him play, and I knew about his reputation.

Q: What did you make of him?

A: Very complex. He comes from a fairly well-to-do background.

Q: I believe he once said that he was the only player in the NBA whose father makes more money than he does.

A: That's probably right. I found him bright, but a bit snarly. He had a very mixed reputation among the students when he was here. He had little time when he wasn't eligible to play, but he finished his degree and went on. And then he had a mixed reputation in the pros, whether he was someone who utilizes talent as effectively as possible. He was not without controversy his whole professional career.

Q: He wasn't Larry Bird's favorite player. Bird got into a fight with him after he more or less mugged Bird from behind in a playoff game.

A: I remember that. I had the highest regard for Bird as a professional athlete. And I think he's been a very successful coach, as I've had an opportunity to watch a lot of his games, since we're both in Indiana. I think for someone who was a superstar at his level and with his commitment and the way he played a phenomenal team game his whole career, that for him to able to bring that out in a team—a fairly old team with no superstar—is remarkable. Most people thought he could never achieve this. I think the question now is, Will he get bored?

Q: How have you seen him get this out of players?

A: I watched the Pacers play enough before he became the coach, and I thought they were not consistent and in big games often would lose by a close margin. I think what Bird has done for them is convince them that they can win. I think his players believe in his system and play as hard as any team in the league. If you took the talent level of some of the other teams and put them in the same mode, I believe they would be a dominating team.

Q: It's my impression that Bird's reserved style is the direct opposite of that of Bobby Knight, and I have a sense that it is no coincidence.

A: Maybe not, since Bird left Knight's program.

Q: What do you make of Knight?

A: I wouldn't want to play for him. He's a yeller and a screamer and a tyrant. I don't sit around thinking what's wrong with Bobby Knight, but I wouldn't want him as a coach here. I just don't like that particular style of coaching, and I think he is very straightforward in his philosophy of coaching and the role that he wants to play, and I don't agree with that philosophy.

Q: Have you had a basketball player leave Notre Dame early to go to the pros?

A: Monty Williams, who went to the Knicks. I had him in class, but I didn't speak to him about the decision. It's a little tricky for a university president to look like you're trying to get too directly involved in specific decision-making.

Q: But how do you feel about student-athletes leaving school early to go pro?

A: I don't like it. I think it's a quick short-term reward for the risk of one's lifetime employment and potential professional success. For some sports, like baseball, it was historically not a college sport.

Q: Players become professional right out of high school.

A: Right, and I think that professional athletics now has taken a short-term solution, and that it's going to end up with a lot of young people on the bench and a few people playing. It's going to inhibit the growth of those players, but I think for the vast majority of them, they're better off, both in terms of maturing socially and academically, by staying in college. They're better suited to go to the pros when they finish that term of their life.

Q: But would you not agree that for some—maybe a minority—it was, and is, a right decision? I think of someone like Stephon Marbury, who left Georgia Tech after two years, and Kevin Garnett, who never went to college at all. Both of them signed contracts in the neighborhood of $100 million. And now for the first time a couple of players are leaving Duke early to try their luck in the NBA It seems to be happening more and more often.

A: You can only tell when someone looks back on his life whether he made the right decision, whether he made a good choice going pro so early. Take someone like Moses Malone, who never went to college. Would Moses Malone's life have been different if he had not made those kinds of choices? I have no idea, but it's probably only in retrospect with a bit of wisdom of age and experience that you can really answer that question for the individual.

Q: Do you enjoy watching pro basketball?

A: As a fan, my favorite sport to watch is pro basketball. The level of ability is so high, and having played the game I appreciate it as a phenomenally interesting game. It can be played raggedly, and poorly, but at its best it's a beautiful game. I was a big Bulls fan when they were good. Because they played as a team. I was a Celtics fan when they were good. You can say we always go for the winners. But I was Celtics as opposed to the Lakers because I liked the Celtics' style better. And I liked the Knicks in their championship years. I like teams that play that kind of style like Utah plays.

Q: Is there a player who reminded you in some way of how you played?

A: I kind of identified with Sam Jones, the Celtic guard from years ago. He was a pure jump shooter and basically an outside shooter more than a driver. He played within a team style. I liked the way he played a lot.

Q: Did you ever meet him?

A: No.

Q: If you had, what might you have asked him?

A: "You banked so many shots off the backboard, did you ever get any lucky bounces that looked like a bank that you didn't intend—because I have." Especially if you bank it from the front of the basket and it goes in off the backboard. If you bank it from the side, you can say, Yeah, I intended that, but if you bank from the front it looks like you just shot it too far.

Q: And what did you say when you banked it from the front and it went in, Father?

A: I said I intended it all along.

Q: How is your game these days?

A: Right now I'm on the injured reserve list. I hurt my shoulder. It was a combination of old age—I'm fifty-seven—and worn-out muscles and bones. But I'm in the process of working my way back. But I still get a lot of pleasure out of playing the game. I've spent a lot of my youth and adult life playing basketball. I enjoy the nature of the game, the capacity to play by yourself, one-on-one, two-on-two, and so on, as well as the normal five-on-five. I like the flexibility of playing indoors or outdoors. And you don't have to have money to play, as long as you have a ball. One of the advantages I have is that I'm basically a shooter. I could always shoot long distances well, so it's possible to still play my style. I wasn't a slasher and I didn't have to drive to the bucket to get a shot off. So it makes it easier to play the game as you get older and your physical skills decline. As long as you can still shoot.

Q: You play in the school gym?

A: There, and also every year in the bookstore basketball tournament at Notre Dame. It's outdoors. Everybody from Notre Dame is eligible—faculty, students, staff. It's five-on-five full-court. Twenty-one baskets wins. There are about seven hundred teams to start with, but there are referees for only the last thirty-two games. If anybody gets hurt, you just drag them off. You can't substitute. I played in that for years. It's rough. My team was named All the President's Men.

In one game, we played a team on which my niece, Maggie Long, was a member. Her team wasn't good at all, but at one point she stole the ball from me. To prevent her from going on a fast break, I grabbed her sweatshirt and tugged it. A picture was shot at that moment and it appeared on the front page of the student newspaper. Here I was holding the sweatshirt of this female trying to go down to the other end of the court. It didn't explain that it was my niece! I got some flack for that. People would see me on campus and say, "I saw you fouling again in the student newspaper."

In another year, there was a game in which I shot eleven for eleven. In the next game I shot zero for eleven. I was asked to explain the difference in the two games.

Q: What did you say?

A: The only thing I could say: the wind was blowing stronger in the second game than in the first.

WALTER MATTHAU

THE first time I met Walter Matthau was on a gray, early November afternoon in 1985 at Aqueduct Racetrack in New York City. He was there to watch and wager on the races in the Breeders' Cup. In the clubhouse, a waiter asked Matthau if he wanted something to eat. "Not now," he said. "Maybe if I have a few winners I'll feel like eating."

Shortly after, Dan Issel, the six-eleven former forward for the Denver Nuggets, came by to introduce himself to Matthau. Issel was with his wife, Cheri, who is about a foot and a half shorter than her husband. "You're a terrific basketball player," Matthau said to Mrs. Issel. Then he turned to Issel. "And what do you do for a living?"

Matthau was born on October 1, 1920, on the Lower East Side of New York, and now lives in Pacific Palisades, California. Matthau has been an acclaimed movie actor for thirty-five years, but he was a Broadway star before he became a movie star. He won a Tony for his stage portrayal of Oscar Madison, the sportswriter, in *The Odd Couple*. His film career began in 1965 when he played the same character in the movie based on the Neil Simon play. He won an Academy Award the next year for his role in *The Fortune Cookie*.

The interview was conducted in mid–October 1999. He had been home for about a week, after spending four months in the hospital for respiratory infections.

●　　●　　●

Q: You have said that sometimes when you're watching a basketball game on television you'll turn off the sound and put on music to watch it by. Why is that?

A: That's absolutely true, but it depends on who the announcer is. Sometimes they talk too much, even if they know what they're talking about.

Q: What kind of music do you listen to?

A: It's got to be Mozart. Practically everything he wrote was magnificent. There's nobody quite like him. And his music is so relaxing, even if the other team, the team I'm betting against, scores a three-point goal.

Q: You can still find a three-point goal against you relaxing?

A: I say, "Oh, shit," and then just go back to the music almost immediately. It's amazing how often the action seems to go in concert with the music. You're hearing a violin concerto or a horn concerto and the players are moving to the music, almost like a ballet. It's most beautiful, of course, when your team is way ahead of the point spread at the end of the game—what's known as a laugher.

Q: Do you observe things differently when you have a bet on the game from when you don't have a bet?

A: I haven't made a bet in over a year, after a lifetime of betting on games. I would say I enjoy the game better if I'm not betting on it. I've been enjoying the games much more. You can really appreciate the artistry.

Last night I made a mind bet on the Boston Red Sox in the playoffs against the Yankees. Now, the Red Sox should have won that game. And the night before they should have won that game. They were two and a half to one underdogs. In a baseball game that means one team is very much the better team. If I was betting on the game and I had the Red Sox, I would get a chemical reaction of pain and stomach distress, spasms, colitis distress. A headache, too. But without betting on the game, it's more pleasant.

Q: Do you truly feel you are working when you are watching a game and have a bet on it?

A: It's terrific stress. They tell me that that's what working is. In fact, I find working—acting in a film—easier than when I'm in the middle of a bet. When making a movie, you can have a number of takes to get the scene right. Whereas in a bet, it's that day, and you either win or lose. There's no fooling around. Yeah, it's a rough number.

Q: Why do you continue gambling?

A: It's in the blood. I'm absolutely addicted to it.

Q: But you've been able to stay away for a year.

A: Mostly I've been in the Intensive Care Unit at the UCLA Medical Center.

Q: But if you had to, you could have still put a bet down, couldn't you?

A: I was on a respiratory machine. It would have been rather difficult.

Q: Is this the longest you've gone without making a bet?

A: Oh yeah.

Q: Do you feel you're missing something?

A: No, because I feel lousy about the dialysis. When you have a lot of things wrong with you, taking antibiotics and all that stuff, and then you wind up with renal failure, it cuts into your other activities.

Q: When you were gambling regularly, and were at home, where would you watch the games?

A: I must have had fifteen television sets throughout the house and in my office, which is in a small building adjoining the house. And I would sit there and get up and walk around from TV set to TV set, and suffer. And it takes substantial bets to do it. One afternoon Maureen Stapleton dropped by for a visit. She's one of my wife's best friends—and she played *my* wife in *Plaza Suite*. Maureen had something she wanted to read to me, a short story. I said, "Maureen, there's two minutes to go in the game! This is work! Later!" She walked out. But I'm working on these games. Laboring. My head is spinning. I'm hollering at the television set, at the umpires, the referees, the zebras: "You damn liar! You're blind, you horse's ass, you crook!" I know these guys are betting on the other team. And then suddenly they'll make a terrific call in my favor. And I'll say, "Oh, maybe these guys are honest." But mostly, they're crooks, thieves. Now, as I've said, when you're winning, everything is quiet, pleasant. So there really isn't much fun in winning.

Q: Do you have a favorite basketball player?

A: I did in high school. In high school the best player I ever saw was a guy named Sol Sherman. We called him Chubby. He played for Seward Park High School, where I went to school. He was a magnificent passer. We said that Bob Cousy came along and imitated Chubby Sherman. He was also a dead shot. He threw the ball up for a shot and it was an accident if it didn't go in. And he was blind.

Q: Blind?

A: Well, he could hardly see. He wore glasses, but only off the court. He just got an idea of where the basket was and threw it up and it went in. Uncanny.

Q: What current players do you like?

A: I like Chris Mullin. When he came to town with Golden State to play the Lakers and I was sitting on the floor in The Forum he would always stop to say hello. He'd ask, "Have you got any new pictures out?" He told me his favorite picture was *The Taking of Pelham 1-2-3*.

Q: He's from a part of New York where that train runs, isn't he?

A: Yeah. He said, "I used to take that train." I liked Michael Cooper, when he was with the Lakers. He was bright. His eyes twinkled. And I loved Wilt Chamberlain. I remember him telling his teammates when he was in the pivot, "C'mon, baby, move. Don't just stand there. Just move. Move, baby." I was with my son Charlie, who was about ten years old at the time. He asked me, "Does he rehearse that?" I guess he thought it was like me doing a movie and working on my lines. And of course Magic Johnson was a treat to watch. He was a guard in a six-nine body. And he could pass the ball like Chubby Sherman. Magic would come by where we were sitting and say to Charlie and me—looking at Charlie—"Hi, guys, want to go for some ice cream later?" Magic has that terrific smile. We never went for ice cream, but it was nice of him to ask.

Q: You watched Kareem Abdul-Jabbar for many years. Did you ever meet him?

A: Oh yeah. I found him very ill at ease. He's from New York and the first time I met him I told him that years ago I played handball with his father. He didn't seem interested. And he stood up so straight. He was determined to make you look at least a foot shorter, no matter how tall you were. I got the impression that it was getting even with the racial state of affairs in the United States for a long time—from slavery days to the discrimination that still exists here. I think he was disturbed about the fact that such a thing has happened, and that he was going to be so dignified that he was going to stand out above all of these humiliating episodes that he had to meet. Personally and historically, both, intertwined.

But one time I played against him in a charity game, the actors versus the pros. And I went into the pivot against him and took a sky hook, the way he did. I missed badly. It was funny. Kareem looked at me and said, "What's the matter? You're supposed to be a great sports figure." I said, "No, that's the sportswriter in the movies." He was confusing fiction with reality.

Q: Is there one basketball bet you had that somehow sticks out in your memory?

A: No. The biggest emotion was when I lost. And when I lost I immediately stored the thought of it in an unmemorable place. Winning is a much smaller emotion. That's because it's pleasant. There is nothing aggravating about it. It doesn't have a large scope.

Q: Is it like reviews? Somehow one seems to remember the bad reviews. Bad reviews have an impact that good reviews don't. Do you find that to be true?

A: Absolutely. I remember a review from Pauline Kael, when she was *The New Yorker* film critic. She said about me in a movie called *The Laughing Policeman*, which was a good twenty-seven years ago: "In this one Matthau plays a black-haired policeman," implying that that's not the color of my hair. She went on: "His hair, like John Wayne's autumnal crop, shrivels his stature." She was implying that John Wayne had a new crop of hair color every autumn. Once a year. When I had a haircut I would send her patches of hair and say, "This is my hair. Why don't you find out whether it was dyed." Never heard back.

Q: By the way, whatever happened to Chubby Sherman? I don't remember him ever playing pro ball.

A: He never went to college, as far as I know. I believe he wound up in the garment center. Worked as a cutter, I heard. I always wondered if he cut clothes without looking, the way he shot those baskets.

WILLIAM GOLDMAN

WILLIAM GOLDMAN, novelist, playwright, essayist, and screenwriter, was born in Chicago on August 12, 1932. His screenplays for *Butch Cassidy and the Sundance Kid* and *All the President's Men* won Academy Awards. Other screenplays include *Masquerade, The Hot Rock, The Stepford Wives, Marathon Man, The Princess Bride, Heat, Misery,* and *Absolute Power.* His novels include *The Temple of Gold, Boys and Girls Together, Marathon Man, Hype and Glory,* and *Tinsel.* He wrote two Broadway-produced plays with his brother, James Goldman: *Blood, Sweat and Stanley Poole* and *A Family Affair* (also with John Kander). His frank nonfiction look at moviemaking and the personalities involved, *Adventures in the Screen Trade,* published in 1983, is still regarded as a classic of its genre.

Mr. Goldman lives in a penthouse apartment on the East Side of Manhattan. At one end of his well-furnished living room, which is lined with books, is a pool table. Goldman, his thick hair mostly gray, wears a yellow sweater, jeans, and sneakers. When speaking about sports, he does so with a decided passion. He has had season tickets to New York Knick games for nearly thirty years.

●   ●   ●

Q: How do you view a basketball game?

A: When I'm watching a sports event and rooting for a team, as I do the Knicks, I'm working, too. I'm in the stands—or I'm watching on television—and I genuinely know that I can control sporting events around the world. I don't know when my power will kick in, though. I think all sports fans believe this. When you get to Madison Square Garden, which is a great arena, and the team is playing well, that's wonderful. It's a very knowledgeable basketball crowd in the Garden, but you still see people crossing their fingers—you know, the mystical things we all do to change the opponent's free throw. I do it all the time, that stuff. And all of it works. I just don't know when. Sometimes I'll chew gum and he'll miss a free throw. I can provably say I put the gum in. It's an if/then thing. I know I did it. [*Laughter.*] But no, I get so crazed and I—I don't know. I think it all has to go back to childhood, but sports has always been a thing for me.

Controlling events around me, ordering a life, is what I do to a great degree in writing a screenplay. I can decide within the context of the story what the characters will do and say. Even who lives and who dies. Like in the adaptation of the movie *Misery*, based on the Stephen King thriller. In the book, the author, played in the movie by James Caan, gets his legs cut off by the crazy fan, played by Kathy Bates. But in the movie, she just breaks his legs. We knew that if we were absolutely faithful to the book, we'd lose the audience. They'd all walk out of the theater. It was too gruesome.

Q: How did you become such a passionate Knicks fan?

A: When they had those championship teams under Red Holzman in the early 1970s. The Bill Bradley–Dave DeBusschere–Walt Frazier–Willis Reed–Dick Barnett–Earl Monroe teams. They were the best team I ever saw. They were the smartest team I ever saw.

I loved Red Holzman. He was an absolutely brilliant coach when they won their championships in 1970 and 1973. His handling of players and situations was masterful. I was having dinner after a game in that period, and it had been a very exciting game. Red happened to be in the same restaurant with a group of people. We were introduced, and I said, "God, that game was exciting!" And he looked at me strange and said, "Was it?" I remember thinking I had said something so stupid and I backed away. I left. Well, he came over a little while later and he said very quietly, "Bill, I'm really glad you enjoyed it. I'm working it. I don't know if it's exciting for you. I'm glad you were entertained, but what I'm worrying about is if I got the matchups right." That's his office. That's when he's working.

I was once talking with Kevin Loughery, who became an NBA coach, but who was a guard on the Baltimore Bullets teams that used to have fierce playoff series with those Knicks. Loughery told me, "We always knew they'd beat us." I asked, "Why?" He said, "If it came down to the last minute, we just knew they were so smart they weren't going to make a mistake, and we would." It was a fabulous team for me because I love passing. If you look at teams today, they don't pass much. I saw Bobby Knight being interviewed on television and he said, "All the players care about today is doing something for the highlight films on *Sportscenter.*" It's this kind of thing that bothers me in basketball now, when I see teams and stars who are essentially inept.

Now, I loved watching the 1998 championship finals between Utah and Chicago, two wonderfully proper teams, with a team concept. And I've always admired John Stockton, the Utah point guard. He's phenomenal because I just never know what he's going to do, but I know it's going to be wonderful. He doesn't go between his legs, and he doesn't go behind his back and all that shit, and that's okay. The point of a pass is to give it to somebody at the right time on the right foot. Not to basically dazzle the crowd. What bothers me now, when I see a player like Chris Webber, who I detest, is that he can really pass when he puts his mind to it, and he can block shots, but mostly he plays like an idiot in this fabulous body. Or Shawn Kemp, who plays a selfish and stupid game. But they are making $100 million on their contracts because they have so much talent, so much potential. So why should they alter their style—but the fact is, it's wrong that anybody should pay them that kind of money because you are not going to win with them.

I think essentially the Lakers are too stupid to win. They got rid of Nick Van Exel, which was a big step forward, but now the team centers around Shaquille O'Neal, who says, "Look at my numbers. My numbers are good, aren't they? I've got twenty-five points, and I had ten rebounds." But his team lost. But O'Neal is making money cutting records as a rap musician, he's making movies. Why should he change anything about his basketball?

What's even worse is when the mediocre players are the highest paid. No one objects to Michael Jordan making a million dollars a game. But Juwan Howard, who has never proved he is a star?

We have an odd thing in Hollywood. I've been doing movies out there for thirty-five years. And the three biggest stars, one could argue, are Jim Carrey, Tom Cruise, and Tom Hanks. They are all hard-working. Carrey is brutally hard-working. He's very nice with the other actors, but vicious with himself about whether he did the scene right. If not, he asks, "Can I do that again? Please! I want to do one more take." And I think basically all three are happy making $20 million a picture, and not making any more. Any one of them could make more.

But when you hear about the ballplayers demanding more and more money, especially when they haven't proved anything, really, and haven't won a championship, and don't even work at their profession the way I believe they should—have you seen some of them shoot free throws, for God's sakes!—then it's a terrible turnoff.

Q: In your view, how does this start?

A: I think some of it has to do with upbringing. Most of the players are black, and for mostly slum kids, there is that disgraceful word which I hope the blacks will rid of their vocabulary as soon as they realize they don't need it anymore, and that's the word "dissed." You know, "You dissed me." You won't be treated as a "man" unless you get—I mean, there was this awful thing with Kevin Garnett, who was twenty years old and offered $100 million by the Minnesota Timberwolves, and it was "dissing" him. He got $126 million over seven years. I contend that there is nothing on earth in that young man's mind in which there is any difference between $100 million and $126 million because you're talking about $13 million and $15 million over seven years. There is nothing you can buy with $15 million that he couldn't buy with $13 million. There is no difference.

Now Jayson Williams of the Nets signed a huge contract and he said just that. What's the difference between $10 million a year and $12 million a year? None. I wish there were twenty Jayson Williamses. He's also clearly become one of the two best rebounders in basketball, him and Dennis Rodman. And he may be better than Rodman, and he's younger, only about thirty years old. He can also run, and he can shoot some, which Rodman can't do.

But this attitude regarding the crazy accumulation of money isn't confined to ballplayers. It sometimes cuts across profession and race. I used to go to a very famous shrink, now dead, and in front of me was an open hour. I saw her once a week, and you'd see all kind of very famous people coming out from the hour that she kept open for consultation. Once, after several billionaires in a row came out, I said, "These guys have so much money, why do they want to make more?" And she said, "Because they have no inner life." I wonder if that's the case with so many of the athletes—after all, from the time they are in the fourth or fifth grade they are being coddled, told how great they are, and able to get away with stuff others can't get away with. I think that many of them, like stars in Hollywood, don't have real friends. They have business associates, who they might think are friends. But ballplayers now have entourages, and that includes their agents. I think the agents are pushing them, and influencing them to equate their manhood with making more money. Of course, the greater the man they are, supposedly, the more the agent gets on his cut, too.

But then you get a guy like Charles Oakley, who I enjoyed immensely. He was not a very appealing player in that he wasn't graceful, but he was like an average talented DeBusschere in the sense that he really tried. You very rarely saw Oakley not kill himself on the court. You want to love these guys, diving all over the place for the ball, blocking out, hustling on defense, doing all the little things that help your team win. And John Starks. Oh, John Starks! He really tested your emotions. You never knew what he was going to do—was it going to be terrific, or was it going to be terrible? I had such mixed emotions when he was traded.

It's that kind of thing, though, that is so attractive about sports, and separates the sports stars from the movie stars. Both have to have big egos, but the difference between Hollywood stars and athletic stars is that Hollywood stars basically know two things: one, that whatever it is that you're seeing, it isn't them. It's not the real person who goes to the bathroom and has trouble with all the rest of the things that we all have trouble with in real life. So we've fallen in love with an image that's perfect. They know it's not them, and they also know it's going to go away soon, unless you're Clint Eastwood, who defies logic. I think probably the only difference I can see with athletic stars is that they have to have worked. You can't fake being an athletic star. You can't fake being a Broadway star. You can't fake being a ballet dancer. You can fake it in a movie. It's like, "I'm a much better dancer than Baryshnikov if you let me near the cutting room."

On the other hand, even the greatest basketball stars can't do it all by themselves. Michael Jordan proved that. He used to call his teammates "the supporting cast," like in the movies. Jordan used to be just a freak, I mean, athletically he was fabulous. But when he was a college player at North Carolina, and they won the NCAA championship, Jordan had Sam Perkins and James Worthy with him. He never had to do it himself. When he got to the Bulls, he felt he had to do it himself. It's true that he didn't have a great supporting cast then, but he was still a selfish player, until Phil Jackson became the coach, and somehow Jackson got it into Jordan's head that he wasn't going to win unless Horace Grant and Scottie Pippen were going to be able to help him. You can't do it alone in a team sport, and Jordan learned it with the Bulls for a second time. The first was when he played at North

Carolina, but then seemed to forget it for a while. The media tries to make it that you can win by yourself, if you're as great as Jordan, but it's moronic to think you can. Jordan was trying to win just as hard in the 1980s as he was in the 1990s. He just wasn't very good at it.

Now that Jordan's retired it will be interesting to see what happens to him. I think he craves the limelight, which is why just as soon as he retired, people were saying he would be coming back soon. I remember Larry Bird making a joke along those lines, but I think underneath it Bird was serious, that Jordan was only taking another hiatus, the way he did when he left to play baseball for a year and a half.

But he's not going to be Michael Jordan when he can't play anymore. Julius Erving is just another tall, bald black guy. Well, he's got hair. But they're not what they were when they could make magic. Now, Muhammad Ali remained a force, a social force, after he retired. So did Jackie Robinson. They both made huge social changes. Jordan has been totally gutless. It seemed that away from the basketball court it was just the making of commercials that drove him.

It's going to be interesting to see what happens to Jordan because everybody says, "Oh, he's different." My perception is, no one is different. I see a sports star's life like a movie star's, in that it's not a good life, at bottom, and very few of them end up happily. Jordan is like a movie star in that he feeds on the adulation of the public. But we only give public figures our love when they are beautiful. One thing that is very painful in the movies is when you see pictures of women that I remembered as being so beautiful—Janet Leigh, Jean Simmons, Elizabeth Taylor—and I don't want to see them in their sixties and seventies because I remember how breathtakingly beautiful they were and how I ached for them. I'm angry—angry at them for letting life etch itself into them, and I think we're going to feel that way about athletes, too.

·

Q: How did you feel about the labor dispute between the NBA players and management?

A: I was angry about it. I wanted the pleasure of the games to be as pure as possible for me—like watching a movie and not caring about the real lives of the actors and actresses in them. It's like the girl you had a crush on in high school and you thought that she really cared for you, and it turns out she didn't at all. It's like the players and owners just didn't care at all about us, and we had given them our hearts.

And some of the remarks that come out of it from the union side especially were incredible. Like Alonzo Mourning saying that there was a race problem because the owners were all white and most of the players were black. But Alonzo Mourning had no race problem when he was getting $100 million for seven years. And he can't pass the ball, either.

But it's also to the players who are ending their careers now, the Michael Jordans, that we must pay attention to. Because the players of the Jordan era are the ones who had to be great to get rich.

Allen Iverson, Kevin Garnett, Shaquille O'Neal, these players are already rich. There is no reason for Allen Iverson ever to learn how to play basketball. That's why I think the NBA is in trouble. They can never put the genie back in the bottle because the money is simply too much now. People like Iverson have gone far by being a star alone in a team sport, so why should they learn to give up the ball? Yes, you're going to get a Tim Duncan once in a while, someone who plays the game in a proper and satisfying way, from the standpoint of a fan—this fan, anyway. I think Tim Duncan is going to be the player of the decade. Or Grant Hill. And as it happens, both of them completed their four years of college. They didn't come out early, like some of the others have. I think that being grounded for four years in college makes a big difference in the way they play basketball and the way they think basketball. Michael Jordan is incredibly rich, but he wasn't when he started.

Derrick Coleman is another great example of someone with great gifts—great gifts!—but totally fucked up. He's been a detriment to every team he's played with. Coach after coach will say, "I think I can make it work." And they can't. You know the story of when Butch Beard was the coach of the Nets and they had a dress code when they traveled. Nothing extravagant, just maybe slacks and a shirt—but no gym clothes. So on the first trip, Derrick Coleman shows up in a jogging outfit. Beard told him he was going to fine him the announced amount of $1,000. Coleman gave him a blank check and said, "Fill it out for all the rest of the road trips—I'm dressing the way I want to." And eventually that kind of attitude affects the team. You can win with a team that hates each other, but I think it's harder. In movies, there are very great movies that have been made under terrible conditions, particularly *The Godfather*. It was a nightmare for everybody. So you can have a wonderful film even when no one is speaking to anyone else. For the most part, it's nice if there is an atmosphere where you feel good about yourself.

I'll tell you what troubles me these days. Here's what's awkward. When I see a movie that I hate, and many other people like it, part of me says they're full of shit, and part of me says, Oh, my God, are you getting so old that you're losing it. I'm sixty-seven years old. And I don't think I'm losing it. I don't mean senility, but I mean, Are you falling out of public taste? Whatever the hell that is.

Like almost any movie this year. Like *Saving Private Ryan*, which I thought was absolutely okay and nothing more than that. I don't understand all the raving about it. And what drives me nuts is, in basketball, watching the players who are detested and the fans cheer. It scares me because I know that the greatest team I ever saw was the old Knicks teams. Those six years in the early 1970s. They were never the biggest team. They were never the strongest team. They were not necessarily the best athletes, although Frazier was a great athlete. But no team ever played with more intelligence. They were simply dogged, and they understood about defense— Red Holzman in a huddle would give them orders about defense and then say, "Okay, what do you want to run on offense, Clyde?" Or "Bill?" Or "Dave?" Or "Willis?" And they understood that they could make an attempt at a play on defense and not worry about being embarrassed because the man behind them could slide over and help. Nobody cared, really, who was the high scorer, but they really wanted to win the game. They were just so smart about playing the game.

Now, one of my daughters lives in Philadelphia and shares season tickets with another person to the Sixers games. And Allen Iverson is a huge star with that team. And I watch Iverson and I think, "Oh, my God! You're so talented. You could be amazing. If only you would learn to play basketball."

As I've said, Michael Jordan did not learn to play basketball until he was almost thirty years old. He was twenty-eight or twenty-nine and we'll never completely know what Phil Jackson was able to do, but he made it clear that Michael couldn't win anything all by himself.

But when we talk about sports, about basketball, as wonderful as it is, as absorbing as it is, as passionate as it is, in the end all we're doing is passing the time till we die. I remember I met a wonderful old TV soap opera director. He was a very bright fellow and he had been doing these shitty soap operas for years. But he was very happy about it. He said to me, "We're just passing time between commercials. That's all we're doing here. Let's try and do it as well as we can." And when you get as excited about sports as I do, you develop expectations and images in your mind of how well a game can be played, and you root for it to be played that way. When it's not, it's disappointing. When it is, it's thrilling. Like life.

JULIA CHILD

JULIA McWILLIAMS CHILD is the longtime hostess of the popular television show *The French Chef*, for which she won an Emmy. She is also the author of numerous cookbooks, including *Mastering the Art of French Cooking* and *The French Chef Cookbook*, and is the recipient of the French Ordre de Mérite Agricole. She was born on August 15, 1912, in Pasadena, California.

●　●　●

Q: Did you ever play basketball?

A: I used to play it in my youth. Of course, I was a center because I was six feet tall. It was at the Polytechnic Elementary School in Pasadena and also at boarding school, the Katherine Grafton School, in Ross, California. And then when I got to college, at Smith, they didn't like me being six feet tall in basketball and that's where they changed the rules. They'd rather throw it in from a distance than leaping for it closer in to the basket. My usefulness was over.

Q: That was too bad. But living in Boston for much of your life, and having had an interest in basketball, you must have enjoyed the great Celtic teams from Bill Russell's era to Larry Bird's.

A: No, I didn't. That kind of killed my interest when they refused me. It was a lot of fun during the time I did it, though. But

I don't watch any sports a great deal. I would rather be in them than watch them. I'm not a spectator sport person.

Q: You must have been aware of some players, like Michael Jordan.

A: I've heard of him, but I haven't paid any attention to it at all.

Q: As a chef, though, can you relate a recipe for putting together a good dish to a recipe for putting together a good basketball team?

A: Of course you need a variety of ingredients, and fixed in a way in which the tastes work together. I can also apply it to putting together a good staff in a restaurant. Or running a television show, as I'm involved in. If people don't work together, you get rid of the bad apples.

Q: That makes sense.

A: And when you're making up a menu, you want to pace the meal. You don't want to overdo in your first course. You don't want to blow it at the start. I can imagine something like that in basketball.

Q: When I interviewed you about food many years ago, you gave me some advice when traveling and locating good restaurants on the road. And on occasion I've shared that with some of the people in sports, like some basketball players, since they travel a lot and some of them are often on the lookout for good and sometimes out-of-the-way restaurants. You told me that the first thing you do when you're checking out a restaurant that you walk by is to look for white tablecloths. Then you see if there are fresh flowers on the table—you said, "Plastic flowers are generally suspect, too kitschy." And third, you liked to poke your head in the door of the restaurant and smell. You said you especially wanted to smell good butter cooking. Since I don't cook, I was not quite sure what the smell of good butter cooking was.

A: Oh yes, you have to smell it. That's very important. Actually, my first criterion is my nose. If it doesn't smell good, you don't go in. And if there is nobody in the restaurant, there is something wrong. I don't go in. Going to a restaurant can be risky business.

Q: So I went to lunch this one time with Bart Giamatti, the former president of Yale University who was then the commissioner of baseball. We went to a good Italian restaurant in midtown Manhattan—a favorite of Giamatti's, who was of Italian descent— and we were standing in line waiting to be seated. And there was this wonderful smell. It had to be the smell of fresh butter cooking. And I told him your criteria. Including good butter cooking. "Bart," I said, "that wonderful smell here has to be good butter cooking." He put his arm around me in a consoling manner. "Ira," he said, "that's garlic."

A: Well, if you were in the south of France, you probably would have been right. There, you want the smell of garlic and olive oil.

Q: So you've never sampled the food at a place like the old Boston Garden, where the Celtics played, or their new Fleet Center?

A: No, but I once went to Fenway Park for a baseball game. I was asked by the *Boston Herald* to comment upon the Fenway franks.

Q: And?

A: They were very good, but the bun had no character.

Q: How's that?

A: The bun was kind of mushy, not very good at all.

Q: Did you try it with mustard?

A: Oh, I had everything on it, but it still didn't improve the bun.

Q: What about the quality of the mustard?

A: Hot dog mustard is different from Dijon mustard, but you have to have hot dog mustard or it doesn't taste right, don't you think?

Q: I agree completely.

A: The Fleet Center probably has the same kind of food.

Q: Ballplayers fly a lot. Are there any tips for eating on airplanes?

A: I hate soft, mushy steaks and limp broccoli and dehydrated mashed potatoes and gravy out of a can. When I fly, I bring my own sandwiches.

Q: Wilt Chamberlain has claimed that he is an excellent chef. And I can't substantiate it because I've never sampled his cuisine. But what advice might you give a tall chef?

A: When you are designing your kitchen, be sure that you have all the work areas high enough to be comfortable for you. Mine are thirty-eight inches. Mr. Chamberlain could probably use forty inches high, or maybe even a bit more than that. After all, the kitchen is for him and not for anyone else. That makes a great deal of difference because you could really break your back otherwise. Now I designed my kitchen myself. It's just right for me, but shorter people don't seem to notice that the counters are higher than usual.

Q: Any other pointers for Wilt?

A: I think tall is an advantage over small in cooking because you can reach everything much easier than most people. You can hang more things higher. But I think the main thing is to learn as much about cooking as you can, and cook with people who are good cooks and get to know chefs at various restaurants. You can often work with them. And have a good time.

Q: Many of the rules of developing your abilities and artistry as a chef seem to easily apply to basketball, such as learning from good coaches and playing with good players.

A: It's the same thing. Oh, and good equipment cannot be overemphasized. Be sure to tell Mr. Chamberlain to get his knife skills going. I think that's very useful. And make sure the knives are good. And he has to have good, solid pots.

Q: Good knives, good pots. Yes.

A: And rememember, it's always a good idea to cook with the pros any time you can.

Q: Do you have a recipe for making a good basketball team?

A: Yes. Lots of tall people.

MARIO CUOMO

THE former three-time governor of New York, Mario Matthew Cuomo is now a member of the Manhattan law firm of Wilkie Farr & Gallagher. Cuomo, who was born in Queens, New York, on June 15, 1932, was sixty-six years old at the time of this interview. Before becoming governor of New York in 1983, he served as secretary of state of New York and lieutenant governor. He has also been on the faculty of the St. John's University School of Law.

He is generally acclaimed as one of America's most effective and distinguished public speakers, and in 1999 the American Academy of Arts and Letters awarded Governor Cuomo a gold medal for "spoken language."

Mr. Cuomo has been an active athlete much of his life, and a college baseball standout at St. John's, where, as a center fielder, he was signed for a $2,000 bonus by the Pittsburgh Pirates. He played part of a season with the Brunswick (Georgia) Class D farm team before a beaning ended his baseball career.

He has also played basketball in organized leagues and pickup games from the time he was a youth until the present. He looks fit, his hair more dark than gray, and is in excellent shape, often playing with men less than half his age.

●   ●   ●

Q: Is there anything about watching or playing a basketball game that reminds you of the political process?

A: I'm a politician. I was the leader of the political unit of New York for twelve years as governor, and the one point I tried to make over and over is, "We have to do this thing as a team. We're all in this together, the rich people and the poor people and the people in the middle, the people who are doing well and the people who aren't, the people who are in trouble and the people who can save them from trouble. Unless we can all play the game together, we are not going to get maximum results. If we all play as individuals, two or three of us may become high scorers, and may even make the all-star team, but we aren't going to win the championship." Basketball says all of that for me.

Q: Was there one player in particular in that regard that you would point to?

A: For me, perhaps the greatest example of a team player was Bill Bradley. If you saw his transition from a basketball player at Princeton to the Knicks, you see what I mean. At Princeton, he was virtually a center, though he may have been listed as a forward. He played essentially with his back to the basket, and he had the ball in his hands most of the time the team was on offense. But there was no way he could go and play for the Knicks with his back to the basket. He was too small. He was too slow. He couldn't jump. And besides that, the Knicks had Willis Reed at center. So Bill Bradley had to change his entire game. He had to invent a whole new game for himself, which was as a kind of small forward.

He passed the ball a lot. He made great use of himself and his body when he didn't have the ball. He was always in motion, frustrating and exhausting the guys who were guarding him. And of course his contributions were invaluable to the great Knicks teams which won the NBA championship twice and made the finals a third time with Bradley starting at forward.

But the way he made the transition from Princeton to the Knicks, I believe he could do it as a presidential candidate. He has so many strengths. When you've played ball yourself, you have a natural admiration for someone who does it as well as he did it. I particularly admired the fact that he performed way beyond his skill level. He has integrity. Whether it's a guy in the old neighborhood, a politician, a priest, or a former basketball player who is a politician, when you find a guy who is honest—as he is—and who has real character, and is no BS artist, then you value him.

What particularly intrigued me about what Bradley made of himself with the Knicks is that you could never have predicted it when he was at Princeton. At Princeton, you'd have to say, "This guy's a chucker." You wouldn't have seen his high intelligence as a basketball player at Princeton. You did with the Knicks. He had tremendous resilience because physically he took a beating with some of those guys much bigger and stronger than he. And I admired his commitment to the idea of "community."

But Bradley was just one of the Knicks players who understood the need for community. They all played that way, which is a testament to their coach, Red Holzman, as well as to the individuals themselves. They won by understanding that five people who are well synchronized, who are selfless to the point where if you have a better opportunity to score, they will give up their opportunity to score so that you will seize the better opportunity, will make it better for the community overall.

If you could apply that kind of intelligence to the United States of America right now, 260 million people, you'd be twice as strong as you are now as a nation. Think about it: Why did they invent games in primitive times that required you to have five, six, or ten people? They did that when they were cavemen and cavewomen. They had team sports. Now they always had individualism as well: Who could lift the greatest weight, who could run the fastest? Individualism is important to our human psychology, and it is important especially to Americans. But from primitive time, they also understood the beauty and pragmatism of being able to do things together in a synchronized, selfless way where you understood that the objective of the whole group is different from your objective individually, and that you must contribute to the whole group. Nobody taught that better than Bill Bradley by his activities on the court.

Q: Would you include Michael Jordan in that assessment?

A: When Michael Jordan was a young player with the Bulls, I don't think he completely understood or accepted this idea. And when he was younger it may have been that it was more important for him to establish himself as a great individual player, before becoming a great team player. When he proved that, and he had the confidence of knowing that he was regarded as the world's best basketball player, then he could give up the ball to a teammate.

Oddly enough, the essence of a team player in America was demonstrated by a man who was crippled. President Franklin Roosevelt. In 150 years in this country, before FDR became president in 1932, the American psyche was one of virtually pure individualism. If you look closely at the Constitution of the United States, the rule book that we play by, it doesn't necessarily say anywhere that Ira has to worry about Mario if Mario is poor. It doesn't say anywhere that if Mario loses his arm in a machine and can't work to feed his family that Ira has to chip in to pay for his children. For 150 years we lived that way. There was no Social Security, no worker's compensation, no unemployment insurance. There was no health care if you were poor. If the private charities took care of you, fine. If not, you were finished. Then along came Roosevelt. During the Depression, he said in effect, "Look, it's a different game. It's a different world. You've got millions of people clustered in small areas. We've been industrialized. We have to compete with the rest of the world. We cannot make it as millions of disassociated individuals. We've got to play as a team. It's the only way to win."

In 1994 a bunch of people in Congress led by Newt Gingrich seized the ship of state, turned it around, and pointed it back to the turn of the last century and said, "This is the way to the future!" They called it a Contract with America. What they wanted to do was go back to that sort of raw, primitive individualism of the first 150 years. I say, No, no, no. You have to play the way Bill Bradley played.

Q: You still play basketball, in your mid-sixties. Why?

A: I play basketball every Sunday morning, no matter what, because basketball is important to me. I liked baseball and signed a professional contract, but baseball never meant as much to me as basketball did. Basketball was always more fun because as soon as you got on the court you were in the game. Even if you didn't have the ball, you were in the game, and even if you weren't scoring, you were in the game. You could defend, you could steal, you could make yourself useful. As long as the game is on. That was not true in center field.

Basketball is still fun, still a diversion for me. You get busy in life and you have a lot of other things that impinge on your consciousness, and sometimes there are things you don't feel like thinking about. How do you block it all out? Well, playing golf you have to think, fishing you have time to think, but get absorbed in a basketball game and while you're on that court you don't think about anything but basketball. An hour, an hour and a half flies by.

When you get to be sixty-six you're not supposed to be able to use your body in a way that's required for basketball. And people are telling you, "Hey, look, if you break a bone you're finished" and "You should be taking it easy." I have a bad back and stitches from dental work. Well, they said that in the old neighborhood— they said that to you all your life: "You can't get to be governor. You can't get to be a lawyer. You're a Jew. You're an Italian. You're black. You're a woman. They won't let you." We have that being thrown at us all the time, and being able to defy it, being able to remind yourself that, "Hey, look, God gave us some extraordinary strengths, and if we use them all we can do wonderful things. . . ." I can even play basketball at sixty-six.

A: I remember you having recalled a game in the Long Island Press league when you were eighteen years old. Your team had only four players show up. The other team—the first-place team—

wanted your team to forfeit, but you insisted on playing. What happened?

A: We played a zone. What else are you going to play four against five? We were all over the place, and in the beginning it was kind of a joke, but it got serious. We beat them 38–36. I was the high scorer with fourteen points. Now, to me, that game was one of the great experiences in my youth. Why? It was astounding— two things happened. Number one, the players on the other team lost their orientation. They couldn't handle it mentally. All they had to do was get their composure and say, "Hey, look, somebody's got to be free. Let's get rid of these clowns."

We were scurrying, running and jumping after balls, cursing and banging. And the adrenaline, the inspiration we got from being the ultimate underdogs and knowing they were losing their composure, lifted us even more.

I tell you, I've never gotten over it because it says to me that you are capable of doing wonderful things if you don't quit. The important thing was the message: You never know; don't quit; keep shooting. The game isn't over.

I wrote a little book some years back titled *The Forest Hills Diary*. I talked about integration in a situation in Forest Hills where the Jewish people and the black people were fighting over a low-income housing project that was being built in Forest Hills. I talked about how hard it was to meld middle-class concerns and poor people, especially when race is a factor. I said, "We are not doing well with it, but we can do better." I finished it by saying, "The game is lost only when we stop trying." I was talking about making a better society. There is no forgiving a failure of effort. That's what that ball game in the Long Island Press league meant to me. That's what every ball game means. That was a great experience.

I had stopped all competitive sports when I was about twenty-five years old. But then when I was in the governor's office and I was around fifty, the doctor said to me, "You're still in good shape." I told him I was doing yoga, about seventeen minutes in the morning and sometimes seventeen minutes at night. It's as close to pure relaxation as you can get. It's magic. And the doctor said, "What do you do aerobically?" I said, "Nothing." He said, "You ought to try running again," which I did. Then I said, "What the hell, let me try basketball again."

I spent three months by myself in the gym with the state troopers. They thought I was crazy. I started very, very slowly. I started just dribbling. I would dribble right-handed around the court and then I would dribble left-handed back the other way. I shot layups. I started shooting foul shots. I did that more and more, and then finally I said I'm ready to play, and I did, and I've been playing ever since.

Q: Have you had any extended talks with Bill Bradley?

A: I had occasion to have a conversation with Bradley when we were both speaking publicly at the Democratic National Convention in Madison Square Garden in 1992. I wanted to talk basketball with him. He said, "Governor, I'll talk basketball with you if you'll talk public speaking with me." I dismissed his proposition and said, "This is foolish." I told him that he knew what it was to speak well. I don't have any special skills. The difference between me and you, I said, is that when I get up to speak, I will do it only if I feel passionate about the subject. When you do that—when you find a subject you're passionate about, like race—all you'd need is to put down four main sentences, throw away the text, get up, and let them have it, the way you played a basketball game when you really meant it.

You don't analyze every move. You don't say before you dribble, "I'm going to dribble three times with my left hand and once with my right hand." That's what you do too often when you deliver your speeches, though. You've got everything calibrated. If you speak from the heart and soul the way you played basketball, you'd always be a great speaker.

For all this, I said he would make a good president. Somebody said to me, "But if he had this difficulty projecting, how could he make a good candidate?" I said, "Because if he were elected president I believe he would do what he had to do. Just as he did for the Knicks."

It happened that four days before that convention, I had been elbowed in the mouth by one of the guys in my Sunday game, and my two front teeth were loose. So I go to the dentist—and I'm the governor—and I say to him, "Can't you rig something so I don't spit the teeth out when I'm giving the speech on Wednesday." He tried, but nothing worked, and then he sent me to another dentist. This guy couldn't do anything, either. It was hard to talk because I kept feeling my loose teeth and thinking they'd fly out. It's a sickening feeling. I gave the damn speech with both teeth loose. Now somehow the adrenaline took over, and with all the people and all the lights, nobody noticed. So all this taught me another lesson from sports: now I wear a mouthguard when I play.

Postscript: Governor Cuomo and I had talked about playing basketball together, and one day in 1997 we did. He had arranged a three-on-three game. He had another lawyer, Andrew Stengel, and his son-in-law, Brian O'Donough, play with him, and he brought Richard Johnson, who writes the Page Six column for the *New York Post*, and Pat Hannigan, a *Post* assistant sports editor, to play with me. The other players were some twenty years or more younger than the governor and I. The governor had T-shirts made for both teams, with the name of the team on the back, our name, and a number. He called his team the "Facts." Our team he named the "Allegations."

We played three games to twenty-one points—one point for a basket scored inside the three-point line, and two points for one scored beyond the three-point circle. He also brought in a referee.

Before the game, I received a phone call from the governor. "The other guys are playing for beers," he told me. "You and I, we'll play for prune juice." I accepted. We played three close games, and his team won the first, the team I was on won the second, and in a game that went down to the wire, his team won the third.

The following day, I went up to his prestigious law office in the Citicorp Center with a paper bag and two bottles of prune juice. I gave them to the governor's secretary, and explained my purpose.

Two days later I received a note from him dated July 23, 1997. He thanked me for the prune juice. "Now," he said, "I can be a regular guy."

Sometime after that I was speaking with Mark Jackson, the point guard for the Indiana Pacers and, like Govenor Cuomo, an alumnus of St. John's University. I told him I had played basket-ball with Cuomo, whom he had met. Jackson asked what kind of player he was. I told him he was a tough competitor, with a good two-handed set shot, and a decent driver—given that he was sixty-six years old when we played, I thought he was extraordinary. I also mentioned that Cuomo was very aggressive on defense.

"There were some photographs when we played," I said, "and in one of them I'm trying to dribble around the governor and he's grabbing my shirt."

"Ah," said Jackson, nodding thoughtfully, "he knows the game."

JOHNNIE COCHRAN JR.

JOHNNIE COCHRAN JR., born in Shreveport, Louisiana, on October 2, 1937, grew up in Los Angeles, where he earned a bachelor's degree from UCLA in 1959 and a law degree from Loyola University in 1962. He practiced law in Los Angeles until 1998, when he moved to New York, where he is a partner in a law firm with Peter Neufeld and Barry Scheck. Both of the latter were on the so-called "Dream Team" that helped defend and win an acquittal for O. J. Simpson in his murder trial. Cochran has also done legal work for such basketball players as Latrell Sprewell, when he was with the Golden State Warriors, and Larry Johnson of the New York Knicks, and Ray Allen of the Milwaukee Bucks. Cochran had season tickets for years to the Los Angeles Laker games, but now subscribes to season tickets to Knick games.

Cochran's new law office is located in the TriBeCa area of Manhattan. He is a man of medium height and is a fastidious dresser, favoring red handkerchiefs that bloom from the vest pocket of his dark suits. On the day of the interview, he sat behind the desk in his eighth-floor law office in a tie and shirtsleeves. On the wall are framed newspaper and magazine articles about him, including a front-page photo of him wearing the dark knit cap, which he donned when making a critical point in an appeal to the jury. The big headline above it reads simply: HE-E-E-E-R-E-'S JOHNNY!

Q: When you as a trial lawyer watch a basketball game, can you relate in any way to the basketball players, to the team?

A: I really can. What it means to me as a trial lawyer is that everybody, I guess, wants to be like Mike. Who want to be the best. Who want to win every time out. Who want the responsibility of taking—and making—the winning basket. When I got called to be part of the Simpson defense team, and ultimately take over the team, somebody said, "Well, why are you doing this?" And I said, "Downtown L.A. is my home court. That's where I feel comfortable. I feel I know the jurors, I speak their language. I know the police department, I know the DA's office. This is like playing a home game for me."

So ultimately, and once I became captain of the team, I felt that in the final analysis when we had to stand up and try to convince this jury, I wanted the ball. I had to stand up there. So when we went through and decided who would do that, Barry Scheck and I said, "Look, we've got to stand there at the end." We really felt that it was like an athlete with the last shot on the line. You spend your whole life trying to get ready for that, and it was the same thing in trying cases. I relate to Michael who wants the ball, like Jerry West who wanted the ball, and I relate to Joe Montana who at the very end of the game when his team was behind and they were driving and had a chance to win and he wanted to be in control. I love that. Any good trial lawyer would feel the same way, I'm sure.

And when I watch a basketball game I think of the necessity of a team approach. When you have a group of lawyers working on a case, you have to have everybody working together for the good of the whole and you have to establish this synergy. You're not running off by yourself doing all this stuff. It's not about ego. On our team that was defending O. J. Simpson, we had F. Lee Bailey—a legend—Alan Dershowitz, Scheck and Peter Neufeld and Henry Lee—one of the foremost criminologists in the country—and Robert Shapiro and me, all men who made a name for themselves in this profession.

When I took over as lead lawyer in the case—O.J. called us all to his jailhouse on New Year's Day, 1995, and said that he wanted me to lead rather than Bob Shapiro—I felt I had to handle this the way a basketball coach would. And Bob didn't take that well because until that point we were working under him, but he had never tried a murder case before.

And when we met soon after I said, "We've got to check our egos at the door when we have meetings together. Let's try to resolve this and do for the client and work for the client together because at the end if we stay together as a team we'll be more successful."

But it wasn't easy to do because Bob especially often wasn't on the same page as the rest of us. And he and Bailey weren't speaking to each other at all. So you had to deal with his ego, and we gave him, among other things, Michael Baden, the forensic pathologist, to examine on the witness stand. We had to give him some plum assignments, but then strictly monitor what he was going to do and stay with him.

But we never let ourselves get down, get depressed—couldn't afford to—even when it seemed things were not going our way. If we had listened to the prognosticators, or some news accounts, saying things like, "The defense really suffered blows today," it was like being behind in a ball game. We never saw ourselves that way. We said, "Look, it's like a daily score—or a quarter score. The pay-off is at the end."

As for the opposition, the prosecution, we had to scout them, like you do in sports. It happened that I knew my opponents, especially Chris Darden. I knew that Darden had these flashpoints. I knew how to get into his psyche. Like in basketball one guy might trash talk to another and say, "You can't guard me." Well, Darden would walk past our table and I'd say, "God, you guys, this is a case of reasonable doubt. You guys are in serious trouble. You're never going to prove this case." And then there was the afternoon he tried to put on those gloves to prove they were O.J.'s and they belonged to the killer. When that turned out to be a fiasco for Darden, I quietly said, "Another bad day for the prosecution." I know I was upsetting him. I know sometimes he wanted to throttle me, the way Julius Erving once did when Larry Bird was scoring a lot of points off him and telling him, "Too late." Bird was one of the best at getting under an opponent's skin.

And then there was Marcia Clark, the lead attorney for the prosecution. She's real sharp and real quick on her feet. And she was good on certain witnesses. But there were times when Gil Garcetti, the district attorney, would come in and take over, and we'd say things like, "God, it's amazing. I thought you guys were in charge? Why is Garcetti taking all the witnesses? He took the coroner for eight days and the jury was about to go to sleep." And it was like Marcia was standing up and looking around like, "Hey, this is my case." And they'd try the reverse on us. So any little thing that kind of keeps them off-balance is part of the proceedings. Your job is to try to win fair and square, but part of fair and square is you get around the guy a little bit, you know?

And the judge is like the referee. You want the referee to respect you. You want the judge to respect you, but they are going to do some things at times and you'll say, "That is the worst call!" But you have to register your displeasure without blowing it for the rest of the game. And that was the problem with us. Sometimes we were losing these motions we thought we should win, but we had to be real careful because we knew we had to come back the next day.

Q: You were called in to advise Latrell Sprewell after he had choked his coach, P. J. Carlesimo, and Larry Johnson, after he had been sued for child support after allegedly fathering children with several women. What perceptions did you make from these cases, if not specifically, assuming client–attorney privilege, but at least generally?

A: I think that very often these days the lives of outstanding athletes have been far different from others, and I think African-Americans are no exception. They are catered to much of their lives, from a young age. And someone like O. J. Simpson even thought he had transcended the African-American culture, and had assimilated into some other kind of world. And there is very often a sense of invincibility among outstanding athletes, a sense of immortality. I saw it. Even the best. I think even Magic Johnson, who has been in many ways a model citizen, had that attitude that he can do things, and there is no way he'll be caught. In his case, it was HIV. But I think power does that, gives this idea of being immortal and invincible. It's a real tough thing. I see that in athletes and it's troubling because they have to realize—part of it is that they are young, too—that one wrong turn, one incident, could change your life around.

You need to understand, you need to have some kind of mechanism or some kind of release that you don't do this, whether it's choking your coach or whether it's going out and doing something really stupid. I think you've got to set them up. If you have a kid who's from a real strong family background, they generally have someone to call. You know, their father, their mother, their big brother, their agent. For me, I call my dad to be grounded. I talk to him. He attended the O.J. trial every day. So you have those kind of processes, and if you don't, if you just abandon them, then when you're out on your own, well, that's when you get into trouble.

As for Sprewell, well, I found him to be a very bright young man. And while some thought the choking incident had racial undertones, a young black and a middle-aged white man, who was an authority figure, I backed away from that. I said, "Look, this has nothing to do with race. Latrell overreacted. These are two guys that got heated over this whole thing. This isn't race. The whole team is black. Does the coach get mad at Muggsy Bogues, at all of them?" And I think Latrell backed off the race issue eventually, too. But I was impressed with him. He had some pretty good insights into it, and I thought they were sensitive. I mean, he understood that what he did was wrong. At his press conference, he said, "I didn't handle it right. I didn't process it right. I didn't stop, I think, between the first time I got angry and when I came back the second time." He left after the initial incident in practice, but came back some twenty minutes later. He realized he shouldn't have come back.

And so he came back to play with the Knicks, who got him in a trade with the Warriors. And I think there is a redemptive quality after having been punished. He was suspended for the rest of the 1997–98 season, which cost him more than $6 million in salary. And when I saw him introduced for the first time in the Knicks first preseason game in 1999, after the lockout, and the fans in New York—really, really tough—cheered him. I said, "What's going on here?" But I think that spoke well for the fans, and I think Latrell will produce. He's a talented player.

Q: And players who have had paternity problems?

A: You read about some athletes fathering a lot of kids with different women. It's totally irresponsible, and it seems to me you've got to support your kids. There should be some old-fashioned kind of coming together. Anybody could be a father, but it takes a real man to be like a dad, to be somebody who's a real parent. Nobody teaches those things, but you've got to some way learn these things and grow up. What kind of society are we going to have when people say, "I'm just going to do whatever I want to do"?

You cannot go through life doing what you want to do and be oblivious to consequences. The intelligent athlete, the one we'd like to have out there on the court, on the field, realizes the consequences.

I think most athletes when they come face-to-face with any problems realize, if they are bright at all—and the ones I've dealt with are bright—that mistakes were made. And I think they legitimately want to make up for those mistakes. And not just because they were caught. You don't always appreciate something until you see it kind of floating away, and the guy who doesn't get it is soon going to be out of the league.

Q: A fourteen-year-old black boy is in the news because he was attacked with baseball bats and was stabbed in the heart by a gang of other black youths on the street after a basketball game in which the fourteen-year-old was a star and helped beat the team of the other youths. The game had been played in the Jackie Robinson Intermediate School in Brooklyn. What thoughts do you have on that?

A: I think about Jackie Robinson himself. I grew up loving Jackie Robinson. And I'm sure that Jackie would blanch at some of the things we see now. There is so much violent culture out there, a kind of strike first and think about things later response, which is unfortunate. Maybe it has to do with people they look up to these days. I don't know. I wouldn't use Dennis Rodman as a model, for example, even though I like Dennis. But I think you need to pattern yourself after someone who demonstrates control over himself, in the tradition of Jackie Robinson. I think Michael Jordan has demonstrated that kind of control on the court.

Jackie Robinson lived in a world where there was racism, yet he let his performance do his talking. This guy understood what he had to do to succeed, and at the end of his career he was able to speak out, but he had a certain dignity and a class about him. That's what I would love to see more of. I think that we're lacking in that. A lot of it has to do with, I guess, immaturity, but I'd like to see a person, an athlete, who can perform at a very high level and carry themselves as gentlemen. They don't take a back seat to anybody, and yet by their conduct no one has to worry about who they are.

I think there's a lack of appreciation by too many of the outstanding athletes—the African-American athletes in particular—for what got them to the place they're at today, of who came before them, and what kind of legacy they are going to leave. You see, they got there because of Jackie, and others like him, but it's not just that they are playing and making all this money. They make more money in a year than Jackie Robinson made in his entire career. And I'm concerned: What do you leave for future athletes?

You see too many of these young black athletes who come

along and are loudmouthed troublemakers who go out and get themselves arrested. You see these articles where many of these guys have felonies and they're still playing. But their bad actions are so unnecessary. These guys are the privileged! These guys are the talented few. These guys are the ones who got the great opportunities. And the other thing that goes along with that is not only how you conduct yourself, but to go back and give something to the communities where kids idolize you. I believe they have an obligation to help others. Some do. Many do. But there must be more. Many more.

There are many good guys, exemplary athletes, on and off the court. In basketball I love Michael, and I think of Grant Hill—who comes from a great family. He may not have all the charisma of Michael but he's a talented, bright young man. He personifies the best in people in sports. I believe Ray Allen, who has a strong mother figure in Flo, is very smart and caring. I think he brings a lot to his team, Milwaukee, and to that community. And besides being an outstanding athlete, he proved a capable actor in Spike Lee's film *He Got Game*.

I like David Robinson and Tim Duncan of the San Antonio Spurs. They are really decent people who comport themselves in a great way, and they make you feel proud.

As for white guys, of course I loved Larry Bird, and I love the way he coaches. He commands respect. People look at him and don't think he's that smart. But he is, and when he was playing he was an assist guy, the consummate team player. And I like Keith Van Horn of the Nets a lot. He's talented and not just a token guy. He can shoot, and he's a very classy player. The man got game.

And I think of Shaquille O'Neal. Let me tell you something about Shaq. Every Thanksgiving Day he takes turkeys into the black community, first in Orlando where he began his pro basketball career, and now in L.A. Bringing turkeys to poor people on Thanksgiving is a nice thing to do, but it could be just a one-time thing, or a public relations stunt. But I think Shaq is more than that, why I think he's a really good guy.

I fought a case for twenty-seven years in which a man, Girolamo Pratt, was convicted of a murder he did not commit. When he was finally released from prison in January 1999, it was a big deal in L.A. And on the day he was released I came into my office and there was a phone call from Shaquille O'Neal. I did not know Shaq. So this was totally out of the blue. He called me because Pratt's mother, who was ninety-three years old—and who basically had refused to die until her son was exonerated—wished to see her son. She lived in Louisiana. But neither he nor his mother had money for him to make the trip. O'Neal called so he could pay for the plane fare for Girolamo.

Another who gives back to the community is Magic Johnson. I was there throughout the Showtime years, the championship Laker teams. And the thing I love about Magic is his never-say-die attitude. He was that way on the court, and he's that way with the HIV virus. And he gives back to the community, like his building these theaters in the black neighborhoods, helping to create jobs and giving an added avenue of entertainment where few had existed. He is a legitimately good guy.

Q: Have you been able to observe Allen Iverson, the point guard of the Philadelphia 76ers? As you may know, he is controversial in that he is very talented but seems to be a street kind of player.

A: I have observed him, and I think he can be a real force in the league. But I think he needs someone to kind of take him under his wing. I don't know much about his background, except I know he was from a poor family in Virginia and raised by his mother, and got into a fight when he was in high school and spent a few months in jail. I think he needs someone to understand his life experiences, to help him understand that he's not invincible, that these are the best years he's ever going to have, and he can make a mark and make things better. He needs someone who will cut through the entourages. I've been around some ballplayers and you see guys around them and you ask, "Who are they?" And you're told, "They're my boys. My boys." And you wonder,

"Where were these 'boys' before the player became rich and famous?" In the old days, you had your family, and if all of us have two or three good friends, we're really fortunate, aren't we? But Allen Iverson needs someone to give him good advice, and he needs to listen to it.

I come back to Jackie Robinson, who paved the way for African-American athletes in all sports—and, I'd like to think, for athletes of any color. He had the talent and the ability, and he got the chance. And he made the most of it. I think that's the message for all of us.

NIKKI GIOVANNI

NIKKI GIOVANNI is the author of thirteen books of poetry, holds the Langston Hughes Medal for Outstanding Poetry, and has been named woman of the year by *Mademoiselle, Ladies' Home Journal*, and *Essence*. For her collection, *Love Poems*, published in 1997, she received the NAACP Image Award.

Yolande Cornelia Giovanni Jr. was born on June 7, 1943, in Knoxville, Tennessee. She has produced five books of prose, including *A Dialogue: James Baldwin and Nikki Giovanni, Racism 101,* and *Sacred Cows . . . and Other Edibles.* She has edited several more books, including *Night Comes Softly: Anthology of Black Female Voices*, and six books for children, including *The Sun Is So Quiet.* Her books of poetry range from *Cotton Candy on a Rainy Day* to *The Selected Poems of Nikki Giovanni.*

Her most recent book, a collection of fifty-two new poems titled *Blues: For All the Changes*, includes "Iverson's Posse," a poem about—and for—Allen Iverson, the controversial guard for the Philadelphia 76ers and the 1998–99 leading scorer in the National Basketball Association.

Ms. Giovanni is a professor of English at Virginia Polytechnic Institute in Blacksburg, Virginia.

•   •   •

Q: Do you see poetry in basketball?

A: I sure see ballet. Because of the moves. So it depends on whether you consider ballet poetry. But definitely when I think of basketball I see ten graceful men in a kind of ballet. They could be wearing tutus as far as I'm concerned.

Q: Any player or players in particular?

A: Oh, of course I'm a Grant Hill fan. Everybody is. I watch basketball games mostly on television, and mostly with my mother, who's a big fan, and naturally a big Grant Hill fan. You can't help but be. Just the beautiful way he plays and the elegant way he carries himself on and off the court. And I'm a big Pat Ewing fan. I'm sorry the Knicks came so close to winning the championship in '99. It's sad—I don't think he's ever going to get a ring. What I like about Pat—and maybe it's my poetry coming out—but whatever he has understood to be the truth of the game is the way he plays it.

Some point guards can stand back and pass the ball. Pat is just the guy that's in the middle, and he has to go to the basket. And he does that. A lot of people would be tired of being hit by now. Kareem got tired of being hit and developed the sky hook so he could stand a little farther back from the basket. But Pat just keeps going to the basket. You have to love that. He's going to get in there if it's possible. Like trying to write a poem and get deep inside the subject. It's Pat's heart that is so captivating. If you're saying to yourself, "I don't feel like writing a poem today," or "I don't feel like giving a speech today," you think, "Well, Pat Ewing will do it." And he does it with such grace. He's not a whiner. You never heard Pat whine.

Now, Grant Hill has a different style. He's fun. I watched him at Duke and I always felt that he was crucial to the Duke victories. I'm not against Christian Laettner or anything, I just always thought it was Grant. And I'm so sorry that Grant is on a bad team in the pros, the Detroit Pistons. I wish he could go somewhere else.

The similarity between Grant Hill and Pat Ewing is that I've seen them both grow and accept their roles. Trying to fit into the team even though they are the major stars of their teams. But look at Tim Duncan. He's a golden boy. He just walks into the league and in his second year—boom!—he wins a championship. Of course it helped that Michael Jordan had retired. And then there's David Robinson. David is not in my opinion a winner—or wasn't. But David knew that when Duncan joined his team that "I've got a way to win now." And he took a kind of back seat—or second seat—to Duncan on the Spurs, and they won. You'd have to credit Robinson with being a winner in that regard.

Q: Have you ever met any of them?

A: No, I don't know any of those people. But I did meet Dr. J. once. But that wasn't like "We're friends."

Q: What were the circumstances of meeting Dr. J.?

A: He was coming through the airport in Cincinnati, where I was living at the time. He was there for an exhibition game. I stopped and said, "Hello, I'm Nikki Giovanni." And he said, "Hi," like, you know, "So?" Kind of "Have a nice day" sort of thing. But he was nice. Some of them won't even speak to you.

Q: Erica Jong said that there is something very erotic about basketball. She said she was "struck by the bodies of these beautiful young black men, wearing almost nothing, with wonderful long muscular legs and great arms." What are your thoughts on that?

A: Well, Erica Jong is all sex and flying. [*Laughter.*] You know, she called them "zipless fucks." And that's fine for her. I went to see *Nutcracker* this year and to me, as I said, basketball is like the ballet. I don't see it as erotic. It's a game of beauty. It's like, "Wow, look at that move!" But I do look at basketball a little differently from the ballet. Oh, God, I hate to say it this way, but I look at it like a mother because I look at the struggle of these young men to get to where they've gotten. It's been a struggle, and I don't care if it's a Grant Hill from a very middle-class family, or Chris Webber, from a working-class family, or one of the others from single-mother or very poor backgrounds.

As a mother, you look at the struggle. I tend to cheer for both sides most of the time, unless it's someone I really don't like. But I tend to cheer for whoever has got the ball because you know how hard it is. You know, these games are coming down to the last seconds, and they all want to win so badly. And they've struggled. I'm talking now about the struggle to get to the top of your profession. I'm talking about Lena Horne. I'm talking about me. I'm talking about anybody who keeps doing something year after year so that they can reach their maximum potential. And that's what you do see. That's why you hate a lazy player. You really do. Someone who is so gifted but seems to be wasting his gifts. You think, "Well, everybody else is out there, giving everything they have." I understood Michael Jordan going off like he used to do because it's like, "Well, I'm giving a hundred percent. What are you doing? Don't stand there and look at me. Get out there and do it!"

So you see people struggle, struggle, struggle. My mother will blame them when they miss a free throw. But I know it's hard at the end of games because your legs are tired.

You know it's just a matter of maybe two points here and two points there between the winners and the losers. So you can end up just full of tears watching. It's like you knew San Antonio was probably going to beat the Knicks in the playoff finals but that didn't stop you from cheering for the Knicks. On the other hand, Tim Duncan is such a quality guy—though I've got to tell you, Avery Johnson gets on my nerves. I mean, learn to speak, Avery. He's got that strange-pitched voice. He's rich, hire yourself a speech coach. And I'm tired of all of that religion coming out of that team. God doesn't really give a damn who wins a basketball game. Everybody wants to thank God, but I've never seen anybody say, "Well, God was against me today." Don't hand me that crap. Just go out and play the goddamned game.

Q: What about the struggle culturally, to rise above mean circumstances in many cases? The struggle to make it out of the inner cities. Do you think about that when you watch these games?

A: No, I think there is a struggle to get out of the suburbs. To me, the struggle would be if the white boys at Columbine High School had rapped or played basketball or did break dancing, they wouldn't be murdering people. I think that the black boys have it made over the white boys, and I think that the black boys know that they have it made over the white boys all day long because they have so many other other outlets for their energy that are life-and-death situations, that are food-on-the-table situations. Whereas white boys are inventing angst, black boys are living it. That's always going to make for good art, and it's going to make for good athletics, and it's going to make for good writing, all of which we're seeing.

Q: But it's also true, is it not, that in the penal system in the United States something like 25 percent of young black men—from ages something like sixteen to twenty-five—are either in prison, on probation, or on trial?

A: Sure, but that's politics. I didn't say that they have it over the politics. That is the decision we've made because Robert Downey Jr. will do cocaine until the day he dies or Charlie Sheen, and they'll keep giving them community service and a black guy will get time in jail. So that's politics. We weren't talking politics. We were talking art. My point only is that we know honestly that black boys and white boys and brown boys and yellow boys get different punishment for the same action.

The unfair meting out of the death penalty to poor people and people of color on one hand and rich people and whites on the other is one issue. But most people don't face that question. Most people face questions of "If I'm late to work and I'm having a joint and driving my car and driving safely, and I'm going to my job which is a basketball player and my name is Chris Webber and they know me and I get stopped by the police and they find seeds, what kind of trouble will I get into—what kind of trouble should I get into?" It's politics and we have crazy laws. And one of which is the illegality of drugs. I'm so against drugs being illegal. But Chris is marked also because he's a big-name athlete. And it's not just blacks who get targeted.

We had a white boy recently here at Virginia Tech who found out he wasn't as white as he once thought he was. That's Jim Druckenmiller, who used to be the quarterback at this school and is now a backup quarterback for the San Francisco 49ers. Nobody in our part of the state believed that he raped that girl. And of course he was found not guilty—that it was consensual sex. But because he was a football player it behooved the girl to ask his lawyer, you know, if you write the check we can make all this go away. We had been talking about black boys coming from the inner city, but we can talk about white boys coming from the country. It's very hard when you make money or people perceive you as making money. It's why I totally admire Allen Iverson.

He's a great player, and he has settled down. He finally looked in the mirror and said to himself, "Oh, I'm a great player, I should act like one." I think he is the next Michael Jordan. And he has begun to take responsibility for that team—to put it not on his shoulders, but to be a leader. This has been a great thing because everybody was on Allen. I mean, every time he sneezed somebody said, "But you put germs in the air and that's against law number such-and-such." The whole thing with the fracas in the bowling alley when he was in high school in Hampton, Virginia, and served six months in prison for it. I was very disappointed with the governor for not stepping in and giving a much lighter sentence to this high school kid who was a first offender and happened to get caught up in something that high school kids could get caught up in.

But Allen has moved beyond that. He's got his $70 million basketball contract. I really hope that he's got a good girlfriend and that he loves her and she loves him.

Q: You had written a poem about your admiration for Billie Jean King, and how she was heroic. Is there a basketball player that does that for you?

A: Allen Iverson is close. One of the reasons he's gotten into trouble in the pros is because of his posse, his close friends. People get on his case because of his posse, and it's clear that he loves his posse. The rappers would call it his crew. It seemed to me that the posse is in the same position as anybody else who loves you. If you love them and stand by them, they should love you and stand by you. So that's the premise of the poem. If they love you, you can make them free because nobody can love you if they're not. I don't know this child, I never met him, so I could write this poem. And in order for the posse to be free, send them to school. You have the money. Send them to law school, send them to the priesthood, send them to medical school, because these are all the things you're going to need. It's better to send them to school than to buy them a Mercedes-Benz. Send them to school so they can be independent. If they go, then you've done something for them. If they don't, get rid of them.

It makes sense to me because one of the things that happens is you have bad friends. And I know he loves his friends because of the way he has stood by them. He's just been such a stand-up guy. Who else would be bothered with those people? We've seen other players where their friends have gotten shot, their friends have gone to jail, and these friends have gotten in the way of these players. But Iverson stood up. He never backed off of them. He knows that there are a lot of people out there who don't care about him. But these guys do. And so he needs to take the next step. And that's what my poem says. Take the next step. Free them. Because if you free them, then you'll always have somebody who not only loves you, but can help you.

When I wrote about Billie Jean, I wrote that "The face in the mirror is not the face in the window" because people have a public life and a private life. I love that line, by the way. I remember when the scandal broke about the relationship between Billie Jean and this girl and I was just very upset. I thought, "Well, what the fuck?" What are they doing to her? At some point something should be private. I don't know Billie Jean King, either. And I never felt motherly to Billie Jean King, but I do to Allen Iverson.* He's only five years younger than my son, Thomas—Thomas Giovanni.

Q: Some players, like Larry Johnson and Shawn Kemp, have admitted having a handful of children with a handful of women. What do you make of the players who father kids and don't take a fathering responsibility for it?

A: What do you make of some of these women having the babies? Be fair. I'm a woman, and these women know what they're doing. They're making decisions based on what they think they can get. I watch Larry Bird—I'm a big Larry Bird fan—and I see him trying to work out a situation with his daughter. Or you can see Dr. J. working out a situation with his daughter, the tennis player, Alexandra Stevenson, and her mother. Neither one of those guys has a relationship with their daughters—or their mothers—except financially, as I understand it. In my opinion, they all handled it badly, but it's something they didn't ask for. And we live in a world that actually has choices. So women have made decisions for whatever reason they make them. I'm saying this as a single mother. I have one child. And one is plenty.

*Iverson was twenty-four years old at the time of this interview in July 1999.

Q: But are you absolving the players of their responsibilities?

A: I'm not absolving them. I'm just dealing with reality. When you make a decision it's your decision. There are other decisions that can and should be made. Everbody wants to bitch and moan about the situation, but look at how many children B. B. King had—at least six, maybe nine—and he's been all over the world. Look at the how many children Bobby Kennedy had, or the king of Siam—he had dozens, at least. So what are we talking? We're not talking children, we're talking who has them.

Q: I don't know about B. B. King, but Bobby Kennedy and the king of Siam presumably had all their children under one roof—theirs. You can't say the same for some of the basketball players.

A: But some of the women have done a wonderful job raising their kids. Like the mother of Jerry Stackhouse of the Pistons. She's a single mother and brought him up by herself. I think she made a wonderful decision to have him because look at what a wonderful kid she got. And they seem to be happy. And in the end, much of the fact of having kids is just sex. The consequences of sex. And sex is a normal thing. So don't pick on the players.

Q: Do any basketball players remind you of any poets?

A: If Grant Hill were a poet, he'd probably be Lord Byron or William Yeats. They are so classy in their approach to their art, and so is Grant Hill. But both of those poets were also a little crazier than perceived. Again, I don't know Grant Hill, but I just know nobody is as nice as he seems to be. And nobody is that polite. There are times when I'm sure he is sick of all of it. We know Byron is so much undercover. Talk about eyes wide shut. I'm not accusing Grant Hill of anything, I'm just saying I suspect there's more to him than meets the eye.

Q: What about Langston Hughes?

A: It's got to be somebody with that kind of jazz feeling. I'm trying to think now who really boogies. I think maybe Penny Hardaway would be Langston because he really boogies, has that loose, easy, creative but controlled way about him.

Q: Have you watched any women's basketball?

A: A little. I'll tell you what I think, but everybody is going to be mad at me. I think they need to lower the basket so the girls can dunk. Right now, it's too high for them. If you lower the basket we'll get all kinds of different moves in their game.

Q: Did you ever play basketball?

A: I'm five-two, and I played in gym class at Austin High School in Knoxville. That's when girls were only allowed to play half-court—they thought at that time that full-court was too strenuous for girls. I went up one time to get the ball and one of the big girls—I don't remember who—pushed me. I fell on my knee and slid. I have a—it's not a bad scar anymore, but it's still there. I got up and there was blood dripping on my leg and I said to Ms. Wynn, the gym teacher, I'm not going to play this game anymore. You can give me an F. Do whatever you have to do. I'm gone. And I limped off the court and I have never picked up a ball since.

Q: So that was the turning point? Instead of becoming a basketball player you became a poet?

A: [*Laughter.*] I like to think I became a tennis player athletically. I still play tennis. But no, in basketball, people hit you. That's why I admire so many of the players. They used to say football is war and basketball is a contact sport. But when you watch somebody like Tom Gugliotta playing with a broken nose in the Olympic Trials and wearing a mask after plastic surgery and then ten days later the boy's nose is rebroken, and you ask, "What the hell was that about?" This isn't war?

I love to watch basketball—and that's the closest I'm going to get to it.

RICHARD MEIER

ICHARD ALAN MEIER won the Pritzker Prize for Architecture in 1984, which is widely held to be architecture's Nobel. His most recent and renowned work is the billion-dollar Getty Center in Los Angeles, opened in 1998. Mr. Meier was born in Newark, New Jersey, on October 12, 1934, and earned his bachelor's degree from Cornell in 1957. He is the founder of Richard Meier & Partners architectural firm based in Manhattan, and has designed a diverse array of buildings throughout the world, from the Museum fur Kundsthandwerk in Frankfurt, Germany, to the City Hall and Central Library, The Hague, The Netherlands, to an office building in Singapore to the Art Center in Des Moines, Iowa, to the Twin Parks Housing in New York City. Other awards presented to him include the Royal Gold Medal from the Royal Institute of British architects, 1988, and the Premium Imperiale, the Japan Art Society, 1998, as well as numerous awards from the American Institute of Architects. He has been a basketball fan for many years, and has a daughter, Ana, who plays basketball for her high school team in New York City.

•   •   •

Q: When you watch a basketball game, is there anything from an architectural standpoint that interests you?

A: The thing that is exciting for me is when you see things that are very clear and direct—similar to a well-made, uncluttered, but artistically satisfying building. If someone is moving down-court and there is a great cross-court pass that's just perfectly timed and directed, I think that's beautiful. It's different from sim-ply the linear play, which is straight up and down. And I love the alley-oop, when a player at the basket jumps to meet a pass that's thrown above the rim, catches at the height of his jump, and slams the ball into the basket. That's really understanding not only tim-ing, but direction, force, and just a perfect comprehension of the geometry of the play.

My daughter was playing in a tournament one weekend down at the outdoor court at Fourth Street and Sixth Avenue in Green-wich Village. The girls are good, but then afterward there was a men's tournament with players that had to have been of pro caliber. Their precision of passing and shooting on that court was unbelievable. It was just a joy to watch how without even talking to one another they were able to take the ball and move it directly, and just in a very graceful manner. Just with extraordinary balance and talent.

Q: There is an adjective that's been used to describe your work, and that's "pristine."

A: I've heard that, but the basketball I'm describing also has a toughness to it when it's well done.

Q: Of the players you have seen in the NBA, which ones please you?

A: Well, there's no one like Jordan. He knew how to move. He knew how to do everything somehow more gracefully and with more precision than anyone. But I think to see people like Latrell Sprewell play is quite a surprise. I mean, the guy is very good. And he's graceful, and at extraordinary speed.

There are a lot of very good players out there. I also think somehow the team brings the players out. It allows a good player to play to the best of his talent.

Q: It was said that with a hobbled Patrick Ewing unable to play in the way he once did, with the ball going into him in the pivot in nearly every play, that the other Knick players began to flourish, which helped land them in the NBA finals in 1999.

A: I agree, and it was terrific to see. The players like Allan Houston and Marcus Camby and Sprewell were able to do it before, but somehow they were suppressed in the system. And that's true about other things as well. Actually, in architecture there are certain people on my team—in my office—who are working under other people, who have a certain capacity, but as long as they're under someone it doesn't come out.

Q: How do you as the coach bring it out?

A: If I get something that's new and small, then I would just try to work with that person rather than the person keeping the structure the way it was. I would find some project where the person can take a stronger role.

Q: In sports, it is often said that a team is "built." When you saw the Knicks in 1999 succeed as they did—the only eighth seed in NBA history to make the finals—did it remind you of any structure you've worked on that surprised you?

A: When anything is finished and it's good, it comes as a surprise of sorts because only about one out of fifteen things that you start gets realized, gets built. Just because you start it, and get all the details together and gather the parts, it still doesn't mean you're going to have a finished product. I've worked on things for two or three years and have the drawings in the drawer. So it's not just getting to the finals—you don't get anywhere! It's a wasted season. I've seen some teams like that, I must say. Not so the Knicks of 1999. Even though they lost in five to San Antonio, they gave a great effort. So in a sense they have their building built. We'll have to see how the building turns out because it can get built and you'll say, "Well, it could have been better."

Q: You mean, the following season a strong wind could blow it down?

A: Right. Take the Getty Museum. That was fifteen years in the making.

Q: Can you draw a comparison between finished products like the Getty and, say, the Chicago Bulls?

A: The Getty is realized and it will be there, but the Bulls team is over. So I'm happier being an architect. [*Laughter.*] At least I can go back and visit it. What do the Bulls have to visit? Memories. I have the reality. But when I saw Jordan play, it reminded me of Frank Lloyd Wright. Jordan had a very long career, as Frank Lloyd Wright did, and a very strong career. And Jordan had some ups and downs—I know he didn't win his first championship until his seventh season in the NBA. But certainly like Frank Lloyd Wright he was the most famous person in his field. And the styles were comparable. Both were inventive. Both of them thought about things differently, but did things in a way that the public could identify.

The public has a stronger recognition of Frank Lloyd Wright than any other architect. And this is a curious thing, both Michael Jordan and Frank Lloyd Wright made their marks in Chicago. But while Wright made his name originally with the Prairie style, buildings with low horizontal lines, Jordan made his reputation early with his extraordinary elevation, creating more or less high horizontal lines.

People from Chicago know about architecture. It's not like people from New York. The buildings in Chicago are fabulous. There is a tradition of architectural history there, and a recognition and an importance to it—from Wright and Louis Sullivan and Burnham and Root to Mies van der Rohe, and famous structures like the Monadnock Building and the Rookery and Wright's Robey House.

And the Bulls built something fine, too, with players like Jordan and Pippen and Dennis Rodman. Fitting all these different parts into a beautiful structure.

Even a New York architectural firm has done its best work in Chicago. Skidmore, Owings & Merrill built the Sears Tower, the Inland Steel building, the Hancock Tower. But I don't think many people know that the Seagram Building was built by Mies van der Rohe, even though it's the best building in New York City.

Mies van der Rohe was a purist as an architect. Reminds me of Bill Bradley as a basketball player. It's someone who has a very clear idea of what he wanted to accomplish, and knew how to articulate that idea and could carry it through.

But I think a stronger analogy with basketball and an architect would be with a coach. An architect has an overall vision the way a coach does, and they both try to bring all the elements together. I particularly admired what Red Holzman did with the Knicks of the early 1970s. He had some very good elements to work with, like Walt Frazier and Earl Monroe and Dave DeBusschere and Willis Reed and Bradley, and made the most of them.

Q: The Lakers in the last few years had great elements but couldn't seem to build on them.

A: What a disaster! It's like most things in L.A. It has good intentions, but somehow it goes bad. Now they've got Phil Jackson as a coach. I think he's a great coach, but he's got his work cut out for him. I also think Kobe Bryant has great potential. He's terrific. He's like a young up-and-coming architect. He's got great appeal, great style. He's very talented and he captures the imagination. As good as he is, he's going to be even better—given the chance, given a decent team. He needs help. He can't do it alone.

Building or rebuilding a team has similarities with architecture beyond just the nomenclature. It's a tough battle in both instances. You have an idea, you work out a diagram of the idea, and then you have to adjust the idea to the contingency of the situation. The more you adjust, the more adjustments that are necessary, however, usually result in the whole not working so well. At least, that's the case in architecture. But I have a sense that it is the same in basketball. Sometimes there are too many outside factors that come into play and that you just don't have all the answers to. It's hard to keep readjusting. I think if the readjustments occur in the schematic design—which is the first phase of the first quarter—then it's okay. If the adjustments continue into the design-development stage, or the second period, it's still okay. But if you're still adjusting in the third period—which is the construction documents—and the fourth period, which is the construction phase, then you're in trouble. Because then it's too late. The elements are just not there.

Like we're doing a city hall in San Jose. So you have the building department, which is the client. And then we have all these public hearings and they want the public to sort of react to the conceptual design. But you just can't take all those comments and incorporate them because they're all over the place. You just have to have someone with a strong idea who is experienced and not let other opinions—maybe in basketball its the media, or even an owner—deter you from the goal, or what you know is best.

And when teams rebuild, it's almost like starting over, though a few elements may be retained from the original structure. But we're really beginning from the ground up. Hopefully, maybe there are some parts that we can salvage or reuse, but if you're really talking about rebuilding, you're talking about starting new. Like the Bulls, after their championship years. What was left? Toni Kukoc and Ron Harper and not much else. So they're going back to build for harmony of the team. A team effort, like an architectural team. It's not an individual effort. The front office and the coach and players. Success in building or rebuilding depends on your structural engineers, on your mechanical engineers, to understand what you the architect are doing because otherwise they'll mess it up.

Q: Of your contemporary architects, can you draw comparisons with contemporary basketball players in regard to style? Like I. M. Pei?

A: Who is the most enigmatic person in basketball? Rodman? No, that's not quite an apt comparison because Rodman is too flamboyant; Pei is much quieter. Pei is consistent. Tim Duncan maybe. Frank Gehry may be more of the Rodman type. But he's less bizarre, to be sure. In the end, Gehry gives you expected high performance. He's extremely talented, very flamboyant, very individualistic. I'd say Gehry's a cross between Rodman and Magic Johnson. And Philip Johnson—he's the Pat Riley of basketball. He's very theatrical and he has great notoriety and is very capable. He's sort of out there leading in a way that the public is aware of.

Q: When we speak in historical terms about architecture and basketball, what are the similarities, what are the differences?

A: The thing about basketball is that it keeps changing. That's a part of its interest. It's never static. A person like Duncan who is a star today, a hero, but who knows where he'll be next year, or the year after. Maybe he'll be there, maybe he won't. But architects, because of the nature of architecture, are around for much longer periods of time. They don't rise somehow to the same notoriety nor do they fall quite so quickly. Like the people who built the Pyramids. Or the Chartres cathedral, in France, or the St. Ivo church in Rome by Boromoni, or the Guggenheim Museum in New York City by Frank Lloyd Wright. These are some of my favorite buildings, and they're still around and will be for a long time. But I think part of the interest in basketball is that we like things of the moment. It's very much a game of the moment. Unlike architecture. But they're both a lot of fun.

I'll tell you what I don't like. And that is seats behind the basket. I once sat there for a game in Madison Square Garden. Now, I like the Garden because you feel a certain proximity to the play. You see it differently at different levels, obviously. But at the Garden you feel a certain intensity among the fans that certainly the players have to react to. The Garden itself is not a very good building. But I think that the arrangement for basketball isn't bad, except from behind the backboard. That's terrible. It's unfortunate for those people who have to sit there, as I did this one time. I think the seating could be better if it were just for basketball, rather than making it a makeshift thing. I mean, it's a multiuse arena, with circuses and concerts and hockey. I wouldn't eliminate those seats behind the backboard, but I wish they were inclined more. Your viewing line is not very good. I'd make it more of a bowl. I don't like seeing a game that way. Somehow the game is meant to be seen from the side. You sit behind one backboard and when play is at the other end, it feels like it's a thing apart. Like looking at a building—if you're too far away you lose the sense of design and the sense of drama.

Q: What did you make of the Twin Towers?

A: I prefer the San Antonio brand to the ones in Manhattan. The World Trade Center buildings are not great architecture. They stand out and are memorable strictly because of their height. And two of the same things in architecture rarely produces esthetic quality. But the San Antonio Spurs pair of David Robinson and Tim Duncan is something else. While they're called the Twin Towers, too, and are seven feet tall, they are each distinctive in their style of play. And they were able to mesh their differences effectively for the team. And that difference conceivably made them strong, and the strength of those differences helped them win, helped them become champions.

ALAN DERSHOWITZ

ESIDES being one of America's most prominent attorneys and a professor of law at Harvard University, Alan Dershowitz also grew up immersed in music and the opera, with both of his grandfathers being cantors, and he grew up immersed in sports. His passion for those areas appears undiminished. Dershowitz was born on September 1, 1938, in Brooklyn, New York. He is a prolific writer and the author of, among others, *Reversal of Fortune: Inside the von Bulow case, Chutzpah, The Abuse Excuse,* and a bestselling murder mystery, *The Advocate's Devil.*

He said, "Lawyers love basketball and opera. Baseball attracts a lot of academics; opera and basketball appeal to the emotional side of the brain, and lawyers are passionate people. When I go to the Met I see a lot of lawyers, especially criminal lawyers."

Before attending Yale Law School, he attended the Yeshiva University High School for Boys in Brooklyn, where he played on its basketball team, including once in Madison Square Garden.

•   •   •

Q: Have you ever gone to a basketball game and had an opera break out?

A: Almost. Basketball is an ensemble, but it's a star system, too. It's like opera. You have the soprano and the tenor and in basketball you have the point guard and the center. You build a team around two or three players, like in opera. The main thing in both, though, is the emotion. You are rooting to see the tenor and the soprano exceed the normal physical skills that anybody can possibly have. I mean, getting up to that top note and the duration. A high C or a D above high C. In basketball, you're constantly looking to see the player exceed all possible human abilities. Of course, Michael Jordan is the paradigm of that. Before Jordan, if somebody ever said, "I'm going to describe to you a player who would do the following things," you wouldn't believe it. Twenty years ago you wouldn't believe that average players can do the things that they do today, just in terms of physical skill, like hang time.

Now, when I first saw the Big O play—Oscar Robertson—I thought, "Oh my God!" Nobody could exceed his physical skills. And Elgin Baylor, of course. When I was growing up everybody said there were certain barriers. Nobody would break the four-minute mile. Forget it. It's never going to happen. Now what are we down to? 3:51? And the long jump. The high jump. And basketball has these incredible individual skills, but no one player makes a team. Three players make a team. You don't need five. The Bulls proved that three players make a team—Jordan, Scottie Pippen, and Dennis Rodman.

Q: And in opera?

A: In opera, it's the same thing. Take for example *Tosca*, which is one of my favorite operas. You must have an extraordinary Pavarotti-type tenor because there are two or three incredible arias that must be sung magnificently. Everyone knows how they're supposed to be sung, and everybody waits to hear whether or not "E Lucevan Le Stelle" can be exceeded. On the other hand, you can't have *Tosca* without a superb soprano who is also a good actress, a Maria Callas–type actress. It also needs a terrific baritone playing the bad guy, the villain. So you can't do it with one, but you don't need thirty. You need three.

You need a core. It's like people say that Larry Bird joined the

Celtics right out of college and turned the team around, from a losing team to a winning team, in one season. Bird was great, sure, but he had help. He had Kevin McHale and Robert Parish. They never had a great backcourt in those days. I never thought Dennis Johnson was up to the talents of the rest of the team, but you didn't need point guards when you had Larry Bird. He had this unique ability to be the floor manager from a forward position. He was the point forward. Johnson just brought the ball up, and brought the ball up slowly.

Q: You have written, "Opera is all about crime, passion, and revenge. It's a busman's holiday." The busman, in this case, obviously being a lawyer. Basketball has passion and revenge, but what about crime?

A: Oh, there's a lot of crime in basketball. I'm not talking only about literally stealing the ball, but part of basketball is what you can get away with. The one thing I don't like about basketball as a lawyer is that I don't like the denial of equal protection. I don't think we have equal rules in basketball for all players. I think some players are treated differently. Rookies and senior people are treated differently. And the rules change. You have, I'm sure, looked at the definition of traveling in the NBA. I give it to my students in criminal law. There's something about the breaking of rhythm that sounds like trotters on horseback now. It's two and a half pages in the rule book. It's incomprehensible.

When I was a kid, you knew you had a pivot foot, and if you moved your pivot foot, the official would call traveling. Now, people shuffle, or someone going in for a dunk takes six steps. Nobody knows what the rule is. As a lawyer, I hate vague open-ended rules. You demand equality. Everybody should be treated equally. And they're not on the court. There's an NBA rules committee and they meet every year and essentially what they say to themselves is, "All right, here's the way Jordan operates. Now let's make sure that's not a traveling violation." So they fit the rules to the player sometimes.

Q: I think it may have started with Julius Erving—Dr. J.— who brought people in the arena to watch him fly through the air to dunk—and of course he had a great literal running start.

A: It probably did. Do you remember the *Saturday Night Live* spoof about "Who's a Jew and Who's Not"? A little old lady is asked about Julius Erving—Dr. J. She says, "Let me think. He's a doctor. His name is Irving. Of course he's Jewish."

Q: Why do you think there are so few Jewish athletes?

A: There used to be many more, in all sports. There's now one in the NBA, Danny Schayes, Dolph's son. The way it works with sports often is this: When you are trying to get out of the ghetto, sports is the way out. For Jews it was sports, it was the violin, it was academia. For African-Americans, sports seems to be the way out. But now that Jews are getting to be much more affluent and more like WASPs in every way, I think many Jews will go back to sports. You're getting to see more of it in tennis. But basketball, I don't know. Basketball is an inner-city game and Jews don't live in the inner city. They used to. What's the joke? A bar mitzvah is the time a Jewish boy learns that his chances of owning an NBA team are considerably better than playing on one.

When I was growing up in Brooklyn Sandy Koufax lived a block away from me. I remember that he was the first guy in the neighborhood who could dunk, and with two hands, and he was only about six-one. He went off to the University of Cincinnati on a basketball scholarship and we all thought he'd make a name for himself in basketball. And of course he ended up making a rather good name for himself in baseball.

I loved playing basketball as a kid growing up in Brooklyn. I grew up in a tiny house but we had an old Ping-Pong table and we put it up on the garage and we had a basketball backboard. I had to be at school, the Brooklyn Yeshiva Academy, at 8:10, but before going, I had a routine. I would shoot one hundred free throws, and I had a baseball and a glove and I would throw one hundred balls up in the air and catch them. And we got permission from our rabbi to play basketball on Shabbos because it was inside. It was gated where we played. We grew up with basketball. I once played with my high school in Madison Square Garden. This was 1954 and it was a game prior to the Knicks playing Syracuse. The Brooklyn Yeshiva Academy versus the Manhattan Yeshiva Academy. I still have the program from that night and my name is of course listed on our team's roster. Well, I didn't play much, because I was a junior and the seventh or eighth man on our team. But it was a thrill, you can imagine.

My life then pretty much revolved around sports and the opera. For me, the two things that bring back feelings of nostalgia are music and basketball. The Met in those days was on Thirty-ninth Street and Madison Square Garden was on Fiftieth Street. Sometimes I would have to choose because I couldn't afford both. And you could get into the Met for fifty cents as a student. You had to carry your libretto, the score, to prove you were a student. So we would alternate. Some of my friends were my basketball buddies and some of my friends were my opera buddies. We'd pick and choose which event to go to.

Q: You've spoken about rivalries in basketball, which you've compared to rivalries in opera. What would they be?

A: I don't think anyone who was at the seventh game of the playoff series in 1988 between the Atlanta Hawks and the Celtics, when Bird and Dominique Wilkins went at it in the fourth quarter, will ever forget it. It was in Boston Garden, and the two of them were just shooting in each other's faces. It was a close game and they were the two stars and when one made a shot, the other countered. It was a real duel. It was so psychological. You just watched them going at each other and this incredible competition for who is the best, and everyone has his fans. When I go to the opera, you have the cliques for Pavarotti and some say, "Oh, come on, Pavarotti is nothing. Richard Tucker is the man."

It was such a game of prima donnas. At the time people were

saying that Dominique was better than Bird as an individual player, and Bird was just not going to dominate. Here was this great chance to prove something, a one-on-one show. Of course, the thing that Dominique was famous for was his moves and his shot. But it came down to Bird almost mimicking him, like "Anything you can do I can do better," the song from *Annie Get Your Gun*. And Bird did. It was close, but the Celtics won and Bird pulled it out.

[*Note*: The Celtics won 118–116, and advanced to the finals of the Eastern Conference playoffs. Wilkins scored forty-seven points in the game, sixteen in the last quarter. Bird scored thirty-four in the game, twenty in the last quarter.]

The big difference between Bird and most others was in the clutch. Bird would win games at the end routinely. Bird played for the last couple of minutes of the game.

Bird understood the drama of the moment like any great opera singer does. Do you know who Bird was like? Bird was more like Maria Callas than anybody. Maria Callas did not have the physical skills that many great sopranos had. If you just heard her on a flat recording, you wouldn't ever get the sense of the greatness of her personality and what she brought to it. She had a sense of the moment. She could make a moment on that stage like nothing that you've ever seen before. The same thing is true of Bird. Let's say there was a tie score and the Celtics suddenly would pull ahead by four or five points with three or four minutes to go. Bird would understand the moment that he could put the game away. He would take the three-point shot when normally you wouldn't take a three-point shot. But it was like he was saying to the other team, "I am now going to devastate you. I'm going to psychologically destroy you."

I think Bird was the best psychological player I've ever seen. The best person to anticipate the interactive nature of the game. The fact that you have to dishearten the other team. And though he wasn't famous as a trash talker to the general public, other players knew that he could say things that could upset the other guys.

And to this day you'll never convince a Magic Johnson fan, say, that Larry Bird holds a candle to him because Bird didn't have anything like the athletic abilities that a Magic had and they're equally smart. And they equally dominated the court. What would have happened if Magic had played for the Celtics and if Bird had played for the Lakers? And you hear that about opera. What would have happened if Pavarotti would have been back in the 1950s where you had to sing more often? What would have happened if Tucker would have been in the 1990s where you traveled more around the world? Could they have upheld the traditions that they had? Did Tucker have a more specific ethnic appeal to Jews and Pavarotti a more general appeal? And so was Bird only the great white hope? Nonsense. He was very popular, of course, among black athletes.

Q: Where does intelligence come in with basketball players and opera stars?

A: I think you have to be smart to succeed in the highest levels of most professions, and that includes sports and entertainment. They used to say about opera singers that tenors are dumb. That's been an old tradition. They said it because tenors were the naturals. Again, it's nonsense. Mediocre tenors may be dumb just like mediocre athletes may be dumb, but great tenors are very, very smart. They know how to save their voice, for example. Pavarotti is very smart. He knows when to give and when not to give. He knows what his audience wants. He's very interactive with his audience, and with other players on the set. But Franco Corelli was a great tenor for only about three years. I don't think he was particularly smart.

And Maria Callas? Absolutely brilliant. Maria Callas is Larry Bird. I mean, Maria Callas couldn't jump either. She didn't have the incredible vocal skills that a Joan Sutherland had or others of her generation before her or after her had. But she used her brain to take her extraordinary talents to the very top, made her the greatest opera diva of her time. I think the same is true of Larry Bird. He didn't have a great vertical leap, but was a great rebounder. He got his rebounds on the floor. It was all positioning.

I remember vividly Larry Bird's first game in Boston. When he came out there were great expectations and then we saw him. He just didn't look the part. He wasn't built like a basketball player. He was six-ten, but he was built more like a baseball or football player. He just didn't have the grace of a great athlete. But soon the normal guy could identify with him, because he was workmanlike. You couldn't identify with, say, Michael Jordan. He was so athletically magnificent it was like he was an alien from outer space. And it has nothing to do with race. It's all about whether or not people have supernatural talents.

Q: Do opera stars get old in the same way basketball stars do?

A: Sometimes. Placido Domingo is one of these guys who realizes that talents change over time. Magic Johnson would be a good example of that in basketball. You can't do as an older man what you could have done as a younger person, and that may be an advantage. Placido Domingo turned that to his advantage. He began to take slightly darker roles, roles that took more maturity and more experience, as opposed to roles that took extraordinary physical talent. I thought Magic in his later years played with even more finesse than he did in his earlier years. He used his experience to not only preserve his strength and stamina, but to utilize the other players better.

Q: Who is Pavarotti like?

A: The thing about Pavarotti is that things come very easily to him. It's pure natural talent. It is Michael Jordan, except that Pavarotti maybe stayed on too long, and Michael Jordan knew exactly when to quit. Pavarotti also quit and came back. He's like Michael Jordan for this reason, too. The last three times I saw Pavarotti it hurt me because I didn't want to remember him that way.

Q: Like Sinatra at the end? Or Dominique Wilkins now, at thirty-eight, sitting on the end of the bench for the Orlando Magic?

A: Yes, struggling. The thing that was so great about Pavarotti in the early days was the ease. He would just throw it off. It would just look like it took no talent. I'm sure it took a lot of practice, but it looked so natural. He was just given this incredible ability and it was beautiful to watch and hear, whereas when you see him now he is struggling. Not so Placido Domingo. He was trying to get up to a talent level and exceed it. For me, it was great to see him do that and to see him manage to overcome physical limitations. Pavarotti had no physical limitations. But now his age has caught up with him.

Q: The Celtics are in a down period as we speak. What expectations do you have for them?

A: There's distress now because people had such high hopes when Rick Pitino came in as coach. He hasn't done it for them. Everyone thought Pitino would be James Levine revitalizing the Metropolitan Opera. But there's no salary cap in the Met, so Levine was able to bring people in from all over.

Q: Is there an opera comparable to what's going on with the Celtics now?

A: Unfortunately, I think *La Sonnambula,* which is an opera about sleepwalking. But I still go to the games. I still cheer them on. And on occasion I've had seats right next to some of the old Celtic players. I've sat with John Havlicek, for one, and Larry Bird. These guys are just geniuses about their game. What sticks out in my mind with Bird is how he predicted plays. How he would sit there and watch from the stands and anticipate what was going to happen moments in advance. He would predict that so-and-so—

a Celtics opponent—would be under the basket, get the defensive
rebound, and be able to fast break. He would say, "Oh my God,
they shouldn't have done that." It was like two minutes before
anybody else could see it he saw what was developing. It was like
a chess player. When I play chess, I can anticipate two moves ahead.
But when a grand master plays chess, he can anticipate six or seven
moves ahead, and Bird was a grand master.

Q: Do you ever play basketball anymore?

A: I'm sixty years old, and three years ago my wife gave me a
birthday present. Unbeknownst to me, she had a full NBA court
built at our house on Martha's Vineyard—outdoors, of course, but
with lines and everything. And we have great games. We play all
the time. My son, Jamin, who is a counsel for the NBA, is a terrific player and my daughter-in-law, Barbara, is also a very good
player. We play two-on-two and three-on-three games. We have
one guy in our neighborhood who is a Buddhist monk, but originally a Brooklyn Jew. He's a Buddhist monk all the time—you
know, at peace with the world—except when he gets on the basketball court, and then the elbows fly!

And a few years ago the Harvard law faculty was challenged
by a group of students to a game of basketball. Now, the faculty
members were a bunch of mostly middle-aged guys. And the team
that showed up were women! Now, this was before the WNBA, or
anything like that. And these women were big. One of them was
Karen Russell, the daughter of Bill Russell, who was about six-
three. And these girls had played college ball. It was no contest.
They whupped us. It was shocking, but to my credit it didn't
destroy me.

I'm back playing ball in my yard.

CHRISTIE HEFNER AND BILL MAROVITZ

THE OFFICE OF Christie Ann Hefner, chairman and CEO of Playboy Enterprises, is on the second floor of a duplex on McClurg Court in downtown Chicago. Modern, button-down, it could be an office on Wall Street. She wears a gray suit and a cast on her left ankle, having slipped off a curb and torn ligaments. Her husband, Bill Marovitz, the former Illinois state legislator and now real estate developer, joined her in the interview.

When Ms. Hefner became chairman and CEO of Playboy Enterprises in 1988, at age thirty-five, succeeding her father, the founder of Playboy, Hugh Hefner, she took over an ailing company. She is widely credited with leading the company back to stability.

Ms. Hefner was born on November 8, 1952, in Chicago, and is a summa cum laude graduate of Brandeis University (1974), with a major in English and American Literature, and was elected to Phi Beta Kappa.

She joined Playboy in 1975 and worked in a variety of jobs there before being named to the board of directors in 1979. She was named president in 1982 and COO in 1986. As chairman and CEO she has expanded *Playboy* magazine to where it now produces sixteen editions worldwide, as well as developing television and Internet interests.

She lives in Chicago, headquarters of Playboy, with her husband, Bill Marovitz, a real estate developer and attorney as well as part-owner of several restaurants, including Michael Jordan's. Senator Marovitz, born on September 29, 1944, has had an extensive legislative career, having served in the Illinois House of Representatives from 1974 to 1980 and the Illinois State Senate from 1980 to 1993. He was the recipient of the Best Legislator Award from the Illinois Public Action Council.

The couple has season tickets to Chicago Bulls games.

* * *

Q: Christie, in your position with *Playboy* magazine, you've had occasion to meet some professional basketball players. What did you observe?

HEFNER: I've met some of the players at various Playboy functions, and they are unusual scenes. Like for the Playboy cigar we launched at Spago restaurant in Chicago a few years ago. The Playmate of the Year was there, Victoria Svlested, a very bright, very beautiful, and very physically imposing woman, and other women, including Playmates of the Month, who have been featured in photo layouts in the magazine. I remember Dennis Rodman was there and numerous other athletes. I don't know if any of them hooked up later, but none of them behaved badly. They are not aggressive. Their language isn't rough. They are not physically grabby. They are actually kind of respectful. Then they may go out and do whatever, but they are sort of—kids. That's part of what people sometimes lose sight of when you see them performing in their sport.

A lot of these guys are in their twenties and they're in these huge bodies and they're incredible athletes, but they're just kids, basically.

MAROVITZ: But when these athletes and these beautiful women come together, it's like an aphrodisiac.

HEFNER: It's a mutual thing.

MAROVITZ: A mutual aphrodisiac.

HEFNER: Oh, absolutely. I think there has always been a strong attraction between gifted athletes and beautiful models and actresses. It's at the essence of maleness and the essence of femaleness in that Darwin "we-were-monkeys-not-too-long-ago" sense of who we are at our core, in every part of the world. It's a classic example of our DNA wiring to perpetuate the life of the species. You can feel the chemistry in the room. It's palpable.

It's like a mating dance. If you've ever gone to Africa and you watch ostriches before they actually mate, you'll see how they sort of check each other out. Someone will get a little too close deliberately, sort of violate the space and brush up against the other. Then they'll back away, and the other one will get a little too close. So there is this constant flirtation and mating dance going on. There was an animal magnetism on both sides.

The dynamics of basketball as a team sport is also fascinating to me. Speaking as somebody in business, one of the things that I find most interesting about the game is the coaching, and putting a team together in a situation that is constantly changing, in which you are constantly having to react to what the other team is doing, to who is on and who is off your team, and what seems to be working, and what isn't. I'm probably as big a fan of Phil Jackson as I am of Michael Jordan. The whole idea of taking a group of people—which is so much of what business is about—some of whom are superstars, and some of whom are just average, and melding them into a team that works is, to me, very intriguing.

I was taken, for example, with the way Jackson handled Dennis Rodman, his ability to integrate someone like Dennis into the team. In the last several years before he joined the Bulls, he clearly did not play as effectively as he did when he came to Chicago. I give Jackson—and Jordan—a lot of credit.

One of the keys in leadership is to understand that you already have power because of the position you are in. The most effective way to wield that power is to lead by showing people what you want them to do and making them want to do that. It means giving people a little bit more freedom, as opposed to using power as a stick in an authoritarian way. Of course, some people have been effective in that way. I guess Mike Ditka and Bob Knight are examples. It's heavy-handed and draws a lot of very limited lines, and when you cross them you get yelled at. Then there is another style of coaching that tolerates a degree of freedom on the part of the players. Obviously for Rodman, that means his need to rebel, his need to sort of break the rules, and to understand which are the rules that are the real rules, and which are the rules that are sort of not real rules.

MAROVITZ: And the real rules pertain to the game, and what's best for the team.

HEFNER: That's right. You must do your job. It's not about how you dye your hair. I think that a tone got set early on by Jackson and Jordan that was a tone of acceptance and respect for what Rodman could bring to the team. Now if Rodman hadn't delivered on that, none of it was going to work.

MAROVITZ: And they never embarrassed Dennis publicly. I think that's an important point. You don't see negative comments in the press, you don't see it on the court when he does his screaming and yelling.

HEFNER: Sometimes Phil or Michael or one of the players will say they are disappointed in something he's done, like miss a practice, or kick that photographer at courtside, or butt the head of a referee. But it's always a remark in a positive vein. It's never heavy-handed or negative. You don't hear Phil say, "Dennis was late again." He'll say, "It's something we will have to address." Or Michael will take Dennis aside and talk to him.

And the team was always willing to publicly give Dennis credit for how much he contributed to the team. I think it's something we all need—but Dennis in particular needs a great deal of it. And

Phil recognized this. Dennis needs to feel appreciated and respected.

Q: Does Dennis make you laugh, or is his act tiresome to you?

HEFNER: Off the court, I don't pay any attention to it. It's irrelevant to me. There are several sides to Dennis Rodman. Dennis has made a science out of rebounding. He's one of the best ever at that—we had an *Playboy* interview with Dennis and I remember how he talked about studying which side of the rim a ball was going to bounce from, or how it angles off the backboard.

MAROVITZ: Rodman is interesting also because of his hermaphroditic essence. I mean, he could pose for *Playgirl* nude, I guess, as well as *Playboy*.

HEFNER: Well, in fact, we did a profile of him before we did the interview with him, and the picture that ran with him was a very sexy, very beautiful picture of him and his girlfriend. He was standing behind her sort of covering her body, and they were both nude. It was a beautiful picture. He's interesting, I think, because he's got this completely theatrical persona that he has cultivated. It allows him to be an entertainer and make money from that and it has nothing to do with his basketball skill.

It's interesting in that when you move to his professional persona, he takes it really seriously. This is not a guy who goofs around. He may occasionally be late for practice, and I'm not saying that's a good thing, but I don't think there is anybody on that team—and, in fact, some of the sportswriters in Chicago have been very critical of him—who works as hard when he's on the court. When he joined the team, it was palpable, the level of energy he brought to the team when it was on the floor. It wasn't just that he was getting rebounds, it wasn't just that he was often better against the big centers than any of our guys because we've never had a great center, it was that he was just giving 110 percent every minute.

So he is very exciting to watch because as goofy as he is off the floor, he doesn't goof around on the floor.

MAROVITZ: And when he does goof around on the floor, it's with a purpose, to take the other guy out of the game, like he does Alonzo Mourning.

HEFNER: It's very calculated. He understands that his counter-culture image is marketable. He's made a lot of money from it, so he continues to cultivate it. I remember when his book, *Bad As I Wanna Be*, came out. I was shopping on the Near North Side and saw a line of people and I'm walking and the line is another block, and another block, and another block. It must have been six blocks of people waiting to get into a bookstore to get an auto-graphed copy of Dennis's book. And then he showed up on a motorcycle and wearing heavy eye makeup and a feather boa. And the people went crazy. They loved it. He has definitely built a cult.

MAROVITZ: I'm friends with Dennis's agent, Dwight Manley. And one day he asked me to fly to New York when Dennis announced that he was going to get married, but held off saying who he was going to marry. Dwight asked me if I would perform the ceremony because he knew I had been in the state senate.

HEFNER: Billy's actually not a judge, but I don't think they registered that.

MAROVITZ: [*Laughs.*] Not that I would have performed the ceremony of that wedding even if I was legally able to do it. Dennis wasn't marrying anybody. If you recall, he married himself.

Q: Beyond Rodman, does basketball have any other appeal for you?

HEFNER: Well, basketball is clearly the sexiest team sport. It's because you see more of the athletes' bodies, see how muscular they are, how strong they are, how fit they are. The truth is, there are plenty of professional baseball players who aren't fit, who you wouldn't want to see their bodies. You're glad that they are wearing uniforms that are big. The same with football players. I'm very happy that William Perry was completely covered up, thank you.

Q: How long have you been going to Bulls games?

HEFNER: Actually, I married into my season tickets. When we first started going out, in 1991, Billy said, "Now this is your seat." The seats are not on the floor but up about fifteen rows up from the Bulls' bench. You see the game from a better perspective than a floor seat, you can see the whole flow of the game from up there. I wasn't that great a fan at first, nothing like Billy. But pretty soon you get into it—the athleticism is an art form, and of course the excitement is enhanced when you're following a winning team, and one with Michael Jordan. It's electric. From the time the lights go down and the announcement starts to the end of the game, it's electric.

Pretty soon you're kind of coaching along with the coach—and Billy. I don't do a lot of screaming, but there are times when you get aggravated, when one of our players makes a poor foul, and allows the shooter to make the basket. I'll holler, "If you're going to foul him, foul him! Don't let him get the shot off!"

Billy and I plan our schedule so that we don't have conflicts with regard to the Bulls if we can help it, and especially during the playoffs. We try not to travel when the Bulls are home. And one conflict I've had to deal with in the last few years is that the finals weekend has been the same weekend as the Playboy Jazz Festival, which is a two-day sellout event at the Hollywood Bowl where I serve as host. So I bring a little watchband or I go to the booth where the artists hang out. I've actually watched the end of the last series, in 1998, with some of the jazz guys standing in the trailer behind the Hollywood Bowl, cheering.

MAROVITZ: Our goal, if the playoffs are away, is to fly to them, wherever they are. I won't miss a game. Our lives, our traveling, our business schedules, all of them revolve around the Bulls. If they are playing, I want to be there. I say to my friends, "What else would I rather do in the city of Chicago than be at a Bulls game with Michael Jordan playing? Is there anything else in this city that you would rather do? I don't care if it's opera, the symphony, a speech, or whatever." There have been times when we've had weddings and bar mitzvahs and stuff like that. I will just leave.

HEFNER: What was the event we went to in black tie?

MAROVITZ: It was the National Football League players' dinner at the Hyatt Hotel in Chicago. I was the chairman, and it was an annual charity event for the Better Boys Foundation. Now, this was the night of a big playoff game with the Bulls at home. And I was introduced along with the players as I walked onto the dais: "And now the chairman of the dinner. . . ." I walk down the platform and right out the door.

HEFNER: I met Billy at the door. He's in black tie, and I'm in a cocktail dress—we had been there for the whole cocktail reception. We got to the United Center just in time for the opening tip and sat through the entire game dressed like that. We did get some strange looks from people. Maybe they thought we were some kind of halftime entertainment. But their focus went quickly to the game—and to Michael.

I actually met Michael years and years before, in 1984. Every year *Playboy* does the All-American College Basketball team. They bring together all the players that they've picked for a weekend, and they do the team picture that runs in the magazine. I've gone to some of those over the years, and I attended the one he was at. In fact, the first time I ran into Michael in Chicago in the 1990s, I was with Billy at a restaurant and Michael couldn't have been more gracious. One of the first things he said to me was what a wonderful experience being a *Playboy* All-American had been, how he really felt it had raised his level of visibility when he was a college player.

If you remember, he wasn't the first player picked in the draft out of college. He sort of blossomed. Not that he was a slouch, but I'm not sure there was the level of belief that he would be, I think, one of the greatest players ever when he was playing college ball.

I've found the players to be very polite, almost—deferential may be the wrong word, but almost shy. I remember Shaquille O'Neal. How can you forget him? I have a picture of him with me from the *Playboy* All-American, so he was obviously still in college. I'm standing next to him. I'm five-seven, and I'm in heels. And I look like a Munchkin from *The Wizard of Oz* next to him. It's very funny.

When he got into the pros Billy and I took Shaq and his manager to dinner. Shaq is not just huge physically but there is a presence about him, it's quite extraordinary. There is basically the shell of this—I don't want to say little boy—but this just-out-of-adolescence young man who was sweet and polite and talked about his family and kind of mostly listened. And he ate twelve times more food than any human being I've ever seen.

Q: What did he eat?

HEFNER: Everything they had. It was at Michael's restaurant and it was like all comfort food—macaroni and cheese and meat loaf and chicken and hamburgers. . . . Then his shoe size! His shoe looks like the kits that kids used to build of aircraft carriers.

MAROVITZ: It's about a size twenty-two.

Q: Christie, do you think you will be as great a basketball fan after the Jordan years and the championship team years? After all, you began going to games at the first of the six championships in the 1990s.

HEFNER: If the team continues to be competitive I think I would definitely continue having a high degree of interest. But when Michael leaves, well, a good deal of entertainment will be lost not just for me, but for a legion of fans. I grew up in a north Chicago suburb and went to New Trier High School and played on the basketball team there. But I didn't really have a great commitment to the sport growing up. My dad wasn't much of a basketball fan, either. His favorite sports going way, way back have been football and boxing. He loves boxing, and he still has fight nights at the Playboy Mansion where he has a bunch of people over to watch a fight on television. And Chicago was more of a football and hockey and baseball town before Michael showed up. But that's changed a lot around here. And what has amazed me about Michael, and many of the others, is not just the athleticism, but the physical stamina that is required to play the game at that level. And a highly strategic game. So that combination makes it more complicated, more interesting, more engaging because as a fan you appreciate it on multiple levels.

And you see Michael make these miraculous shots, but I also have come to appreciate how he can sublimate his phenomenal talents for the benefit of the team, how he helps move the ball, how he uses his other players.

From a physical standpoint, I also have enjoyed watching Scottie Pippen, the picture of grace. And I like watching Dennis. He runs like an antelope. He has a very interesting kind of lope to the way he runs down the court. And I love watching some of the little guys, like Muggsy Bogues. He's five-three and you cannot believe he's actually playing on the same court with people who are two and three feet taller than he is. But he's so quick that it's funny how some of the other guys are afraid to put the ball on the floor when he's around, because he just picks it off.

I don't like watching a lot of those big centers on opposing teams. I find them awkward-looking. It's like they're muscling their way under the basket, and of course they are always traveling. They never get called for it, which pisses me off.

Q: Billy, which players have been your favorites to watch, beyond the Bulls?

MAROVITZ: Magic Johnson, Isiah Thomas, but I think my favorite was Larry Bird.

Everything Bird could do from his passes, his assists, to the position that he'd get for setting up other players. He was always at the right place at the right time. One of the saddest things I've ever seen in sports was the last time that Larry played here, in 1992. His back was really hurting him. He wasn't the same Larry Bird. They'd take the ball away from him. He'd throw the ball away. He couldn't keep up with team. It was really sad to watch.

HEFNER: That's what we don't want to see happen to Michael. We want to see Michael go out on top.

MAROVITZ: I remember when he retired the last time, when he went off to play baseball. It got frustrating for us.

HEFNER: Like the game when we happened to be sitting with friends at courtside. I never shout negative things at the players, but Billy will. Who was the guy who almost came across the floor? I thought you were going to get into a fistfight.

MAROVITZ: Pete Myers. He was supposed to be the new Michael Jordan. And I was yelling at Myers. This was one of those, if you're going to foul a guy, don't let him get a shot off, and the guy hit a three-pointer! Plus a foul! He pushed him instead of really taking him out of the shot.

HEFNER: But you were yelling insulting comments.

MAROVITZ: I don't know what you mean by insulting comments.

HEFNER: Like "You—"

MAROVITZ: Oh, no.

HEFNER: Oh, yes. Yes, yes.

MAROVITZ: Well, in the heat of the game.

HEFNER: [*Laughs.*] Sometimes we both may have gotten a little carried away with it.

SEIJI OZAWA

SEIJI OZAWA began conducting the Boston Symphony Orchestra in 1973, the longest tenure of any music director currently active with a major orchestra. Mr. Ozawa is also director of the Boston Symphony's Tanglewood Festival and the Tanglewood Music Center in Lenox, Massachusetts.

While working with Herbert von Karajan in West Berlin, Mr. Ozawa came to the attention of Leonard Bernstein, who appointed him assistant conductor of the New York Philharmonic for the 1961–62 season. He was music director of the summer home of the Chicago Symphony Orchestra at the Ravinia (Illinois) Festival for five summers beginning in 1964, and then became music director of the Toronto Symphony, then music director of the San Francisco Symphony, and then to Boston.

He has received two Emmys, the first, in 1976, for the BSO's PBS television series, *Evening at Symphony,* and the second in 1994 for Individual Achievement in Cultural Programming, for *The Dvorak Concert from Prague: A Celebration,* with the Boston Symphony.

Mr. Ozawa announced in 1999 that he would be leaving Boston to take the position of conductor for the Vienna State Opera. He was born September 1, 1935, in Shenyang, China, to Japanese parents, and studied at Tokyo's Toho School of Music.

He regularly attends home games of the Boston Celtics.

●　●　●

Q: You are considered a conductor with a great degree of energy, artistic energy. Have you seen a similar kind of energy in basketball?

A: You see it in a good way, and in a bad way. When everything is going good, great. But when it is going wrong, you know that somebody has lost concentration. And the power goes out of the movement, in basketball as well as music. And it can bring all the other players down. Sometimes the problem is caused by the coach, or the conductor.

And sometimes the good players can cover someone who loses concentration. Say the French horn goofs. That happens. He just misses it. Then who else can carry this moment? Usually a clever composer covers things. He doesn't leave things naked. For instance, there's another instrument covering the part. Viola and second violin are playing the same thing as the French horn. So if the horn player is lost, I go with the violin or viola. Then three bars later, or ten bars later, the French horn will catch up from there.

But the difference in basketball is that the coach can call time-out and fix things. He cannot do it himself. The conductor is different from a basketball coach. The conductor has to do it himself.

Take *The Rite of Spring* by Stravinsky. It's a very complicated score. We spent a lot of energy to study it, and we know it. So professional people like me and my group, we can do it. However, even in the Boston Symphony, mistakes happen. Just recently during a performance of *The Rite of Spring,* the bass drum did not play. Everybody thought the timpani had caused the problem. Of course the timpani was affected, but it was the bass player who lost his way. He just miscounted, I think, or lost his concentration. It's really a concentrated moment. You can't be thinking about dinner tonight, or some personal problem. This man didn't play. It's like when you step down and one stair is not there. You know how you feel? That happened. And then he recovered, but he hit the wrong note! That threw everybody, including me. But we are a very professional group, and three or four seconds later we're back.

Everybody gets wet. [*Laughs.*] It's very bad for the heart. I'm sure in basketball, that moment is a time-out call.

One day I'm watching the basketball game and one of the Celtic players was obviously not playing on the same level with the others. When he came in, immediately something happened. The whole team came down. You felt it even in the stands. It completely leveled the place. I don't know if he was not in good shape or mood or what. I said, I know that feeling when one person screws up like that. And in basketball it's more obvious because you don't have a hundred players on the court, you have only five. But Rick Pitino knew it right away, and called time-out and took him out. I wish I could do that sometimes.

When I watch the basketball games on television, I like watching Rick Pitino, how he coaches the Celtics, and on television you get the close-ups of his face that you don't quite get when you go to a game. At a game, you're too far away. I think we can read him more than the usual person. He looks like he's very emotional, but I'm sure he controls the overreaction of a player, and he can go wild or he can be cool, depending on the situation. But I think sometimes he really goes off. He looks that way.

You can see from how the team plays that they must be able to practice with concentration. And in music, practice is everything. For a conductor, the performance is really too late to do anything except make sure everything is okay and some emotional direction is observed. Everything happens during rehearsal.

So in a way it's a very strange profession. The conductor of the orchestra is in front of the audience the same time as the player, but 90 percent of the work is before I appear in front of the audience with my tails. I have to do work with the practice time. I'm sure it's the same in basketball. Most of the work is in practice, and at game time not as much.

Q: When did you first get interested in basketball?

A: I came to America twenty-five years ago, and for the first ten years I didn't pay attention to basketball. I thought basketball was easy. The ball comes and you throw it back. When I learned how difficult it was, how quick you have to be, I was taken by it completely. The action, the quick reaction, is like in music. And while it seems like reflex, it takes concentration and practice. Like Michael Jordan. What I appreciate so much in him, what is so remarkable, is his concentration at the moment, not five seconds before or after, but right in the second that is necessary. It lasts just a second, but that concentration that is also critical for a musician.

Many people think music is easy. No. The music, the notes must happen at exactly the right moment. Not just before or not just after, or not too short, not too long. It has to be there at that moment. Pinpointed—even more than pinpoints. Otherwise when you listen it's not good. If you are a little bit late, a pinpoint late or a pinpoint early, it will not be comfortable to listen to.

There's a big difference between an amateur musician and a professional musician. A professional musician practices for that right second in which to put the note in the right moment, and the right pitch. That takes concentration.

And in an orchestra, like in basketball, one musician cannot do it alone to effect beautiful music. You have to work as a team. Like on the fast break. You practice and practice, and then in the game, it is the eye contact which says, Here it comes. Like in an orchestra, there must be eye contact. From what I have seen, I believe it is the same in basketball. An orchestra has a lot of eye contact. Just before they play I establish eye contact with the solo player. Then the next moment he hits the note. On the other hand, a bad player doesn't do this. They just avoid the conductor and play. But the best, they watch the conductor and the moment you hit the note, you find the partner where the pass goes—the next instrument to pick up the music—and he picks it up right at the precise second. Not a second before or after.

If it is a slow movement, you have to put one timpani—*boom*—like with strong feeling at the precise moment. Like Beethoven's Ninth Symphony. It is a slow movement, like, how do you say, a wave over the ocean. Not hitting the beach, but a wave rising in the water. It is very difficult to hit the point exactly at the crest of the wave, but Beethoven asked for the timpani to come in at that very moment. And then it is immediately answered by the wind instruments. And then the timpani with the contrabassoon pizzicato.

Now, while the timpani is the leader at that moment, the rest of the orchestra is of course still watching me, watching my baton. The audience usually doesn't see it. And when it all goes right, it is fantastic.

When I watch basketball, I see it in two ways. One is the philosophical. I cannot imagine otherwise when something goes very well. When one thing breaks down, everything goes wrong. But a good wave goes, and a good mood, and then the offense is working in synchronization, very smooth and effective. It was like nothing extraordinary happened, but there was a right point and somebody was waiting at the right place and right time and the pass goes just right.

On defense, the same thing. Five players working in harmony. The difference between basketball and music is that in music, we at least have a score to work from. [*Laughs.*] We don't work toward a score, like in basketball.

But in music, the composer really plans it, and we the orchestra have to define or recreate sound from the score, from the music he wrote already. We have to find out how to make sound again. In basketball, I'm sure the coach has plays, but everything is much more improvised.

And of course in an orchestra you don't have a defense that's trying to stop you from completing the score.

Q: You were in Boston when Larry Bird was playing. What impressions did you have of him and his team?

A: Many times I watched Larry Bird play and also the big guy.

Q: Parish?

A: Yes, Robert Parish and Kevin McHale. I was once even brought backstage to the changing room to meet them. They were wonderful. And I thought Larry Bird had an inner fire. He didn't show much but he always had the fire inside him. That I enjoyed very much. It reminded me of the pianist Christian Zimmerman. A musician who doesn't show too much. He looks so peaceful and in control. But the music has fire, and you know it comes from within. You would see Bird drive to the basket with such force, the way Zimmerman plays.

Both have a lot of drama. And for me, seeing the movements of the basketball players, I find it amazing what a body can do. But of course I know there must be a lot of practice.

In music, we know how much practice we need. Practice, practice, practice, practice. Just to put your system and your muscles together. And when you go to the performance it just has to come naturally. You can't think. For musicians, when you play real music for the audience, you cannot think when is what and what is when—no, then it's too late.

I also look at the faces of the players. Shaquille O'Neal's face I like. You know how it goes this way, his eyes are almost crossed, and seem to be looking in two different directions. I'm not sure how he sees the basket.

I watched a game recently with Houston and Pippen doesn't do so well. He cannot do anything. It's like a different guy from when he played with the Bulls. I think Michael Jordan made all the other players better, including Pippen.

But there are musicians who make other players better, too. We have a new flutist, and the flute doesn't make a big sound, and we have a hundred instruments, but everybody feels very good because he is able to lead. He can set the intonation, or the pitch. It's amazing. I think he's the best flutist in the world. The Michael Jordan of flutists.

We do a lot of eye-to-eye contact. I don't have to wave my arms. I just look at him when necessary and he knows then that it's his show for the next ten bars. It's a beautiful feeling, it's trust. And that's what makes our life so good, so rich. If a conductor has to conduct everything, it's terrible.

Q: Some basketball coaches say that they are many people in one. Sometimes they are the coach, sometimes the father, or a policeman and a psychiatrist. Can a musical conductor relate to that?

A: It's the same thing, though we don't say it openly. But in an orchestra everybody comes from a different school, even a different country, so it's a different mentality or orientation. Beethoven's symphony is the same score, but everybody is reading with a little bit different perspective from Russia, from Germany, from France, from Japan and China. Each country has a tradition.

The tempo—and the attack of the notes—may be different in different cultural interpretations. All this is not well written in a score. The musicians have learned in various schools, but every school is different. So when they arrive in Boston they have to play music at the same time and that is sometimes where the ensemble is difficult. You can see how it is when different basketball players come from different schools and coaches. The coach has to bring these different styles into one cohesive team. Sometimes quite difficult.

It's like a family dynamic. If you spotlight each individual person, you'll find they are all different.

And of course the conductor has to do more than just lead the musicians. My musicians don't say it, but inside they are looking toward Papa. Psychologically, if somebody is really having a problem, playing-wise or family-wise, I have to know because it could affect their music, and the whole orchestra. If we help this way, the result is wonderful. And things are at a very fine level here. If you are not a good musician, you cannot get into the Boston Symphony. Competition is so high. It's the same as the NBA. The basic standard is very high. So how you use this talent to build one unit of sound is my job. It's not so easy. I think I can clearly relate to what Rick Pitino does, and I wouldn't be surprised if he can relate to what I do.

And if there is a mistake, or someone is not going in the precise direction the rest of us are going, then sometimes you have to talk with the person. And musicians—both men and women—can be very fragile. Some can have thick skins, but most do not. You have to be sensitive to them.

Q: As the conductor, it seems that you may not run quite the risk that a basketball coach might these days, after one player choked his coach.

A: Sometimes a conductor wonders how popular he is with the players, but you try to have a good working relationship. And just because you are the leader of the orchestra, it is maybe natural that they come to look at you like Papa.

But conducting can be dangerous. I'll tell you what happened to me last October. We had a concert on a Thursday here. My soloist, a big Canadian tenor—Ben Heppner—who is this high. He's more than six feet—maybe six-four or six-five. He's a big guy and a Canadian. Wild Canadian. And his music stand was this high, about up to my chest. Just before the music starts, he moves his stand to the right, which was close to me. I didn't like it because it took up my room, but I thought I won't use this area. I'll just stay this way. I went to give a cue at one point, to say, "Hey, you come in." I didn't have to do it, because he knows the music, but I did it. And I had my head down and I raised my hand and then brought it down forcefully, and my small finger banged against the music stand. And there was so much pain. Everybody in the orchestra noticed, but I had to conduct for the next fifty minutes with this hand. It wasn't bleeding, but it was very painful. I had to put ice on it afterward.

So the next day they wanted me to go to the doctor, but I didn't go. I went to conduct in Vienna and the finger became inflamed. But I still didn't go to a doctor. Finally in Japan I couldn't stand the pain any longer. The doctor told me, you have cut a ligament in the finger and if you don't have an operation now you will lose this finger completely. I had the operation.

This was in January. I was so stupid to delay. Someone told me, this is like when Ray Nitschke used to play football on broken legs.

I know there is a saying in sports, "playing hurt." It is a badge of honor. So I was conducting hurt. But next time I go to hospital.

DR. ISAAC STEVEN HERSCHKOPF

THE bearded, six-foot-tall Dr. Herschkopf has a private practice as a psychiatrist in Manhattan and is a faculty member at the New York University School of Medicine, as well as being an attending physician at both Bellevue and University hospitals. He was born on April 28, 1950, in Manhattan, was graduated Phi Beta Kappa from Queens College in 1971, and was valedictorian of his class at the New York University School of Medicine in 1975.

He has played basketball on a recreational level for much of his life, and continues to play in games in gyms and schoolyards near his homes in Manhattan and Southampton, New York, where he lives with his wife and three daughters.

•   •   •

Q: When you watch basketball, do you ever find a correlation between a game and your practice of psychiatry?

A: Often. One that occurs frequently is the need for deceleration in a crisis.

Q: Deceleration?

A: In psychiatry, when things get really tough for the patient, when he's sitting in my office, or in the hospital, and there's a real emergency—maybe the patient is suicidal, things have gone terribly wrong in his life—those are the times when you try to decelerate the process. You have to slow things down, to stop and think. The more of a crisis there is, the more you have to decelerate. In that respect, it's very much like basketball.

Q: You don't panic?

A: Right. In basketball your adrenaline at that moment can be working against you. In psychiatry, your adrenaline also works against you. You're trying to calm the situation, rather than what your adrenaline does, which is the fight-or-flight mode—the crisis.

Q: Can you give an example of a game in which you observed this phenomenon working, or not working?

A: I guess I notice more when things fall apart. As a psychiatrist, you are more attuned to pathology—you're attuned to the Hemingway definition of courage: grace under pressure.

I always notice when people don't respond with grace under pressure—your players or coaches, and you see that all the time. You have a player who loses his cool in a game. The most obvious example was the departed, not necessarily lamented, Dennis Rodman. When things would go badly in a game he would often literally and figuratively lash out. This was a perfect example of someone decompensating physically—a psychiatric breakdown in the middle of a game, whether it's kicking a photographer on the sideline, whether it's head-butting a referee, or just saying, "You know what, I'm not playing. I'm taking off my sneakers. I'm going home." Or deliberately provoking a situation where he'd be thrown out of a game. This was someone who was basically saying, "I can't deal with the pressure. Get me outta here." In some ways, it was almost like an adolescent crying out for help. But in a self-destructive, and ultimately team-destructive, manner.

Q: But in other instances he really was good, wasn't he, and good for the team—getting rebounds, playing a good team game.

And he was an important contributor to five world championship teams, two with the Pistons, three with the Bulls.

A: I never thought he was good for the team. I always thought that even in his prime, when he played his best ball when he came up with Detroit, it was because he had a very clear father figure in his coach, Chuck Daly, and he was trying to please him. Once Chuck Daly was no longer in his life, even when he won championships with the Bulls, I never thought he was a particularly great player. He was a great rebounder, but not a great player. He wasn't part of the flow. Basically, he was almost like an onlooker, a scavenger, who would pick up the rebound and in that sense contribute to the team, but you never got the sense that he was part of either the offensive flow or the defensive flow. Certainly toward the end—especially with the Lakers—I thought he was enormously self-serving. Like when a ball was going out of bounds off the other team, and he was hustling after it, he grabbed the ball and the TV announcer remarked, "Well, Rodman really wanted that rebound." I said to myself, "What did he want that rebound for?" His team was getting the ball anyway. If anything, he cost the team time because instead of getting the ball out of bounds, he saved it and sent it back. It cost his team seconds off the clock. What he was clearly doing was diving for his statistics.

Q: Is there a player or players that you might contrast with Rodman?

A: John Stockton, for one, or, one of my favorite players of all time, John Havlicek. Marvelous team players. So is Charlie Ward, of the Knicks, who gets a lot of criticism, but I think he is first and foremost a team player. I'm impressed with the timing of Karl Malone. He looks like he should be the archetype power forward who just bullies his way into the basket, but he scores most of his points on an elegant pick and roll with Stockton. He moves beautifully without the ball. He and Stockton play together as though they are twin brothers who've played together their whole lives.

Q: They've played together for about fifteen years.

A: In basketball terms, I guess that's about a lifetime. . . . When I watch a basketball game, I rarely look at the ball. I usually look away from the ball. I look to see who's cutting without the ball, who is setting picks, who is setting the low-post pick, who is playing defense. To me, that's the best part of the game. The teams with the most of those type of players, I think, tend to be the teams that win the most.

Q: What in your view would be the defining characteristic of this kind of player?

A: I think it's character. I think part of it is also sacrifice, the idea of being able to subjugate your own needs for the needs of the team. In other words, knowing that, for example, unlike Rodman, it's less important that I get the rebound than for someone on my team to get the rebound. If by boxing out my man it means that someone on my team will get the rebound, even though I don't get it, then I've done my team a great service, even though I have one less rebound on the stat sheet.

Q: In what category would you put Charles Barkley?

A: Barkley is an interesting player in that on the court I'm not as impressed with him as I am off the court. There is a refreshing intellectual honesty about the man. He'll say things that other people would think, but would never think of saying, and there is something endearing about him. Like the way he spoke about Allen Iverson. He talked about Iverson not being a team player— but more so even when he talks about himself. He'll be very blunt in terms of assessing both himself and his team's chances.

He reminds me, ironically enough, of someone else who I have equally mixed feelings about—Howard Stern. Again, both of them can be offensive and crude and vulgar and immature—that's probably the prominent word—and undisciplined. But at times both will say the one thing that everyone else is thinking, but wouldn't dream of saying publicly. There is something engaging about that.

Q: Tim Duncan?

A: I love watching him play. Even though he is a spectacular one-on-one player and almost unstoppable, what's interesting is to watch him in the flow of the game. It's also interesting—and again, here it's in terms of dynamics—the deference he always shows David Robinson, his veteran teammate and front-line partner. It's quite possible, in fact, it's probably the case at this point in time that Duncan's game has eclipsed Robinson's, and yet Duncan always treats Robinson, both on the court and, I understand, off the court, with a certain deference befitting Robinson's senior position. I see it frequently in the picks he'll set for him. I see it, for example, when they are both going for a rebound. There are times when Duncan could clearly get the rebound, and yet will just as soon let Robinson have it. I've seen it where on a fast break Duncan will give up the ball—at times, even ill-advisedly—to Robinson. An extra pass at times is unselfish, and at times just increases the possibility of something going wrong. It's giving the defense a chance to get back. Something could go wrong that could mess up a pass. But that kind of deference I find admirable.

Q: Does it have anything to do with upbringing?

A: It can. He plays well with other campers. This was a kid who knows how to share. On the other hand, I always liked watching the huddles during a time-out, particularly the team that called the time-out because the other team has just run off a string of points. It's fascinating. Watch what happens when they come back to the bench. Who do they look at? What do they say? You can't overhear what they are saying, but the body language speaks volumes. Do they look at the coach when they sit down? Do they listen to him? Do they give the coach the respect of looking at him when he's speaking, or do they look away—or, like Rodman, sometimes, do they take off their sneakers as if they don't even want to be part of the game anymore? I read in the papers that one game recently the Lakers were self-destructing and there was a huddle and the coach—Kurt Rambis—wasn't even a part of it. It was almost like a players' meeting. That to me is incredible. Twenty, thirty years ago it would have been unthinkable. Can you imagine a player telling Red Holzman or Red Auerbach, "No, I don't want to guard him"?

Q: Do you think this reflects a change in society?

A: It does. I think our culture has moved too far in the direction of individual rights. I think there was a time in our culture, and life in general, where society dominated at the expense of the individual, and rightfully so. We said, "You know what, yes, there is a majority rule, and yes, society has its rules, but we have to respect the rights of the individual." We've done that, but unfortunately, as with everything else in life, the balance has swung a little bit too far in the direction, at times, of the individual rights. For a player to tell a coach, "I'm not going in the game"—that's destructive to the whole.

Q: Like Allen Iverson swearing at his coach, Larry Brown, or the famous incident in which in the last seconds of a crucial play-off game, Scottie Pippen tells Phil Jackson that he is not going into the game because the play is not designed for him to shoot?

A: And Phil Jackson was a strong coach. So is Larry Brown. But, yes, that's exactly what I'm talking about. No matter how strong the coach is, there's going to be a handful of players on the team who everyone knows—or believes—are more important than the coach. They are making more money than the coach. They have a longer contract than the coach. I don't know if there is a coach left in the league—with the possible exception of Pat Riley, who also has ownership rights—in which this is not true.

Forty years ago, the paradigm for society was the army. In the army, there was a hierarchy, and you followed rules. And in those days, World War II—often referred to as The Last Great War—the army was respected. The General of the Army came back to be our President.

Nowadays, Vietnam and later, the army is perceived as bad. To say you are a general in the army is not something that gives you respect. On the contrary, it is often met with derision and condemnation. And the whole idea of hierarchy and answering to it is amazing, too. When I went to medical school, you treated your professors with a certain amount of deference, and, for the most part, it's still there. But strange things now do go on. I remember giving a lecture and a student comes in late and picks up the *Times* and starts reading it in the middle of the lecture.

Q: Was the case of Latrell Sprewell choking his coach an aberration in our society?

A: I don't think it was an aberration. I think it was just the tip of the iceberg. It was the first time that we know of that a pro player tried to actually choke his coach, but Sprewell had attacked two or three other teammates before this. He attacked Jerome Kersey with a two-by-four. If that had happened on the street, he would have gone to jail. The problem is, there were no ramifications to the incident. I doubt if anything happened to him. So why should he think anything would be different this time? In fact, what was his response to all the hoopla? Subsequently, he sued his agent on the grounds that the agent should have had the foresight to negotiate a clause in his contract to make sure that he wouldn't be held culpable if he physically attacked his coach. In other words, there was no shame. There was no sense of, "Oh my God! I lost myself and I feel so remorseful and I'm embarrassed and humiliated." Instead, there was, "It's my goddamn agent's fault. He should have had the foresight to protect me in a case when I went off and did something like this."

Q: And Sprewell also sued the league.

A: He said a year's suspension was too much for physically assaulting another human being and leaving choke marks around his neck.

Q: But for losing part of his salary during the fourteen-month suspension, it did cost him something like $6 million.

A: Based on what? How much is he making this year?

Q: He's in the stratosphere.

A: I seemed to remember something like a $30 million contract. He probably lost more money on his endorsements than he did on the year's salary that he lost.

Q: And then he got a huge sneaker contract.

A: Unfortunately, often the people who do get the huge sneaker contracts are those who represent the rebel—the Rodmans, the Iversons, the Sprewells. They represent the outsider. Adolescent boys identify with that kind of anger, with that kind of anti-establishment "screw you" tone. "I can do anything I want and if you don't like it's too bad because I'm talented, I'm extraordinary, I'm this special, and there's nothing you can do about it."

Q: But a lot of adolescent boys don't have the talent that some of those ballplayers do. But they still view themselves that way, or is it just being a rebel for the sake of being rebellious?

A: All adolescents want to rebel. All adolescents want to individuate. At times, it reaches unhealthy proportions. All adolescents view themselves as simultaneously special and worthless. That's part of the angst of adolescence. It's part of finding yourself, and every adolescent goes through it. And there are some adults—some ballplayers—who seem never to get out of the adolescent stage. They're pampered. They're put on a pedestal. They are never forced to grow up. But once they finish with the game they have a difficult time adjusting to the world beyond the basketball arena.

Q: Can you tell by watching them play basketball who will be able to make the adjustments after their playing careers?

A: I believe you can tell more about a person in the way he plays the game than in almost anything else he does. Oscar Robertson and Magic Johnson and Bill Bradley are perfect examples of the positive side. Oscar held the record for assists for years, until Magic Johnson broke it. Both were superstars, but both were known for their great passing and team play. Not coincidentally, both have succeeded as businessmen in their lives after basketball. Bradley was one of the best at moving without the ball that I've ever seen. He set picks, he was always in the flow of the game. He was dwarfed often by the people he was playing against, both in terms of talent and size, but he played intelligently. And he's certainly made what you'd have to call an impressive adjustment in his post-basketball life.

I remember playing ball with a classmate in high school. He was a charming guy off the court. Years later, a friend of mine who ran a business asked me for advice about hiring this guy, since he knew that we were classmates. I said, "I wouldn't hire him, he cheats at basketball." My friend said, "When was the last time you spoke to him?" I said, "It doesn't matter. If he cheated when he was sixteen, he is likely to continue cheating. I wouldn't trust him."

My friend hired the guy, and years later he discovered that the guy had embezzled several million dollars from him.

Now, some people can change. Absolutely. I think you can even see this change on the court. A great change by a player was Michael Jordan, who learned to be a team player after several years in the league—he discovered that he wasn't going to win a championship unless he involved all of his teammates on the floor. And he changed as a player in a physical sense, too. He was famous for his high-flying slam dunks, but what made him a phenomenal player was the fall-away jump shot that he developed later in the pros. He wasn't jumping toward the basket, he was jumping away from the basket. It was unstoppable, and added an element to his game that was unbeatable.

Q: Do you observe the use of psychology by coaches in a game?

A: I always watch that. It's always interesting to see when a coach chooses to take a player out and put him in, the message the coach is trying to get across and how the players react. I watched Larry Bird, one of the greatest players of all time, take out Mark Jackson for defense in the fourth quarters of Pacers games. The Pacers were doing well with that, yet Jackson was pouting. He'd come to the bench and he wouldn't look at Bird. You could see him sitting on the bench and moving his lips and grumbling. I find that that can be extremely deleterious to a team. Part of character is whether or not you can come back when you're down, and teams that are self-destructive—like the Pacers and the Lakers— lack that certain character. Does the player who is going in pat the guy who is replacing him on the rump, as encouragement? It rarely happens nowadays. It happened much more previously. Does he give the coach the silent treatment when he comes out? One of the things I decry about the state of the game is this total self-involvement. And it's probably unfair, but I blame a lot of it on Pat Riley. He fines players if they have the audacity to help up an opposing player who has fallen—even if you had knocked him down. That's terrible. Is that something to teach? Is that what society should be about? Does Riley mirror society? I fear nowadays he does.

Q: Gary Payton is supposed to be a great trash talker. What about trash talking?

A: He's truly a great player. I've seen him at times take over a game. Yet I can't feel positively about him because he never looks like he's having fun on the court. Either he looks like he's gloating when he's doing well, or he looks like he's sulking when he isn't. He never looks like a professional. He doesn't look like he does this for a living. It would be nice if some of these players who are making more money in one year than most of us make in a lifetime would act like a mensch. Act like a professional. And there is no excuse for trash talking. On the playground level, I understand it, but I think it's a terrible thing. Certainly on a professional level, when you dunk in someone's face and then you stand over him and taunt him. It makes me sick.

I remember not long ago I was playing a three-on-three game outdoors. I was guarding some kid. And I'm an old man—forty-nine years old. The kid might have been fifteen or sixteen. He makes a good move on me and scores. Fine. As the ball goes through the hoop, he turns to me and sticks his nose so that it's literally touching mine and screams, "In your face, motherfucker!" I had never seen this kid before in my life. I'm old enough to be his father. And he says this to me. As it turns out, I outweigh him by about twenty pounds. At first I laughed at his remark, but then I was infuriated. I had simply been trying to play a nice game. From then on he never got within fifteen feet of the basket. I boxed him out beyond the foul line. Finally at one point he looked at me as if to say, "What's the matter, old-timer?" Like, "What did I say to piss you off?" He didn't even realize what he had done.

When I was growing up, trash talking wasn't acceptable. If you did it, you were ostracized. Now it has become socially acceptable. When you see people on TV—the pros—doing it and not being reprimanded, but idolized, it becomes acceptable to kids when they play in the schoolyards or playgrounds. Sure, you can make good-natured fun of someone, like, "Where did you get that shot?" And we used to have rank-out contests—"In your wildest dreams, you never made a shot like that." But it was something you grew out of. It was considered an immature trait. It was acceptable as an adolescent. Later, hopefully, your put-downs became wittier. More subtle. In adulthood, they hopefully have disappeared. In the NBA, players often take pride in acting like they're fourteen years old. I think that's unfortunate. Remember

Shawn Kemp and Derrick Coleman playing for the United States all-star team in Canada, and grabbing their crotches in front of the audience? This is an acceptable way for our sports heroes to act? The commissioner of the NBA, David Stern, had to fly to Toronto to explain to them that this behavior could hurt the image of the league.

Q: What would Freud have made of basketball today?

A: [*Laughter.*] Well, tying together Freud and Dennis Rodman, for instance, Freud said, "If you feel like your mother's favorite, you can accomplish anything." So I'm reminded of the relationship Rodman had with his first coach with Detroit, Chuck Daly, though in this case it would have been his father's favorite. On the whole, I think Freud would have been outraged at the tenor of basketball. Freud was a very private person. He was very uncomfortable with public displays of emotions, despite the fact that he did more toward our understanding of them than probably any human being who's ever lived. Freud was so uncomfortable with his patients, for example, that he created the analytic framework so that they wouldn't look at him while they were talking.

Can you imagine someone coming over to Professor Freud and standing nose-to-nose and saying, "In your face, motherfucker"? Well, motherfreuder. I think Freud would have taken great offense at this confrontation. But I think he would have been fascinated by the use of the term *mother*fucker. How Freudian!

Q: Would Freud have been charmed, for example, by Rodman's nose rings?

A: Freud was a very formal man. This was a man who probably wore a three-piece suit to the beach.

Q: He wouldn't have dyed his hair technicolor?

A: I doubt it. I don't think Freud would have been charmed by any of it, but I think he would have perceived most professional ballplayers nowadays as being, in effect, adolescent rebels acting out their temper tantrums on the court. He certainly would have been fascinated by the Oedipal aspect of their relationship with their coaches. He could have written volumes about the Sprewell–P. J. Carlesimo incident.

Q: Might Freud have gotten any pleasure out of basketball?

A: He didn't really seem the athletic type. He was more ruminative. The part of basketball that might have appealed to him, though, was putting the ball in the basket. Freud was so into sex he probably would have seen the act of scoring a basket as carnal. I'm sure he would have seen scoring a basket as a form of penetration. Especially the dunk. He would definitely have seen it as a sexual metaphor. The score and then the celebrating and the adulation. The orgasm, the climax.

Q: Would he have been right?

A: Probably. He knew a thing or two.

SHARON STONE

HARON STONE won the Golden Globe Award for best actress and was nominated for an Academy Award for Best Actress in 1995, both for her role in *Casino*. She was born on March 10, 1958, in Meadville, Pennsylvania. She attended Edinboro (Pennslyvania) University before becoming a model with the Eileen Ford Agency. Her first film was Woody Allen's *Stardust Memories,* in 1980. Other films include *Total Recall, Scissors, The Quick and the Dead, Diabolique, Sliver, Celebrity,* and *Intersection.* One of her most memorable films, however, was *Basic Instinct,* in 1992, co-starring Michael Douglas. It is a steamy, explicit thriller in which she plays a character named Catherine Trammell, sexy, villainous, and riveting.

She is married to Phil Bronstein, the executive editor of the *San Francisco Examiner.*

The following interview was conducted by telephone in July 1999, while Ms. Stone had taken a break during the filming in Vancouver, British Columbia, of *Beautiful Joe.* I had requested an interview with her though her agent, and I was told that Ms. Stone would call me. And she did, picking up the phone in her personal trailer one afternoon and dialing the number.

●   ●   ●

Q: I had been told by Lon Rosen, Magic Johnson's business manager, that you had studied Magic's moves on the basketball court for your role in *Basic Instinct.*

A: It's true. I loved to watch Magic Johnson play basketball. He was genuinely magical. He had such generosity of spirit, and was in such control. It was thrilling to see, for example, that no-look pass. He knew where everybody was—he *sensed* in his bones where everybody was—and he invariably threw the pass to the right person at the right time. This is the quintessence of magic, isn't it? But beyond that, even, I appreciated how he extended the grace of his own energy to the other players. When he wanted to slow things down, to get order on the court, so to speak, he would raise up the palm of his hand. Not in an authoritarian manner, but in a collegial spirit. And yet there was no doubting by his teammates who the leader, the respected leader, was out there. They understood that this was not an ego thing with him, but it was done solely to get a basket, a step to winning the game, which was paramount for him. He was controlling the pace of the game. And as a spectator, you're drawn to the aura, both physical and spiritual, of the performer.

Now, Magic inspired and captivated others with the innate goodness of his heart. When I acted in *Basic Instinct,* I played an adversarial role, as opposed to Magic's being a good guy for his team. But all the moves, the body gestures—the control of a situation—are precisely what Magic Johnson demonstrated in basketball and which I had in mind when I made my moves, my body gestures, when I hoped to exude a control of a situation, a total confidence. And a true professional integrity.

Q: As when you sat in the chair during the interrogation room in the police station and lit up a cigarette? And the assistant district attorney told you, "There's no smoking in this building, Miss Trammell," and you said, "What are you going to do . . . charge me with smoking?"

A: Yes.

Q: And what about the no-look pass?

A: There are moments when, like when I'm chopping the ice with the ice pick, that I don't see the Michael Douglas character—Nick—because he is behind me as we talk. But I *sense* him and his attitude. And the audience, I hope, knows that I do. There are times in life when without speaking we know something is happening, or going to happen, or that two people in distant places are thinking of the same thing, or of each other. It's a phenomenon, but it's real.

Q: In the interrogation room, there is one of the most famous scenes in recent moviemaking, when you're wearing that short white skirt and are sensually smoking a cigarette and then uncross your—

A: I've gone over that so many times now and I don't want to talk about it again. It's been done to death. I've said I felt exploited, and the director and I have since talked it out and I just want to leave it alone. I'd just like to talk about my love for basketball.

Q: I would imagine that exploitation is not limited to movie stars.

A: No, I know that athletes are often exploited. I mean, the fans often always want more—one more autograph, one more interview, one more something. And you want to be accommodating, but sometimes you do it at your peril. Sometimes it seems you just can't give enough.

Q: Magic always got the best out of his teammates. Can you learn anything from that as an actress, in regard to performance?

A: I think as an actor or actress you have the responsibility to know and respect your craft and know your lines, to act professionally. That's the way you help the picture along, help the other actors and the director. But I think the way to help the picture in another way is to have a generosity of spirit with the crew. They aren't staying in a princess trailer, and they have to schlep stuff all over the place. Why should they want to do that for you? So you try to say things, or do things, that will make their jobs easier. Just like in basketball, there are the little things that result in the big things.

Q: What about relationships between actor and director? Can you draw a comparison to that of player and coach?

A: In some instances, yes. I thought Magic Johnson and Pat Riley had a special kind of relationship. They had shared goals. Magic knew what Riley wanted him to do, and Riley knew that Magic wanted to do it—and would. But there are special relationships like that in filmmaking, like Robert De Niro and Martin Scorsese, and Barry Levinson and Dustin Hoffman. They are just such winning combinations, and their finished product has a glow to it. I've had that with a few directors, most particularly with Mark Rydell, who directed me in *Intersection*. He's a highly intelligent, earthy man who brings a sensuality to his direction, and creates a positive atmosphere in this regard for his actors.

Q: Have you seen much of women's basketball?

A: Some, not a lot. I haven't followed it that closely, but I like it very much. The women play with a kind of purity that is sometimes lacking in the men's game. They play with such enthusiasm for the game itself. I think men sometimes are so wrapped up in their machismo that it overwhelms their performance. They'll display an aggression that I think masks an anger, some deep-seated fear of something, maybe not being as macho as they'd like people to think they are. All that rough stuff, and that chest-bumping, covers up other feelings.

Q: Do you have a favorite team?

A: My favorite teams are the ones who get me seats at court-side. [*Laughs.*]

Q: Any specifically?

A: I love the Knicks. I just love the Knicks. They come at you flat, I mean flat, with power, like a tidal wave. And I love the Heat. It seems to me that they play in a kind of mist, but with lightning. There's a lot of electricity there. I haven't been as taken with the Lakers. I find them rather ethereal, too jazzy, too individualistic. You can be jazzy, but you have to play off your other band members, your other teammates, too. And they haven't. We'll have to see what Phil Jackson can do with them, if he can coach them as suc-cessfully as he did the Bulls.

Q: You loved the Knicks, and the Knick players?

A: Yes.

Q: What are your thoughts on Latrell Sprewell? He had an out-standing playoffs with the Knicks, after being traded from Golden State. Now, I understand you live in San Francisco, so you as a bas-ketball fan and resident there must have been aware of Sprewell and the choking incident with his coach at Golden State, P. J. Carlesimo, after they'd had an argument in practice. What did you make of that?

A: [*A throaty, kind of ironic laugh—which sounded, over the long distance wires, as though she might be able to identify with it.*] Choking! I wasn't living in San Francisco then, but of course I know about it. When you do something that takes so much physicality, you can get to an emotional state where everything is bound up inside you and you need some kind of outlet, or release for the emotions. And sometimes it gets out of control. Sprewell is obviously a highly charged individual. You can see it in the way he plays, with a lot of emotion and physicality and force. So I can understand how the incident occurred.

Q: Do you justify it, then?

A: Oh, no. No one should ever choke anyone else. I don't justify it, I just say I can understand it. [*A voice is heard speaking to her nearby.*]

A: Oh, I'm getting distracted. Sorry. I'm being called to the set. I'll have to wrap this up. Goodbye, and remember, don't exploit me. Now don't fuck me!

Q: Ms. Stone—my intentions are strictly honorable! Good luck with the movie, and thank you.

SAUL BELLOW

S AUL BELLOW was born on June 10, 1915, in
Lachine, Quebec, Canada, and moved to Chicago
as a young boy and grew up there. His novels include
*Humboldt's Gift, The Adventures of Augie March, Dangling
Man,* and *Mr. Sammler's Planet.* He was awarded the
Nobel Prize for literature in 1976, has won a Pulitzer
Prize and three National Book Awards, and was awarded
the 1990 National Book Foundation Medal for distinguished contribution to American letters. He currently
is on the faculty of Boston University, where he has the
title University Professor. He is also the founder of the
recently launched periodical *The Republic of Letters,*
designed to encourage unknown writers.

Following is a telephone interview conducted with
Mr. Bellow on March 17, 1999.

•   •   •

Q: Hello, Mr. Bellow.

A: Hello, Mr. Berkow.

Q: How are you?

A: Not so bad.

Q: Well, you sound good.

A: It's an illusion, but I'll let you keep it.

Q: I understand you're a basketball fan.

A: I'm not a huge basketball fan, but anybody who went to high school in Chicago in the 1930s was a basketball fanatic. I used to watch the Taylor Trunks. Do you remember them?

Q: No, I don't.

A: Taylor Trunks was a suitcase company on Wabash Avenue. This was women's basketball.

Q: And you watched this?

A: Yeah.

Q: Oh. Did you watch it for the basketball or for the women?

A: [*Laughs.*] Listen, there was no—as the boys used to say, "They were too strong and healthy for me."

Q: Have you followed basketball over the years?

A: I got a revival of my interests when the Bulls became prominent.

Q: And you were still in Chicago?

A: I was.

Q: What did you make of that at that time, and why was your interest piqued?

A: Those guys were all virtuosi. They were very accomplished athletes, especially Jordan, who is a kind of genius at this game. His displays are just wonderful to watch.

Q: I understand you watched Jordan's retirement news conference on television. I don't know if you read Louis Lapham's editorial in the March issue of *Harper's* magazine, but he writes at one point about the impeachment proceedings in Congress against President Clinton: "In the corridors behind the press gallery, the reporters were talking mostly about Michael Jordan whose retirement from basketball had been played as bigger news on the front page of that morning's *New York Times* than had the commencement of the President's impeachment trial. At least five hundred correspondents had crowded into Chicago's United Center. Not as many as one hundred were seated in the Senate. The deference to Jordan accurately reflected the society's order of values. . . ."

Do you agree?

A: I think that's just journalistic exaggeration.

Q: But what did you make of "society's order of values"?

A: I think all of this sports business in the U.S.A. is extremely important, to be sure, because it's sort of an old-fashioned measure of manhood, like the Westerns in the movies.

Q: Do you mean that Jordan has taken over for John Wayne in the American consciousness?

A: In a way, except that there is much more skill involved in what he did, and much more thought. Mind-body thought. Mind-body connection. It's visible in him. It's wonderful.

Q: Can you recall a particular moment when watching Jordan?

A: That last great deed of his when he stole the ball in the last minute of the last game of the finals and won the game. I watched on television. Jordan looked for a moment like he was lost in thought, and he noticed that the guy had the ball under his arm and Jordan just poked it out and dribbled away. Is that luck? It's just this marvelous presence of mind that he had, this terrific alertness and keenness about what he was doing.

Q: To return for a moment to there being just one hundred members of the press in the Senate for the start of the presidential impeachment hearings and five times as many for Jordan's retirement announcement. What does that say to you, if anything, about the country?

A: That they've given up on politics. As they should. They know it's a low, lousy game, and they just sort of turned their backs on it. When the chips are down they'd rather watch a good basketball game.

Q: How did you feel about it when you watched the retirement announcement?

A: I thought he was doing the right thing. There was no reason why he had to pursue his golden career any further. He had reached his prime. It's up to him to decide when he no longer has anything to prove to the American public. He had shown everything he could do. It was just marvelous.

Q: What about the pure pleasure of playing, of continuing on when he was still the best player in basketball?

A: I don't know. I never met him, so I have no particular insight into him, except as a spectator.

Q: You once touched on playing racquetball in a novel. Is that correct?

A: Yeah.

Q: But other than that I can't recall you ever writing about sports. Have you?

A: No, not that I can think of. I was never really much good at it. I was one of these injured children who had to beef himself up. I ran around Humboldt Park until I developed my muscles. [*Laughs.*] But I was on the track team in high school. Tuley High School.

Q: What did you run?

A: A mile.

Q: How did you do?

A: Persistent. That's all. Just grinding along.

Q: Have you seen sports grow more important in this country?

A: I don't know that they're more important. The old-timers will tell you that standards have fallen and fallen and fallen. It's like a bottomless fall into the pit. Ring Lardner used to complain that the baseball in his day had been corrupt.

Q: And there are people today who say sports like basketball are corrupted by people like, well, Dennis Rodman. Does Rodman interest you in any way?

A: He's just sort of a very clever clown, and he's an oddball. He's a sardonic personality. He doesn't look it, but that can be the only source of his behavior. And he likes to play the sophisticated bisexual angle. He's all right. Associated with a great team, he had more resonance. I don't know what he's going to do now.

Q: Have you read the Updike books about the Rabbit Angstrom character who was a basketball player?

A: No, I've never read that.

Q: Do you go to any games?

A: I go occasionally. I went to see Jordan play here in Boston when they lost to the Celtics. It reminds me of the old times. But I'm not a great maven.

Q: As a novelist, are there storylines that you see sometimes in basketball that strike your imagination?

A: I enjoy reading sports stories if they're written by Ring Lardner. I swear by stories like "You Know Me Al." I love them. I read Lardner as a child, and was fascinated by him. And I'm loyal to my childhood impressions.

Q: Are there any other thoughts you might have about basketball?

A: Just that I'm impressed with those great jumps to the basket. And Jordan, what he does amounts to genius.

Q: I once asked a Celtic player named Ed Pinckney if Jordan was the best jumper in basketball. He said, "No, there are others who can jump higher. But Jordan is the best floater in basketball."

A: Aha! That he can sustain himself once he got up there.

Q: He stays up there.

A: How does that happen?

Q: I don't know.

A: That's a feeling you do get from him. He's a great virtuoso and he has very special gifts that most people don't have. The vast majority of us don't have them, and even the people in the sport don't have it.

Q: Is there a writer who you might in some way compare to Jordan?

A: I would say Stephen Crane. He had some of that.

Q: Of what?

A: It's just this ability to project himself. You know, Crane wrote *The Red Badge of Courage* as a boy. He really didn't know anything about it. And what you feel in Jordan is that there is some imagination at work in what he does. This is unusual in athletes, I think. At least I've talked myself into it. *Se non é vero, é buon trovato, dev' essere proprio una buon' idea*, as the Italians say.

Q: Which means?

A: "If it isn't true, it's really a good idea." [*Laughter.*]

Q: Thank you, Mr. Bellow.

A: Thank you, Mr. Berkow.

About a week after this interview I wrote Mr. Bellow, telling him that there was another question I wished to ask. And that is, "Do you find anything in basketball or a basketball player—Michael Jordan or otherwise—in which you, as a writer, might identify (that is, in regard to, say, technique, or emotion, or focus, or economy, etc.)?"

One week later, on Boston University stationery, I received the following, dated March 31, 1999:

Dear Mr. Berkow,

Jordan soars towards the basket and at the required elevation does not drop the ball as lesser men would—he remains aloft and seems to be waiting for the ordained moment when the shot will be complete. I do identify myself with this power to hang in the air.

Yours,
S. Bellow